Clash of the Little Giants

ALSO BY ARNE K. LANG

The Nelson-Wolgast Fight and the San Francisco Boxing Scene, 1900–1914 (McFarland, 2012)

Prizefighting: An American History (McFarland, 2008; paperback 2020)

Clash of the Little Giants

*George Dixon, Terry McGovern
and the Culture of Boxing
in America, 1890–1910*

ARNE K. LANG

McFarland & Company, Inc., Publishers
Jefferson, North Carolina

Unless otherwise noted, all photographs are provided by the Boxing Hall of Fame Las Vegas (President Steve Lott) in association with Official Boxing Gods.

LIBRARY OF CONGRESS CATALOGUING-IN-PUBLICATION DATA

Names: Lang, Arne K., author.
Title: Clash of the little giants : George Dixon, Terry McGovern and the culture of boxing in America, 1890–1910 / Arne K. Lang.
Description: Jefferson, North Carolina : McFarland & Company, Inc., Publishers, 2022 | Includes bibliographical references and index.
Identifiers: LCCN 2022033600 | ISBN 9781476688732 (paperback : acid free paper) ∞
ISBN 9781476647005 (ebook)
Subjects: LCSH: Dixon, George, 1870–1908. | McGovern, Terry, 1880–1918. | Boxing—New York (State)—New York—History—20th century. | Boxing—United States—History—20th century. | Boxers (Sports)—United States—Biography. | Boxers (Sports)—Canada—Biography. | BISAC: SPORTS & RECREATION / Boxing
Classification: LCC GV1132.D538 L36 2022 | DDC 796.83092 [B]—dc23/eng/20220811
LC record available at https://lccn.loc.gov/2022033600

BRITISH LIBRARY CATALOGUING DATA ARE AVAILABLE

ISBN (print) 978-1-4766-8873-2
ISBN (ebook) 978-1-4766-4700-5

© 2022 Arne Karl Lang. All rights reserved

No part of this book may be reproduced or transmitted in any form or by any means, electronic or mechanical, including photocopying or recording, or by any information storage and retrieval system, without permission in writing from the publisher.

Front cover: Boxers Terry McGovern (left) and George Dixon (Library of Congress)

Printed in the United States of America

*McFarland & Company, Inc., Publishers
Box 611, Jefferson, North Carolina 28640
www.mcfarlandpub.com*

Table of Contents

Acknowledgments   vii

Introduction   1

1. George Dixon Coming of Age   13
2. George Dixon's Boston   20
3. George Dixon: Champion of Three Continents   26
4. Coney Island: Sodom by the Sea   38
5. Young Griffo and the Kentucky Rosebud   47
6. Eastern Precincts and a Wild Goose Chase   52
7. The Horton Law and the Broadway Athletic Club   55
8. Highs and Lows on Opposite Coasts   59
9. Terry McGovern: The South Brooklyn Comet   64
10. 1899: The Year of the Deluge   71
11. Tom O'Rourke and the Other Guy   84
12. Dixon vs. McGovern: The Championship Fight   96
13. Terry McGovern: High Times and a Shocking Reversal   102
14. George Dixon's Second Act: A Career on the Skids   115
15. Terry McGovern After the Fall   123
16. Little Chocolate in the Autumn of His Years   137

Table of Contents

17. Terrible Terry's Psychopathology	140
18. Funerals and Monuments	143
19. Necrology	146
Appendix I. Key Fights in the Boxing Career of George Dixon	157
Appendix II. Key Fights in the Boxing Career of Terry McGovern	160
Chapter Notes	163
Bibliography	177
Index	181

Acknowledgments

I would like to dedicate this book to the memories of the late John Luckman and his brother, the late George Luckman.

An unassuming man partial to flannel shirts and khaki pants clenched with suspenders, John Luckman founded Gamblers Book Club in 1964. This was no club, not in the sense of a membership club, but, rather, a retail book store, a little shop tucked away in a quiet, if somewhat sketchy, neighborhood near downtown Las Vegas. John, who collected antiquarian gambling books, preferred "Club" because he envisioned it as a clubhouse of sorts for people with a common interest.

In time, John's business boomed. Books about gambling in its various manifestations were joined on the shelves by books on such subjects as magic, the mob, con artists, Las Vegas in general, and so forth. The inventory was nothing if not eclectic. Where else could one find a gaggle of football tout sheets within an arm's reach of a book on probability theory by a noted mathematician? But through it all, even as the mail-order component of John's business expanded in lockstep with the global expansion of casino gambling, John's little store maintained its hot stove league ambiance.

I wasn't an employee of the store, but it was there at a desk in the back room that I cobbled together my first book with an advance from John Luckman. It was a modest effort, a little primer on sports handicapping interposed with a loose history of bookmaking and sprinkled with sports gambling ephemera, but it was a start; I had found my niche, working with words.

John Luckman's kidneys eventually failed him. After months of dialysis, he died in 1987. His brother George Luckman came over from southern California to help John's widow Edna run the store, returning to California after she died in 2003.

George, who was as laid-back as his brother, happened to be a hobbyist boxing historian. Before he left Las Vegas, he gave me a box of old boxing magazines. Nestled among the magazines were a few IBRO

Acknowledgments

journals, correspondence from the International Boxing Research Organization. Each issue contained career records of selected old-time fighters whose ledgers were haphazardly compiled by previous enumerators.

I knew that those "authoritative" record books that were published by *The Ring* had many missing pieces and that some entries were mislabeled, but the full extent of the omissions didn't hit home until I chanced upon these send-outs. They whetted my curiosity to learn more about the lives of fabled boxers whose careers hadn't been fully fleshed-out by early biographers. An upshot is this book, my third published with McFarland. I am indebted to the folks at McFarland, in particular my editor Charlie Perdue, who welcomed this tome and offered many helpful suggestions.

In 2016 I accepted an appointment as editor-in-chief of TheSweetScience.com, one of the oldest of the online boxing magazines. It's been a privilege to work with a fine ensemble of writers, whose names I won't mention for fear of leaving someone out.

The photos in this book were provided by Steve Lott. The images were part of a treasure trove of boxing memorabilia bequeathed to Steve by his mentor Jim Jacobs. It pains me to write that Steve passed away as this book was being readied for publication; he died after a fall at his home. I am eternally grateful for his generosity.

Having yet to master all the functions of technological tools at my disposal, I was lucky to have a safety net in the form of Shane Langvad, whose assistance was invaluable. Shane and his mother, my wife Kitt, were my rocks of Gibraltar. And while I'm at it, as a confirmed library rat, here's a shout-out to old Andrew Carnegie.

About those early biographies, both stand-alone and those incorporated within broader histories, many were splattered with folklore. But to point this out in a haughty manner, as some have done, would be unfair as early writers lacked the resources of those of us who work in the digital age and have a wealth of primary materials right at our fingertips.

The book *John L. Sullivan and His America*, by the late Michael T. Isenberg, is a work that is breathtaking in its scholarly rigor, and yet Isenberg, the most dogged of researchers, felt compelled to add this caveat: "Sullivan's life is so filled with apocrypha and hyperbole that patent untruths and downright lies have doubtless crept into this biographical study."

I kept that caveat in mind as I explored the lives of George Dixon and Terry McGovern. It was important to filter out the folklore. However, I can't promise that my filter was faultless, and the buck stops with me. Ergo, if there are any errors in this book, the fault lies with the author.

Introduction

In the foyer of a recreation center in Halifax, Nova Scotia, there are two portraits of George Dixon hanging on the wall. The panel on the left shows Dixon as a boy. He appears to be about 11 years old. The photo is of the sort that one might find in a school yearbook, except that it covers a bit more of him below the shoulders, showing the top buttons of the vest that matches his charcoal-colored suit jacket. Obviously taken in a photography studio, the portrait undoubtedly marked a special event in his life. Confirmation Sunday at his church, perhaps? Who knows?

Dixon may well have been older than 11 years. Shorter and slenderer than most of his peers, George Dixon would always look young for his age, even as his hairline receded, until late in his short life when his silky coffee-and-cream complexion turned sallow, and his eyes betrayed the look of a man beaten down by too much hard living.

This premature decline was almost inevitable as the occupation he had chosen had a high risk of debilitation at an early age; he was a prizefighter. But George Dixon was no ordinary prizefighter. He was the first boxer one could fairly call an undisputed world champion, recognized as such on both sides of the Atlantic and in Australia, the first to win titles in three weight divisions, and simply the best boxer of his generation, if not the best of all time.

None of these distinctions is universally accepted. Other boxers have claims to being the first undisputed champion, the first to hold titles in three weight classes, the first this and first that. Identifying George Dixon as the best boxer of his era, if not the best of all time, is obviously a subjective opinion. But his name certainly belongs in the conversation. And although he's been largely forgotten, it's inarguable that he was famous. Dixon was held in such esteem, said a newspaper writer in 1901, that no one, barring perhaps the great abolitionist Frederick Douglas and the great educator Booker T. Washington, did more to advance the cause of his people.[1] The author did not elaborate on why he felt this way. Dixon wasn't a newsmaker who leveraged his fame

Introduction

to stump for racial justice. He was a prizefighter extolled for his ring accomplishments but also for his comportment, a man who eschewed ostentation and was a square shooter in a sport overrun with fakers.

George Dixon had a remarkable career with a few speed bumps and eventually a setback that fractured his career to such an extent that he was never the same or looked upon in the same way again. On one fateful night, he was reduced from a lord of the ring to a has-been.

There was nothing unusual about this. Many great prizefighters devolved into run-of-the-mill journeymen as they continued fighting beyond their "expiration date." But while George Dixon's career arc was fairly typical, his story is yet compelling because he was such a brilliant boxer, because he was a man of color competing at a time when racism was unapologetically rampant, manifested in a spate of lynchings and the expansion of Jim Crow laws sanctified by the U.S. Supreme Court, and because he came along at a time when professional boxing was undergoing a great transformation, a fitful process in which eras overlapped and there was little uniformity from one jurisdiction to another. (Had major league baseball been subject to the same geographical disconnect, the number of innings that constituted a full game would have varied from one city to another.)

It has become common for professional boxers to enter the sport with a ready-made nickname. Historically, however, a boxer usually had to show that he was a cut-above before someone would be inspired to invent a *nom de guerre*. Little Chocolate was the sobriquet fastened upon George Dixon. An earlier prizefighter of note who sprung from the same soil, a bigger man named George Godfrey, came to be called Old Chocolate, and Dixon's nickname sprang from it. As is often the case with nicknames in sports, his career was well under way before the nickname found favor with sportswriters. It really didn't become firmly affixed to him until after he retired, and his extraordinary career came fully into focus.

The man that toppled George Dixon from his pedestal, reducing him to a journeyman, also had a nickname. Terry McGovern was called Terrible Terry. It was a hackneyed nickname in common with most euphonic nicknames, but it fit for he inflicted terrible punishment on his opponents when he was going well. During one stretch, he achieved 19 consecutive knockouts, and this in an era when knockouts were far less common than they are today. "No one before his day and no one since, in any era of the game, punched into the history books an array of spectacular performances that remotely approached those of

Introduction

McGovern," wrote the syndicated sportswriter and noted sports historian Frank G. Menke in 1929.[2]

George Dixon vs. Terry McGovern transpired on January 9, 1900. "It was the most significant meeting between featherweights to date, and astonishingly, it almost inarguably remains so today," wrote the noted Scottish boxing historian Matt McGrain in 2015.[3]

Both combatants in this historic fight are the focal points of this book; we hover longer over George Dixon because his career, which began at an earlier point in time, was meatier. Moreover, Dixon had a manager, some would say a Svengali, who was one of the most influential figures in the sport, a man who commands more attention than any of the key people around Terry McGovern. One could not write the life story of Elvis Presley without acknowledging the influence of his manager Colonel Tom Parker; likewise, one could not write the story of George Dixon without taking into consideration the role played by his manager Tom O'Rourke.

A writer rummaging through old newspapers to learn more about prizefighting in George Dixon's era frequently runs across stark discrepancies in prizefight reports. It's more than an annoyance; it forces the writer to make a judgment about which summary was more truthful and leaves him questioning whether he has captured an honest portrait of the scene that he is describing. Judging a fight is a subjective exercise. Eyewitnesses to a crime scene often see things differently, so it should not surprise us that the scorecards submitted by ringside judges often lack uniformity. But here we're talking about something more than selective perception; we're talking about something ignoble. By way of illustration, check out these descriptions of the November 10, 1903, fight between Joe Walcott and Sandy Ferguson at the Criterion Athletic Club in Boston: "There was nothing to it. It was Walcott's decision by a big margin. He beat the heavy-weight from start to finish. It was the worst verdict ever given in this city when Referee Dan Donnelly decided Joe Walcott a loser.... Indignation is at a high pitch among the sporting men who saw the bout, and they threaten dire things if Donnelly presides at any more meetings as referee." (This summary appeared in the next day's *New York Evening World* under the headline "Referee Gave Verdict Against Joe Walcott.") The story in the *Boston Globe* told a different tale. The ringside reporter gave Ferguson eight of the 15 rounds, scoring three rounds even, and wrote that Ferguson "finished in a whirlwind fashion and had [Walcott] hanging on in the final round." His story ran under the headline "Ferguson Wins Bout. He Clearly Outclasses Joe Walcott."

Introduction

The summary that appeared in the *Brooklyn Times-Union* also deviated from the *New York World* report. The story said the decision in Ferguson's favor met with the approval of the crowd.[4]

In Dixon's day, the stringer covering an out of-town fight was often a member of one of the fighters' camps. The colorful boxing manager Dumb Dan Morgan, dubbed "Dumb" Dan by a whimsical reporter because of his loquaciousness, regaled fight writers with stories of rushing off to the nearest telegraph office at the conclusion of a fight to send off his summary to out-of-town papers. He needed to rush so as to get there ahead of the rival manager whose story would tell a different tale. Back at the newspaper office where typesetters were working under a tight deadline, the first story that came in was usually the story that made it into print. In these days before the advent of radio, even incorruptible fight writers were prone to let personal feelings bias their ringside reports, cognizant that only those who were actually at the fight could take umbrage.

An inordinate number of post-fight stories back in those days opened with the words "In the fiercest fight ever seen around these parts...." This was especially true of dispatches from the hinterland. Another commonly-found introduction was "In the most scientific fight ever seen around these parts...." This testimonial served a dual purpose. Extolling the skillfulness of the combatants served to build interest in their future engagements, and it was a riposte to the pesky reformers who railed against the brutality of the sport, seeing every match as a slugging contest devoid of a cerebral component.

Boxing writers circa 1900 were often involved in the sport in ways that went beyond just writing about it. Sportswriters moonlighted as referees and other kinds of fight functionaries, and some were actually involved in negotiating the terms of a match. Also, betting on the fights was far more common back then, among aficionados and among sportswriters too. "Because these newspaper people bet money and established a conflict of interest, and had personal venom and exhilaration through each second of the contest they covered, stories were horribly biased and always a thrill to read," wrote Jimmy Breslin in his jaundiced biography of Damon Runyon.[5]

Breslin's distinctive style was given to flights of exaggeration, but there was a kernel of truth in his piquant observation. Hyper-ventilated specimens of sports reporting do indeed pop up now and then in old newspapers. And some of them were repackaged by Nat Fleischer for inclusion in his famous magazine.

Introduction

Fleischer, the self-described Official Historian of the Ring, co-founded *The Ring* magazine in 1922 and served as its publisher and editor until his death in 1972. Under his stewardship, *The Ring* clobbered the competition. It was a must-read for people in the industry, but Fleischer was very conscious of the need to attract young readers, and young male readers were partial to adventure stories of the sort found in Western dime novels. An issue rarely went by with at least one embroidered story about an old-time fighter or an old fight. Some old fights were certainly ferocious, while others were impressive displays of ring artistry. The best of them were an amalgam of the two, but in the re-telling they became even more extraordinary.

An obsessive collector of all things pugilistic, Nat Fleischer likely knew more arcane facts about prizefighting than anyone alive, but he wasn't averse to playing loose with the facts so as not to despoil a good yarn. And because Fleischer acquired the aura of an unimpeachable authority, future generations of sportswriters were prone to embrace his accounts of events as if they were gospel. Since 1972 the Boxing Writers Association of America has given the Nat Fleischer Award for Excellence in Boxing Journalism at their annual confab. Crackerjack wordsmiths Red Smith, Jim Murray, and John Schulian—to name just three—are among the former honorees. The great irony is that as journalists go, Nat Fleischer was a hack.[6]

It would be audacious of this writer to think that he could fully apperceive all the slings and arrows that left scars on the psyche of George Dixon—as the saying goes, one had to walk a mile in his shoes—but what had to be especially dispiriting to him is that save for one time very late in his career, he was always the "road team" when his opponent was Caucasian, even when he was a matched against a foreigner and despite all the nice things that white sportswriters had written about him. In a sport so heavily dependent on tribal loyalties for commercial success, one would have hoped that nativity would have trumped pigmentation, but not so. When Dixon fought, the audience was always racially mixed, but whites were invariably in far greater abundance. When Dixon and a white opponent entered the ring, the cheers, save for that one occasion when his glory days were well behind him, were always louder for the white guy.

The boxing gym was a different world. Inside these walls, young men of different races and ethnic groups interacted as equals, and men of color were often looked up to as mentors. This was true in the bare-knuckle era in England, it was true in George Dixon's day, and it

Introduction

remains true today. There is no other interracial community on earth where social equality reigns to such a degree as the boxing gym.

Dixon and McGovern came along at a time when a reduction in the workday gave laborers more leisure time, a development that coincided with a greater emphasis on masculinity. Powered by the Muscular Christianity movement, a philosophical perspective that held that building strength and stamina was a byway to building good moral character, the "cult of masculinity" first flowered in England and reached its zenith in America in the closing decades of the 19th century.

"There is character as well as strength in muscle, and little of either in flabbiness or lard," asserted John Boyle O'Reilly. "Take the colloped [sic] fat from the under chin and jowl of a young man and put it on his arms, trunks, and legs in the shape of firm muscle, and, other things being equal, you improve his moral as well as his bodily health." A renowned poet, newspaper editor, public speaker, and Boston's most prominent apostle of physical fitness, O'Reilly placed boxing with soft gloves at the very pinnacle of all salutary manly exercises in his 1888 treatise *The Ethics of Boxing and Manly Sport*.[7]

Beyond its value as an exercise that promoted good health, boxing was also deemed to have benefits to society. "It is an established fact that a man skilled in the noble art of self-defense scorns to attack the weak and defenseless, and he is too confident of his muscular power to resort to the pistol," said an editorial writer for the *New York Sunday Mercury*.[8]

Boxing's boosters, by and large, were careful to make a distinction between boxing and prizefighting. The terms conveyed different imagery. The difference was somewhat akin to that between fencing and dueling.

Inside athletic clubs, boxing instructors—"professors" as they were invariably called—emphasized defense. When their students sparred, they sparred with the aim of improving their mastery of the basic principles they were taught. The blows they struck were not meant to be concussive. A prizefighter, however, was in the hurt business. Mastering an opponent meant not just flustering him, thereby sapping his pugnacity, but beating him up to where he was physically incapable of continuing.

Prizefighting, although seen as a healthy sport by a certain segment of the population, was viewed by the great majority as a perversion of the art of self-defense, as something unwholesome as expressed in this 1889 editorial in the *Portland Oregonian*: "[Boxing] teaches a man how to use both hands with equal readiness, makes the physical carriage erect, the movement of the limbs graceful, and best of all is an object

Introduction

lesson in diet and exercise, since excellence in boxing demands a bodily condition incompatible with intemperance in the pleasures of the table and the wine cup.... But boxing is not prize fighting. Prize fighting is inexcusably barbarous and absolutely immoral."[9]

Prizefighting was condemned not only for its brutality, but because it contravened the amateur ideal and because of its close link to gambling. True, all sports were vehicles for gambling. But in boxing, unlike team sports, gambling was actually codified into the rulebook. The revised rules of the London Prize Ring, issued in 1853, in addition to spelling out the rules of combat and addressing such concerns as ring size and glove weight, specified that if a fight were interrupted, it had to be resumed within the same week for betting purposes, or else all bets were off. John Graham Chambers, author of the transformative Queensberry overhaul, left the rule in place.

Although they could not point to any passage in the Bible that specifically condemned gambling, Protestant clergymen were overwhelmingly inclined to see it as a sin. "Whatever we have not found or earned or received by gift or realized from legitimate investment, is stolen, whether we got it by burglary or betting," said the prominent Methodist clergyman the Rev. Dr. Elbert R. Dille, expressing a sentiment that was widely shared.[10] Lurid stories of men who had lost their fortunes gambling, wrecking their home life, intensified the condemnation. "90 percent of defalcations, embezzlements, forgeries, and breeches of trust were caused by gambling," insisted a writer for the *Oregonian*.[11] The labors of a professional gambler contributed nothing to society and inverted the Victorian ideals of frugality and hard work.

Gambling games that were not fastened to the law of large numbers were puzzles that tested a man's acuity at problem-solving. Horseracing and human team sports were prime examples. These competitions attracted handicappers who gathered data with an eye toward identifying the most relevant variables and then would weigh each of them accordingly, a primitive algorithm. But all gambling games also attracted so-called "sure thing gamblers" who would seize the opportunity to pre-arrange a competition if the opportunity presented itself. Gamblers of this stripe fed the stereotype of gamblers, and their ranks were thought to be especially thick among prizefighting insiders, a perception that had more than a kernel of truth, notwithstanding the fact that the public was too quick to assume that the fix was in if a fight had an odd ending or did not conform to expectations. Because there were only two principal participants, and only one had to be complicit, a prizefight

Introduction

was far easier to rig than a sport that required the cooperation of more people.

Disturbances outside the ring were commonplace in the bare-knuckle era, and these were often fomented by gambling disputes. Here was more reason to outlaw prizefighting, more evidence that the sport was atavistic, the domain of ne'er-do-wells and brutes. The line between prizefighting and boxing, however, was never rigid. Many public "sparring exhibitions" in the gyms of athletic clubs turned bloody. Retired prizefighters, and some who were still active, found work as professors of boxing in these clubs and many played an instrumental role in arranging bootleg fights. The amateur ideal was an upper-class paradigm that held little sway with the immigrants and children of immigrants who became immersed in the affairs of the ring.

They were overwhelmingly Irish, and the Irish were also greatly over-represented among the ranks of America's gambler-businessmen, especially bookmakers and poolroom operators. Among the most prominent was James Patrick "Big Jim" O'Leary, whose Irish-born mother Catherine would be blamed for the Great Chicago Fire, supposedly started when a cow she was milking kicked over a lantern. Big Jim became nationally known for his "winter books" on America's richest thoroughbred horseraces.

O'Leary never ran for political office, but he could not have become the czar of gambling on Chicago's southwest side without first building alliances with men at the top of the city's political pyramid. In America's largest cities, these men increasingly shared O'Leary's ethnicity. John Morrissey's saga is instructive. Morrissey, who first attracted notoriety as a bare-knuckle boxer, became a pet of Tammany Hall, New York's notoriously corrupt Democratic political machine, and with its support became a two-term United States Congressman. Then, when a schism developed in Tammany over the pay of New York City's municipal workers, he declared himself the workingman's candidate and was elected to the New York State Senate. This is the same John Morrissey who parlayed his ownership of a chain of New York gambling dens into an opulent gambling house in the upstate New York village of Saratoga where he played an instrumental role in the establishment of the iconic racetrack there.

The Irish Americans who seized control of the political machinery in many of America's industrial cities were looked upon with great disfavor by those whose family roots in the new world ran deeper. The anti-prizefighting movement in America in the late 19th century was

Introduction

thus two-pronged. Those that were repulsed by the brutality of prizefighting, seeing it as a remnant of a less civilized age, were joined in their crusade by reformers roused to sunder The Machine. For these people, notes historian Meg Frisbee, "prizefighting was just one symptom of a dangerous social and political disease, not the pathogen itself."[12] A need to overturn the political applecart, hobbling the incumbents who were prizefighting's biggest enablers and thus setting the wheels in motion to replace them with men deemed to be more virtuous and thus better role models for the youth of the city, was the driving force behind the campaign to purge prizefighting from Coney Island, a subject that will be addressed later in this book.

There evolved natural destinations for prizefights as the sport grew in popularity, enabling organizers to hold their events in auditoriums rather than outdoors in semi-secret locations. Prizefights naturally gravitated to places that were free-and-easy, places characterized by a *laissez-faire* approach to human foibles. New Orleans, which sports historian Randy Roberts called America's original Sin City, and San Francisco, which at the turn of the century still had remnants of the Gold Rush days when the culture of the city was shaped by hordes of rough-hewn fortune-seekers going to and from the gold fields, were obvious examples.

Free-and-easy cities tended to have large populations of Irish Catholics and all that this implies. With their knack for political organizing, the Irish were quick to wield political power. (San Francisco elected an Irish mayor in 1867—14 years before an Irishman was elected mayor of New York.) A welcoming approach to prizefighting by a good-sized segment of the population counted for nothing without the support of men at the top of the political pyramid. Moreover, Irish Catholic men tended to marry late, and bachelorhood was more common among the Irish than among other ethnic groups. When single Irish men gathered in saloons and in social clubs and during lunch breaks at their workplaces, sports were often the major topic of conversation.

It's important to note, however, that no city, no matter how libertine, could keep the opponents of prizefighting permanently at bay. There was a continual tug-of-war and at various times, such as in the aftermath of a fatal fight, they had the upper hand and succeeded in shutting things down. They won many battles, but ultimately not the war as prizefighting became less brutal (or at least the perception of it) and the informal tenets of the Muscular Christianity movement became ingrained, profiting sports of all stripes.

Introduction

The Muscular Christianity movement, which brought about a greater appreciation of athletic prowess, was manifested in a big spike in the number of athletic clubs. In the United States, they were springing up in such profusion, said a *New York Tribune* writer in 1887, that it was impossible to enumerate them all: "In the large cities, there are from five to twenty-five, sometimes even more."[13]

In these establishments, virtually all of which were for men only, many different kinds of athletics were taught, the exact mix a product of the surrounding topography, local sentiment, and the club's resources. Boxing, the "manly art of self-defense," was embraced in large part because it was the most commercial. Monthly dues were usually insufficient to keep a club in the black; other sources of revenue were needed. Members were usually charged a premium to attend a boxing competition. In many places, these events were open to the general public (perhaps for a one-time "membership fee"), and they drew crowds far in excess of what turned out for other kinds of offerings, such as a gymnastics competition or track meet. The situation was akin to what one finds today at many large American universities where the revenue sports (typically football and men's basketball) subsidize the non-revenue sports.

Between 1890, when the Queensberry rules in the main took hold and prizefighting became less of an outlaw sport, and World War I, boxing in the United States, amateur and professional, was the near-exclusive domain of athletic clubs. Many of these clubs, at their founding, were designed to serve the upper class, but in some cities competition between rival clubs grew so fierce that young men who gave evidence of developing exceptional athletic prowess, regardless of their social rank, were not only welcome, but wooed. The best boxers were often pressed into teaching other members how to box, for which they received a stipend, the equivalent of a scholarship. And the best of the best attracted financial backers and—abetted by a fast-growing cadre of sportswriters whose ranks expanded in concert with a burgeoning body of tabloid papers—spread their wings and became nationally known.[14]

Dixon and McGovern were products of a subculture that nurtured and encouraged their chosen callings, and that subculture took on a somewhat different tint in Brooklyn, McGovern's hometown, from that in George Dixon's Boston, where Blacks played a much larger role in the athletic life of the city. Indeed, Boston, the Hub as it was then often called, spawned a greater profusion of good Black boxers than any other city, a development obscured by the towering figure of John L. Sullivan,

Introduction

the Boston Strong Boy, the first American athlete who could fairly be called a superstar.

Much has been written about racial discrimination in boxing. Contrarians point out that boxing produced a Black heavyweight champion more than three full decades before the integration of major league baseball, but that argument rings hollow. Good Black boxers were routinely underpaid relative to their white cohorts, and that has been true in every era. A white boxer thought to have the potential to go far is a prized commodity, able to attract well-heeled backers who would be less inclined to invest in his future if his skin were darker, and that is especially true of a heavyweight. Down through the ages, some of the best fighting men—heavyweight Peter Jackson and middleweights Sam Langford and Charley Burley—were not afforded the opportunity to fight for a title. Bob Armstrong, a top-shelf heavyweight during the prime years of Dixon and McGovern, undoubtedly made more money as a sparring partner than in the sum of his actual fights.

Boxing, it has been noted, is an unforgiving sport. The glovemen who keep at it for a considerable length of time, answering the bell for many rounds, more often than not leave the sport with incipient cognitive issues that will burden their loved ones as they grow older. The boxing literature is full of cautionary tales. This book fits the genre but strives to be something more. The goal in chronicling the rise and fall of both George Dixon and Terry McGovern was to learn more about these little giants of the squared circle, but the larger consideration was to acquire a deeper understanding of the "culture of bruising" in the years straddling the birth of the 20th century.

CHAPTER 1

George Dixon Coming of Age

George Dixon was born on July 29, 1870, in Halifax, Nova Scotia, the youngest of five boys born to Charles Dixon and the former Maria Dulliver. In those days, the maritime province of Nova Scotia had the largest per-capita population of Blacks of any province in Canada. Many were descendants of U.S. slaves who were assisted in re-settling in Canada by British sea captains who arrived in America during the war of 1812. A few were descendants of domestic servants who were brought to Canada by their employers, wealthy British sympathizers who left New England for Nova Scotia during the Revolution. Their ranks were augmented by runaway slaves escaping to Canada by the Underground Railroad, a development that picked up steam when the second (and more stringent) Fugitive Slave Act was signed into federal law in 1850. Many would return to the United States after the Civil War.

Black immigrants to Halifax encountered many of problems they thought they had left behind. Discrimination in housing trapped many in a settlement that would take the name Africville, a neighborhood that after decades of municipal neglect was condemned as part of an urban renewal project. George Dixon is thought to have spent the early years of his life in Africville.

One of Dixon's grandparents was reportedly white, an assertion concordant with his pigmentation. In news reports he was sometimes called a mulatto. A few, such as Nat Fleischer, boxing's foremost popularizer, used an even more archaic word: quadroon. When writing about Dixon, however, sportswriters were especially partial to "dusky," an adjective that struck a finer distinction than "colored" or "negro," the standard denominations. But the blatantly racist term "coon" does turn up occasionally. The term had wide currency. Vaudeville shows featuring blackface minstrels were frequently advertised as coon shows. Whatever the nomenclature, rare was the story about Dixon that did not make passing reference to his "negro-ness," even after he was pictured in newspapers so often that he became one of America's most recognizable sports personalities. Black and white prizefighters of the era, notes British sports historian Brian Dobbs, were dichotomized in the papers as if they were different breeds of cattle.

In *A Lesson in Boxing*, an 1893 instructional manual written under his name, Dixon says that he was about eight years old when he came to Boston. Other accounts differ, including attestations attributed to Dixon himself, and since the book was obviously ghostwritten, perhaps with little or no input from the nominal author, as was commonplace in those days, one can't say with certainty what age he was when he became a full-time Bostonian.[1] There's reason to think that the Dixons did not leave Halifax all at once but as a chain, with some emigrating before other members of the family and periodically returning home to Canada for long stretches. Regardless, what we do know is that little George was in Halifax on November 1, 1886, for on that date he had his first documented fight, knocking out a fellow novice identified as Young Johnson in the third round. Dixon would have then been 16 years old, and he was 10 months away from the first recorded sight of him in a Boston ring.

Before he embarked on a professional boxing career, Dixon worked as a "go-fer" for Elmer Chickering, who ran a locally famous photography studio at 21 West Street. All the notable fighters in Boston went to Chickering's studio to be photographed. They often came accompanied by their manager and trainer. Dixon delivered Chickering's photographs to newspaper offices and athletic clubs and came to know all the major players on the Boston boxing scene.[2]

George Dixon's name first appeared in a Boston daily paper on September 22, 1887. The previous evening, a new athletic club presented a boxing show

The earliest known portrait of George Dixon, undated but likely taken in 1892.

Chapter 1. George Dixon Coming of Age

at their gymnasium. Dixon opposed fellow Bostonian Elias Hamilton in an eight-round affair, the opening bout of a four-bout card. This was a hard fight between two gentlemen of color, said the writer for the *Boston Daily Globe*, who concurred with the referee that Dixon had the best of it.[3] The weights were not announced, but Dixon then carried about 105 pounds on his five-foot-three frame.

Dixon didn't fight again the rest of the year, but he was a busy young man in 1888, appearing in 12 bouts at various athletic clubs in the city. The most prestigious of Boston's athletic clubs were the Cribb Club and the Athenian.

The Cribb Club, whose name paid homage to the venerated British bare-knuckle battler Tom Cribb, was organized in 1881. Membership was limited to 150, of whom four went on to become Boston police commissioners. Poet John Boyle O'Reilly who was perhaps America's best-known and most admired Roman Catholic layman, was one of the original "25" and for a time served as the club's president.[4]

The boxing instructor was Professor Tim McCarthy, who also arranged the fights and served as the referee. McCarthy was credited with being the first man to see the potential in Jake Kilrain, who fought John L. Sullivan at Richburg, Mississippi, in 1889 in the last great bare-knuckle fight on American soil. Kilrain worked as McCarthy's assistant prior to becoming a big name in the sport and would take the name Cribb Club with him when he opened a boxing school in Baltimore.

The walls of the gymnasium were decorated with portraits of notable fighters. In the center of the room was a 24-foot boxing ring around which were gathered all sorts of athletic equipment: foils and masks for fencing, Indian clubs, weights, rowing machines, trapezes, and so forth. On boxing nights when all of the equipment was pushed up against the walls, the capacity was 400.[5]

With the success of the Cribb Club, athletic clubs began to spring up in Boston like mushrooms. "So many," said historian Stephen Hardy, "that it would be an endless task to enumerate them all. Indeed, many undoubtedly lived and died without leaving so much as a trace in the historical record."[6] Among those that were not oriented around a particular sport such as cycling or rowing, the most prominent was the Athenian Club. "It stands without rival in all of New England," said a reporter for the *Globe* in 1887. "The men enrolled as members are all prominently identified with the leading interests of the city."[7]

The Athenium Club was founded by David Blanchard. A wealthy

merchant born in Nottingham, England, Blanchard was a noted big game hunter, angler, and turfman, but locally he was best known as a boxing man. "Of all the admirers of the manly art in this city," said the *Globe*, "probably the most enthusiastic is David Blanchard."[8]

Blanchard invented a set of rules that modified the seminal Queensberry code. Blanchard's "Fair Play" rules, widely used in New England during his day, stipulated that a boxer had 12 seconds to rise after suffering a knockdown, but upon rising he had to come unaided to a circle three feet in diameter drawn in the center of the ring and resume his fighting pose. This modification, needless to say, never caught on, but another innovation credited to Blanchard, padded ring posts, would become standard.

Dixon's first appearance at the Athenian Club came on February 17, 1888. His match with Barney Finnegan, slated for eight rounds, was the opening fight of a four-bout card. Although out-weighed by seven and a half pounds, Dixon had the best of it from the start in a crowd-pleasing mill that went the full distance. "The little colored fellow's clever work won for him many warm friends," said the reporter for the *Globe*.[9]

The following month, Dixon engaged in his first 15-round fight. It was staged in the gym of a new organization, the Tremont Athletic Club. In the opposite corner was Paddy Kelley, a fighter from neighboring Cambridge, Massachusetts, who fought as Jimmy Conley's Unknown. This proved to be a very hard fight for Dixon. He was hit by a punch in the fourth round that damaged his left eye, and by the start of the ninth round, it had closed completely. He stayed the course, and at the end the referee declared the bout a draw, a decision deemed fair. Little George was then four months shy of his 18th birthday. Kelley was reportedly 10 years older.[10]

A 15-round fight would come to denote a title fight, but during the 1880s not necessarily so. Some jurisdictions had laws that set a ceiling on the number of rounds, but in other places the duration was whatever the combatants agreed upon. This would be the first of many fights that would enter George Dixon's ledger as a draw. Where decisions were allowed (we will get to that later), the referee was judge and jury. As a rule of thumb, he gave the nod to the fighter who looked fresher at the conclusion of the bout, assuming there wasn't a clear-cut disparity in the level of skill. By pronouncing a relatively even fight as a draw, the referee was playing it safe. With so much money changing hands in bets, a fishy decision put him at greater risk of being assaulted when he left the ring. Moreover, the Articles of Agreement sometimes stipulated

Chapter 1. George Dixon Coming of Age

that a match would be deemed a draw if both men were still standing at the final bell, and the referee was obligated to adhere to the agreement. (Some veteran turn-of-the-century fighters finished their careers with more draws than wins and losses combined.) Dixon and Kelley would fight again in January of 1889, a 10-rounder in which Dixon was judged the winner.

Prior to this bout, Dixon had three consecutive bouts with Hank Brennan, the first of which was staged at the Pelican Club, an establishment that took the name of a famous athletic club in London. This was a newly chartered club, but the man behind it, Thomas Earley, a former British booth fighter who had toured with the legendary Jem Mace, was one of Boston's best-known sports personalities.

Born in Roscommon, Ireland, Hank Brennan had come to Boston with his parents as a young boy. One year older than George Dixon, he was every bit Dixon's equal despite having no regular trainer and being somewhat less experienced. Dixon–Brennan I, the first installment of what would be a great intra-city rivalry, came off on June 21, 1888. The match was scheduled for 12 rounds but went 14. The referee was unable to determine a winner after 12 and ordered two additional rounds. The fighters protested; this was like being asked to work overtime without the promise of extra compensation. However, the referee was following the *Police Gazette* rulebook, which gave him the authority to order up an additional round or two if he could not come to a decision. The *Police Gazette*, boxing's greatest popularizer in the post–Civil War years leading up to World War I, had considerable sway in pugilistic circles, although this modification of the Queensberry rules did not achieve wide acceptance or last long. The referee was still unable to separate Dixon and Brennan after the extra sessions, and the bout went into the books as a draw.

A rematch slated for September 28 at the Pelican Club fell out when Dixon and Brennan played hardball, insisting on more money than the club was willing to pay, but the Athenian Club had deeper pockets and reeled in the rematch. Dixon–Brennan II was scheduled for seven rounds and came off on December 4 in a show headlined by a contest between Boston-based featherweight Ike Weir, the Belfast Spider, and Tommy Danforth. Their second meeting also went to "overtime," producing a nine-round draw, and two subsequent meetings, 15-round and 26-round battles, yielded the same result. The 26-rounder, the last of their four meetings was slated for 25. Although Dixon forged ahead after knocking Brennan to the canvas in Round 22, the referee yet ordered two additional rounds. After one additional frame, a police captain demanded that the bout be halted. According to Nat Fleischer, all four of the Dixon–Brennan fights were "hair-raising affairs."[11]

Fistic rivalries that continued beyond four encounters were common in this era, but Hank Brennan had only one more recorded fight (another draw) before abandoning boxing for employment as a brakeman on a gravel train. On March 28, 1896, he was crushed between two empty freight cars when one of them lurched as he was inspecting an air brake, killing him instantly. He was only 27 years old. He never had a manager or full-time trainer. Had Brennan been taken in hand by responsible people, said a reporter, he would have been a phenomenon.[12]

The Queensberry rules, named for the Marquess of Queensberry (John Sholto Douglas), were introduced in 1867, but the road to the universal adoption of the key features—a fistfight with gloves contested over a predetermined number of rounds with a one-minute break between each round—was a slow and bumpy road. In the credo of the old guard, the true measure of a title fight was that it had no ceiling, lasting until one man was unable or unwilling to continue. When George Dixon arrived on the scene, gloves (often skin-tight) had replaced bare knuckles, but fights-to-a-finish hadn't yet faded into antiquity. Indeed, an outstanding prizefighter circa 1890 could not fully cash in on his name as an attraction on the vaudeville circuit without winning fights of this nature. And getting there required a backer as there was little money, if any, to be gained from gate receipts in a fight-to-the-finish as it was by necessity a hush-hush affair in which the principals were subject to arrest. A fighter, if victorious, was entitled to a portion of his backer's gambling winnings.

Although he had once again been denied the satisfaction of having his hand raised in triumph, Dixon emerged from his fourth meeting with Hank Brennan with something more valuable: a wealthy backer. Dixon was backed by Athenium Club founder David Blanchard (who may have taken in junior partners in his "investment," as was common). Blanchard was so high on Dixon that he wanted to send him in against American bantamweight champion Cal McCarthy straightaway, but was persuaded that George should first test his mettle against Eugene Hornbacher, who had given McCarthy a very difficult fight in September of the previous year before succumbing in the 22nd round. Prior to this engagement, Hornbacher, a Harlemite, had attracted national notice with a 25th-round stoppage of "Loi" White, a well-regarded campaigner from Brooklyn. They fought wearing skin-tight gloves with the

Chapter 1. George Dixon Coming of Age

fingers cut off on a barge in the Hudson River opposite Yonkers before an intimate and "unusually fashionable" gathering.¹³

Hornbacher's backer nixed the idea of holding the fight in Boston, and Blanchard was likewise averse to fighting on Hornbacher's turf in New York. They found a willing host in New London, Connecticut, roughly equidistant between the two cities, and the fight materialized there on December 27, 1889, in a large room on the second floor of an inn. This was a private affair in which each party was allotted only 75 admission badges, and the location wasn't revealed until the day before the fight to minimize the risk of police interference.

George Dixon (left) with Tom O'Rourke, ca. 1890.

The fight was a terrible mismatch. Dixon knocked Hornbacher down four times in the opening round. Hornbacher was still groggy when the second round began and in short order would be knocked out cold, Dixon turning the trick with a straight right hand to the cheek. It took several minutes before poor Hornbacher came to his senses. "Boston Has a Pugilistic Phenomenon" read the first sentence in the report of the fight in the next day's *New York Evening World*.¹⁴

Tom O'Rourke had fastened himself to George Dixon prior to Dixon's fourth encounter with Hank Brennan. O'Rourke accompanied Blanchard and Dixon to New London to serve as Dixon's chief second. Thus began a relationship that would endure through the remainder of the century and into the dawn of a new one. David Blanchard peeled away from George Dixon, exploring other interests, but O'Rourke was omnipresent.

Chapter 2

George Dixon's Boston

Looked at from afar, the Commonwealth of Massachusetts, and Boston in particular, was a haven for people of color. Slavery was abolished in Massachusetts in 1781. An 1843 act of the state legislature prohibited the arrest of fugitive slaves. Massachusetts was the first state to admit Black children to previously all-white schools. Boston was the cradle of the abolitionist movement. An African American was appointed to the Boston Police Department in 1878.

However, Blacks in Boston were held back by the same roadblocks that handicapped their brethren in other cities. In antebellum Boston, note the historians James Oliver Horton and Lois E. Horton, "Blacks were restricted by 'Jim Crow' accommodations on public transportation, isolated in schools that were rapidly deteriorating and scholastically inferior, excluded from juries, and seated apart in white churches, lecture halls and places of entertainment.... [Moreover] blacks were not safe in some parts of the city."[1] Conditions improved after the Civil War, but before Dixon's career was finished, there was a general calcification of anti–Black prejudice. Many establishments that previously served people of all races—hotels, restaurants, ice cream and candy stores, etc.—took to turning away Black patronage.[2]

At one time, Black families were clustered on the north slope of Beacon Hill where large homes had been converted into boardinghouses. Many white immigrants fresh off the boat also took shelter there. The first great wave was from Ireland. In 1849 alone, almost 30,000 immigrants arrived in Boston from the British Isles, the overwhelming number of whom were Irish. (After the Cunard Line established a terminus in Boston in 1842, it became cheaper to emigrate to Boston than to New York.) By 1855, there were 50,000 Irish in Boston, almost all natives of the southern and western counties. Thirty years later, the Irish made up over 40 percent of the city's population, outnumbering native-born Yankees.[3]

Anti-Black sentiment among the Irish reached a fever pitch during the Civil War. In July of 1863, New York and to a lesser extent Boston were roiled by bloody riots following the imposition of a draft lottery by President Abraham Lincoln. The rioters were disproportionately Irish, and the civilians that bore the brunt of their rage were overwhelmingly Black. However, things steadily cooled down in Boston as the Irish climbed up the social ladder and came to dominate the political life of the city.

In 1884, Hugh O'Brien, who arrived in Boston with his parents at the age of five, became the first of Boston's many Irish Catholic mayors. He served four one-year terms. In 1895, the Charlesbank Athletic Club, a rival to the Cribb Club, was described as the strongest and most popular professional boxing club in Boston. The members were predominantly men with Irish names, of whom 42 were said to be "prominent members of the city government and other city authorities."[4]

The friction between Black and the Irish residents dissolved inside the sanctuary of a boxing gym, where young men of different races and ethnic groups interacted as equals, and men of color were often looked up to as mentors. For reasons not entirely clear, no city produced as many good Black boxers circa 1890 as did Boston. Boston-bred John L. Sullivan famously drew the color line, but interracial matches were never verboten in Boston as they were in many other places.

George Dixon was never hobbled in securing lucrative matches because of the color of his skin, although it mattered greatly that he was a man of small stature. By contrast, Black boxers who competed in the heavyweight division, such as George Godfrey, were at a disadvantage. Throughout most of his career, Godfrey was referenced as a heavyweight despite rarely weighing more than 170 pounds.

Other Good Black Boxers in Boston in Dixon's Day

George Godfrey

Born on Prince Edward Island, Canada, George Godfrey was 17 years older than George Dixon, but he came to boxing at a relatively late age, and their careers intersected. He fought primarily in Boston where he and his brother James operated a gymnasium and boxing school. George Dixon apprenticed there, so to speak, and the Godfrey brothers worked the corner of several of Dixon's fights as George was coming up the ladder.

Godfrey's signature win came in a fight-to-the-finish on the outskirts of Denver where he halted McHenry Johnson, the "Black Star," in four one-sided rounds in a bout packaged as America's "Colored Heavyweight Championship." This was hardly the first fight to be painted with this imprimatur, but it was the first to be widely accepted as the real McCoy. Godfrey and Johnson had met twice before in Boston in four-round bouts that were called draws.

Godfrey never officially defended that title, but informally lost it when he was stopped in the 19th round by Peter Jackson in San Francisco. The most celebrated of the Black heavyweights during the reign of John L. Sullivan, Jackson was eight years younger than Godfrey and had a 30-pound weight advantage.

Godfrey rebounded by stopping Denver Ed Martin in Hoboken in the 23rd round of a 25-round fight in a three-sided ring; the fourth side was a brick wall. (Martin was very good. He would go on to give the great Jack Johnson a whale of a tussle in a losing effort in a humdinger of a 20-round fight in Los Angeles.) But age was beginning to catch up with Godfrey, who would soon acquire the cognomen "Old Chocolate." Subsequent fights with Jake Kilrain in San Francisco, Joe Choynski at Coney Island, and Peter Maher in Boston, ended with Godfrey knocked out or too exhausted to continue. His match with Kilrain was a fight-to-the-finish that lasted almost three hours.[5]

In retirement Godfrey continued to run his boxing academy while living comfortably in Revere, Massachusetts. His death in 1901 at age 48 was attributed to heart failure and dropsy. He reportedly left a substantial sum of money to his survivors, his wife and six children.

George Byers

Byers, like George Godfrey, was born in Prince Edward

George Godfrey, ca. 1887.

Island. The product of an interracial union, he had his first documented fight in Boston in 1895 and was active through 1904, competing mostly in New England.

An undersized heavyweight even by the standards of his era, akin to Godfrey, Byers had three fights with Chicago's Frank Childs that were billed for the Colored Heavyweight Title. Byers won the first fight, outpointing Childs across 20 rounds in New York. The second meeting, a six-round contest in Chicago, where six rounds was the limit, was ruled a draw. Their final encounter, in Hot Springs, Arkansas, ended with Byers knocked out in the 17th round of a fight slated for 20. But Byers' opponents were primarily Caucasian, including such well-known boxers as Jack Bonner, Tommy West, George Gardner, Jack Root, Mysterious Billy Smith, and, late in his career, Philadelphia Jack O'Brien.

Ed Binney

A coal heaver by trade, Ed Binney, the "Boston Black" (sometimes billed as Edward Phinney or simply Pinney), was born in Washington, D.C., but had his first documented bout at Boston's Cribb Club and 21 of his 27 documented fights in Boston. On November 31, 1891, he claimed the Colored Middleweight Title (a hollow title; like many secondary titles today it was seemingly always vacant and seldom defended) by defeating Harris Martin, who quit on his stool after 25 rounds. This match, contested in San Francisco, was a big upset. Harris was vastly more experienced, and Binney wasn't provided with the funds to bring his own trainer with him.

Binney's last two fights were with Dick O'Brien. Their first meeting, contested in Boston at a weight of 145 pounds, was billed for the New England Middleweight Title. A former world title challenger from Lewiston, Maine, O'Brien packed a hard punch but had a questionable chin. However, Binney, whose effort was lackluster, never reached his chin, and the referee waved the fight off after 14 rounds. Binney retired, but returned two years later to meet O'Brien in an eight-round contest at Bangor, Maine. This bout, Binney's last documented fight, was ruled a draw.

Billy Hill, Muldoon's Pickaninny

Some Black fighters were identified in promotional materials and in newspaper stories only by their ring name (Black Pearl, Black Cyclone,

Black Demon, etc.). This was the lot of many journeymen Black boxers. Billy Hill, whose fighting weight ranged from 115 to 140 pounds, was too good to have his name totally obscured by his nickname, but his name seldom appeared without the words "Muldoon's Pickaninny" attached to it.

Hill was born in Wilmington, North Carolina, and had his earliest pro fights in New York, but he fought out of Boston for most of his career and had more than half of his documented fights in Massachusetts. His most notable win, however, came in London, a 14th-round stoppage of Arthur Callan at the National Sporting Club on a card in November of 1896 that also included California featherweight Solly Smith. Hill promptly claimed the 134-pound world title, which opened a few more doors for him on the vaudeville circuit.

Billy Hill, who honed his act as a street performer in Boston, dancing and performing acrobatic stunts, was quite the showman. "He is one of the cleverest buck dancers in the world, and not to hear him on the mouth organ is a crime," said a letter writer to the *Brooklyn Citizen* who caught Hill's act at a London music hall.[6] Hill never fought at Madison Square Garden, but he appeared there in cake-walking contests where the contestants competed for a cash prize and a medal awarded by the *Police Gazette*. Terry McGovern served as a judge at one of these competitions in which Hill appeared, a Christmas night show at the Garden in 1903.[7]

About that nickname: Muldoon was William Muldoon, the champion Greco-Roman wrestler who conditioned John L. Sullivan for Sullivan's famous 1899 fight with Jake Kilrain. When Muldoon was touring the country, a troupe of young Black boxers served as his warm-up act, a troupe that took the name "Muldoon's Pickaninnies." Legend has it that Billy Hill left his job as an oyster shucker at a Washington, D.C., restaurant to join the ensemble where, besides performing in Battle Royals, he would "take on all comers." (Battle Royals, on the vaudeville circuit, were well-choreographed and thus a form of slapstick comedy.)

"Pickaninny" is derived from the Spanish phrase *pequeno nino*, a little child. It undoubtedly rankled Hill to be saddled with such a demeaning nickname, but he chose to embrace it as he could see that it enhanced his marketability.[8] (Ironically, William Muldoon was openly opposed to interracial matches during his tenure on the New York State Athletic Commission, which lasted from 1921 until his death in 1933.)

Chapter 2. George Dixon's Boston

Professor Andy Watson

BoxRec, the invaluable record-keeping web site, lists Andy Watson's record as 5–21 with 44 draws. This tally suggests that Watson was never more than an Opponent, the term for a journeyman whose value to a promoter lies in the fact that he won't despoil the record of the man he is matched against. But look inside the numbers, and you will find that Watson—Professor Andy Watson, if you please; Watson ran a boxing school in the city's West End—fought a slew of tough guys on even terms in long fights and never failed to go the distance. Eleven of his draws were in fights that lasted 12 rounds, 12 went 15 rounds, and two went 20 rounds.

Born in Georgetown, British Guiana, Andy Watson came to Boston as a sailor in 1890 and had his first fight two years later in Philadelphia where he was sent in against Joe Walcott in a four-round bout underneath a six-round contest between George Dixon and Walter Edgerton, the Kentucky Rosebud. Late in his career, he had six fights with up-and-comer Sam Langford, a fellow Bostonian (via Nova Scotia) who would come to be recognized as one of the all-time greats despite never owning a world title.

During his long career, Sam Langford was largely relegated to fighting on the so-called Chitlin' Circuit where good Black boxers fought other good Black boxers over and over and over again. Andy Watson had one foot in this subculture. He fought globetrotter Bobby Dobbs five times and had six matches with Billy Hill. But Professor Watson also had deep rivalries with several of New England's top Caucasian fighters. He had six matches with Charlie O'Rourke, five with Tim Kearns, and three with Patsy Sweeney. These 14 fights consumed 201 rounds.

In 1903, as his career was winding down, Watson was appointed the coach of Harvard's intramural boxing team. Several of Boston's pro boxers had the job before him.[9]

Joe Walcott

If there were a Mount Rushmore restricted to prizefighters from Boston, Joe Walcott would be there along with George Dixon, Sam Langford, and the larger-than-life John L. Sullivan. Dubbed Barbados Joe Walcott by boxing historians, so as not to confuse him with the future heavyweight champion who borrowed his name, Walcott toiled in the shadow of Dixon, his bosom buddy, but was a great fighter in his own right. He too was managed by Tom O'Rourke, and he will turn up frequently in the pages of this book.

Chapter 3

George Dixon: Champion of Three Continents

Cal McCarthy was the pride of the Scottish-American Athletic Club in Jersey City, an amateur boxing powerhouse where he also excelled as a harrier; i.e., long distance runner. He turned pro in 1888 at age 19 and claimed the Featherweight Championship of America (the bantamweight division wasn't yet established) after defeating Eugene Hornbacher before a handful of aficionados at a private resort at the northernmost tip of Long Island. He was reportedly undefeated in 28 fights when he consented to risk his title against George Dixon. Speculation was that the bout would be held somewhere near the midpoint of New York and Boston, but it ultimately came to fruition at the Hub in a hall over a bank in the far southern part of the city. As a fight-to-the-finish, the February 7, 1890, event was by definition an invitation-only affair.

Contested with two-ounce gloves at 114 pounds, the match was a spirited contest with many twists and turns. It reportedly consumed seventy rounds, lasting four hours and 40 minutes. Long after midnight, the stakes were pulled, and the match was declared a draw by mutual consent.[1]

Barely a month after this fight, negotiations were underway for a match between George Dixon and Birmingham's Edwin "Nunc" Wallace, the British 114-pound champion. The match, with a 30-round limit, came off on June 27, 1890, at London's Pelican Club, England's foremost boxing establishment (a distinction it would soon yield to the National Sporting Club). Dixon finished up his training in England at the country estate of Hugh Cecil Lowther, the 5th Earl of Lonsdale, whose titular name would be memorialized on the belts awarded to British champions, a practice begun in 1909. Tom O'Rourke made many friends while in England and would have many dealings with British sports promoters in the ensuing years.

Chapter 3. George Dixon: Champion of Three Continents

Dixon vs. Wallace was contested in a 24-foot ring with four-ounce gloves. That was an advantage to Dixon as Wallace, two years older than George, had done his best work in bare-knuckle bouts, but the odds were yet tilted in favor of the Englishman.

The fight was one-sided from the opening bell. It ended late in the 19th round when Wallace, who was being pummeled against the ropes, raised his arm in a token of surrender. By then, both of Wallace's eyes were nearly closed shut, and his face was badly bruised. By contrast, Dixon left the ring with hardly a scratch.[2] The match played to a full house with many members of Parliament (including Lord Randolph Churchill, father of Winston) in attendance. The U.S. contingent included *New York Herald* publisher James Gordon Bennett, Jr., who said the "Corinthian gathering ... [was] unparalleled in number and enthusiasm at that swagger resort."[3]

The various weight classes had not yet been standardized. Most reports credited Dixon with winning the world bantamweight title, but some reports denominated him the new featherweight champion. Regardless, with his victory, George Dixon became the first American fighter of the Queensberry era to launch his title reign in England.

Dixon remained in England through the last week of July, giving sparring exhibitions and attending banquets in his honor. His first match upon returning to the United States came against Johnny Murphy in Providence, Rhode Island, on October 23, 1890. A protégé of Jake Kilrain, Murphy had been inactive since fighting Cal McCarthy in March of the previous year. In that contest, he had all the best of it until breaking the ulnar bone in his left forearm in the third frame. He stayed one more round before his corner pulled him out.

Murphy worked with Harvard's intramural boxing team, and many of his students reportedly made the short trek to Providence to wager on him, bringing wads of dough they willingly placed at 5/4 odds. To their dismay, it became evident early on that they had miscalculated. Murphy was a glutton for punishment, and the fight lasted more than two hours before his corner threw in the sponge. When it was over, said a reporter, Murphy was "a pitiable spectacle, blood streaming down his face, and his breath coming in short spasmodic gasps." Dixon had a bruised eye but was otherwise unmarked.[4]

Dixon's first fight with Cal McCarthy, a 70-round marathon with an inconclusive ending, was the sort of mill that begged for a rematch. McCarthy was certainly bullish on it. In their fight, McCarthy had fractured his wrist in the third round when a punch landed awkwardly on Dixon's head, or so it was written.[5]

Dixon–McCarthy II was set for 25 rounds and went to the Puritan Athletic Club, a new organization whose cozy wood-frame amphitheater in Long Island City sat a short walk from the ferry terminal at Hunter's Point across the East River from Manhattan. On February 5, 1891, the day of the battle, the ferry boats leaving 34th Street in the late afternoon were jammed with fight-goers. The passengers, said the *New York Sun*, included members of New York City's swankiest private clubs plus "stock brokers, racing men, gamblers, bookmakers, race-track touts, jockeys, trainers of race horses, owners of race tracks, State officials of New Jersey and New York, and the general sporting riffraff."[6]

The operators of the club had received an assurance from the mayor, Paddy Gleason, that there would be no police interference. But Gleason had enemies, several of whom were prominent members of the Jeffersonian Club, an established club in Long Island City with a more WASPish membership. They succeeded in getting the district attorney to swear out arrest warrants for Dixon and McCarthy, and although no arrests were made, the threat forced the show to be cancelled.[7]

When the police arrived with their warrants, a large crowd of people was huddled outside the entrance. Some stragglers "hung on like grim death hoping against hope that it might be 'fixed up' with the sheriff," said the *Brooklyn Eagle*, and when the doors finally opened, they rushed inside, which served only to temporarily shelter them from the chill on a very cold night.[8]

The ostracized event found a home in Troy, New York, a wealthy industrial city on the Hudson River near Albany, where it materialized on March 31 at the indoor bicycling oval of a bicycle racing club. Three of America's most celebrated bare-knuckle boxers—John Morrissey, John C. Heenan, and Paddy Ryan—had spent their formative years in Troy at a time when the city housed a large community of Irish immigrant navies imported to work on the Erie Canal. However, by the time Dixon and McCarthy fought there, the city was far less woolly. There was considerable opposition to the fight from community leaders.

Several days before the fight, the odds were "even" in New York, but a rumor spread like wildfire that McCarthy hadn't been taking proper care of himself, and there was a surge of Dixon money. The rumor had substance as McCarthy, who purportedly spent 48 hours in a Turkish bath to come in at the required weight, had none of his old steam. In Round 22, McCarthy's corner tossed in the towel, but referee Jere Dunn paid it no heed and waited until the round was over to wave the fight off.[9]

A story about the fight in a Troy paper said that 10 minutes before the fight, the air was so thick with tobacco smoke that one "could almost cut it with an axe," which led referee Dunn to request that all cigars and pipes be extinguished. Sixteen days after the fight, a mass meeting was held in Troy for the purpose of shaming the authorities into preventing any further events of this nature. The upshot was that Dixon and McCarthy were indicted for disturbing the peace. It was a moot point as they were never tried.[10]

Three weeks after disposing of McCarthy, Dixon fought in Chicago. The city of big shoulders, as Carl Sandburg described it in his famous 1914 poem, hadn't yet become a major destination for important boxing matches. As America's passenger rail hub, however, it was a major point-of-departure for prizefights in outlying areas. A case in point was the 1889 fight between Jack McAuliffe and Billy Myer, a world lightweight title defense for McAuliffe. The match was staged in North Judson, Indiana, a little town where several railroad lines converged, but most everyone got there by way of Chicago. The bout, a stalemate that lasted four hours, was co-promoted and refereed by Mike McDonald, Chicago's most notorious gambler-businessman and reputedly the boss of the city's corrupt Democratic machine. The match was allowed to go forward after McDonald greased the skids with the county sheriff and the town marshal.[11]

If Chicago was a beat behind other cities in making the transition to the modern era, that would quickly change as the Windy City had the requisite human infrastructure to become a major factor in this sport. Five men in particular left a big footprint: Charles (Parson) Davies, George Siler, Lou Houseman, Malachy Hogan, and Harry Gilmore.

Charles "Parson" Davies

Parson Davies, homeless in New York after being orphaned at age 13, followed an older brother to Chicago and entered the liquor business. He did so well that he was able to purchase Mike McDonald's poolroom, an establishment the locals called The Store. In his first foray into the world of sports, he managed the affairs of the renowned long-distance race walker Dan O'Leary. Davies was best remembered for his association with boxing's "Black Prince" Peter Jackson, with whom he barnstormed the country in *Uncle Tom's Cabin*, the dramatization of Harriet Beecher Stowe's famous anti-slavery novel with Jackson as the featured performer. He was never far from the boxing scene in the years that straddled the new century, whether arranging tours, establishing athletic clubs in various parts of the country, or networking with managers and promoters in the role of a facilitator. (Davies always dressed in funereal black, which gave him the appearance of a clergyman. His handle, "Parson," was conferred on him by the Prince of Wales, King Edward VII, or by the great shipping magnate Cornelius Vanderbilt, or by the Rev. Henry Ward Beecher. Accounts differ.)

George Siler

George Siler toured the country giving boxing exhibitions before settling in Chicago in the late 1880s where he opened a boxing school. He earned his spurs refereeing fights in places like Roby, Indiana, an untamed hamlet just across the Chicago line and became nationally known when he was tabbed to referee the Corbett–Fitzsimmons fight at Carson City in 1897. He was America's most prominent turn-of-the-century boxing referee, traveling far and wide to officiate important matches, and for a time, he may have been America's most widely read boxing writer. His columns in the *Chicago Tribune* were widely syndicated.

George Siler, ca. 1899.

Lou Houseman

Lou Houseman was the sports editor of the rival *Chicago Inter Ocean*. Like many in his position, he was also a promoter of sporting events and a manager of prizefighters. The *Inter Ocean* had looser standards than the *Tribune*, and whenever Houseman was involved in a prizefight, he laid the hype on thick in his column, "Talk of Boxers." His lasting contribution to boxing was the introduction of the light heavyweight division, the only one of the eight standard weight classes born in the United States. Houseman invented the division for his fighter Jack Root when Root outgrew the middleweight class. Root's 1903 bout in Detroit with Kid McCoy would come to be recognized as the first world light-heavyweight title fight.

Malachy Hogan

Malachy Hogan wasn't as well-known nationally as George Siler because as a referee he had a tighter geographic circumference, never venturing outside the Great Lakes region, and also because his byline appeared in a far less important newspaper, the *Chicago Record-Herald*. But Hogan, busier than Siler in Chicago rings, was an important cog in the city's boxing apparatus. His saloon at 75 South Clark Street in Chicago's loop was a favorite among the sporting crowd and the site of frequent weigh-ins. In common with Parson Davies, Hogan was born in Ireland and came to the United States as a young boy.

Harry Gilmore

Harry Gilmore was recognized as the lightweight champion of Canada before moving to Chicago in 1889, where he established a boxing school in the city's gashouse district, an Irish settlement that became a leading incubator of world-class fistic talent, particularly in the lower weight classes. The greatest of Gilmore's pupils was little Jimmy Barry. Active from 1890 to 1899, Barry won world titles at 105, 108, and 110 pounds and retired undefeated. Barry and many of his stablemates had their first documented bouts at McGurn's, a handball court where Gilmore conducted his classes after his original gym became too small for his needs.

* * *

Several Chicago fighters would figure in George Dixon's life story, but his first Chicago fight, on April 20, 1891, was an all–New England affair. His opponent, Martin Flaherty, hailed from Lowell, Massachusetts, a mill town that would become known for its strong boxing tradition. Held in a National Guard armory, the match was restricted by law to six rounds.

Dixon was superior from the start, but fought at a leisurely pace until suffering a bad cut over his left eye near the end of round five, the result of a head butt. In the next round, he fought with the fury of a wounded animal. The bout had almost run its course when a police lieutenant leaped over the ropes and shouted, "That's enough," denying Flaherty, who was in bad straits, the satisfaction of lasting the distance. The police had everyone involved in the promotion on a short leash as there had been a ring fatality in the building the previous year.

The attendance was estimated at 3,500. The faces of the multitude "resembled a vast checkerboard," said a reporter, "every alternate face being black, for Chicago's colored population was out to do honor to the valiant conqueror of Nunc Wallace and Cal McCarthy."[12] Dixon and Flaherty would meet again five years later.

When George Dixon defeated Wallace, it was a great feather in his cap. It made him the champion of two continents. But there was another continent where boxing was making great headway as a mainstream sport, and that was Australia. The island nation was in some ways comparable to a new sanctioning body seeking parity with the two established "organizations," namely England and the United States. And Australia couldn't be brushed aside as it was producing some of the best boxers in the world, the vast majority products of Larry Foley's academy in Sydney, which circa 1890 had no peer in cranking out world-class fighters.

Fighters from Australia, with very few exceptions, had their first U.S. fights in San Francisco, where they first set foot on U.S. soil, arriving from Sydney on the steamship Alameda. San Francisco was then America's eighth largest city and the third largest west of Pennsylvania, trailing only Chicago and St. Louis. The city was wide open. A vestige of the Gold Rush days, it housed an abnormally high percentage of unmarried men, and the Irish exerted considerable sway over the cultural and political life of the community. In a nutshell, San Francisco had all the ingredients to be a strong fight town.

In San Francisco, the California Athletic Club, the premier athletic club in the city, founded in 1886, was the leading destination for big fights. It was here in May of 1891 where native son James J. Corbett, who had come to the fore in a bare-knuckle fight on a barge with Joe

Chapter 3. George Dixon: Champion of Three Continents

Choynski, had his celebrated fight with Peter Jackson, an immigrant from Sydney (by way of the Virgin Islands), who was on the staff of the CAC as a boxing instructor. Corbett vs. Jackson was a fight-to-the finish (it went 61 rounds, ending in a draw), but under Queensberry rules. The California Athletic Club, the National Sporting Club in London, and Larry Foley's academy in Sydney were the three most influential entities in popularizing the Queensberry rules, which transformed prizefighting by purging, or at least moderating, its most objectionable elements.[13]

Nine weeks after the Corbett–Jackson affair, the California Athletic Club rolled out the welcome mat for George Dixon. He was matched against Abe Willis, recognized as the bantamweight champion of Australia. The skinny on Willis, who was stockier than Dixon, was that he was most adept at in-fighting and, in common with most boxers from Australia, was an excellent body puncher.

The purse for the fight, reportedly $5,000 with $4,250 to the winner, was said to be the highest ever for a bantamweight fight. Assisting Tom O'Rourke in Dixon's corner was John L. Herget, who was better known by his ring name, Young Mitchell. A San Francisco native who had toured Australia with a troupe of boxers and was then billed as the Australian Comet when he returned to the city of his birth, Herget was a middleweight of considerable renown who retired undefeated to pursue business interests but kept his hand in the sport in various capacities. Herget would go on to be elected to the San Francisco Board of Supervisors, the equivalent of a City Council, where he chaired the police committee.

Abe Willis went at Dixon like a tornado, but he wasn't in Dixon's class. George knocked him down with a right to the jaw in the opening round and smashed him to the canvas twice more in the fifth frame. The second knockdown, caused by a left to the jaw, left Willis flat on his back, unconscious. "In his boxing and vigor of execution [Dixon] showed himself a veritable wonder and an artist of the first order," said the ringside correspondent for the *Australian Star*, a Sydney paper.[14]

Unlike their counterparts from the British Isles, boxers from Australia tended to stay in the United States for a considerable time, with many becoming permanent residents. But not Abe Willis, who returned to Australia and was never seen in these parts again. As for George Dixon, by adding the scalp of the Australian champion to his figurative bedpost, where also resided the scalps of the British and American title-holders, he completed the "hat trick." He unified the title, and as the first man of color to become a true world champion, he would be badged—many years after his death—as the Jackie Robinson of his sport.

* * *

Eleven months elapsed before Dixon engaged in his next title fight, but during the interlude, he and his handler Tom O'Rourke raked in steady coin on the vaudeville circuit. The George Dixon Athletic and Specialty Company was no penny-ante operation. There were 30 first-class variety artists in the troupe, said a September 1891 blurb in a Philadelphia paper. In addition to Dixon, the headliner, the bill of fare included sketch comedians, acrobats, a contortionist, a man with a trick dog, and a female song stylist who, it was said, had achieved a large measure of fame in England. When the troupe moved on to Montreal, the opening night of the week-long engagement at the Lyceum saw the theater, the largest auditorium in the city, "packed to the doors with a sweltering mass of humanity."[15]

Dixon's act varied a bit according to the circumstances. He ordinarily sparred with a hired hand, after which he issued a defi to "take on all comers," which meant that he would fight a volunteer from the audience who would receive a certain sum, perhaps $50, if he could last four rounds. The volunteer was sometimes a man with a local reputation seeking to make a bigger name for himself and occasionally a name fighter determined to re-kindle a flagging career, but often the volunteer was a plant.[16]

Legitimate or not, danger lurked. On January 11, 1892, the *Boston Globe* reported that Dixon's hands were in bad shape. "Such work [meeting all comers] will injure the best of a fighters' hands," said the writer.[17]

When Dixon returned to the prize ring, it was to accept the challenge of Fred Johnson, an Englishman who made his mark in amateur tournaments before winning British titles at various weights that stamped him a featherweight. They met at Coney Island on June 27, 1892, in what would be the first of Dixon's five big fights at the seaside resort. It was, however, a bout that occurred 10 weeks later that would get more attention in the history books by virtue of being noosed to a historic event.

The September 7, 1892, heavyweight title fight at the New Orleans Olympic Club between John L. Sullivan and James J. Corbett would come to be seen as the watershed fight that birthed the modern era of boxing. The match was likely witnessed by more sports journalists from more papers and disseminated by a leased Western Union wire to more

Chapter 3. George Dixon: Champion of Three Continents

locations than any sporting event that had come before it. Sullivan–Corbett was the grand finale of a three-fight, three-day pugilistic festival billed as the Carnival of Champions. Dixon's match with Jack Skelly was the middle fight of the festival, sandwiched between Jack McAuliffe's rematch with Billy Myer and the big wind-up on the following evening.

The name Jack Skelly did not resonate beyond New York for the very good reason that his contest with George Dixon represented his pro debut. But as an amateur, he won a slew of metropolitan tournaments, and his work was so impressive that a backer emerged willing to meet Tom O'Rourke's terms, which included a $5,000 side bet at even odds. The bet on Skelly's behalf was posted by William H. Reynolds, an energetic 24-year-old real estate developer who would be one of the co-founders, along with Tammany bigwig "Big Tim" Sullivan, of the Jamaica Racetrack in the New York City borough of Queens.

After the match was signed, Arthur T. Lumley was brought in to supervise Skelly's daily affairs. Lumley was the publisher of the short-lived *New York Illustrated News* and a former editor of the *Police Gazette*. Lumley also had a connection to McAuliffe, the Napoleon of the Prize Ring, who successfully defended his world lightweight title with a 15th-round stoppage of Myer, the Streator (Illinois) Cyclone who had battled him on even terms in their previous encounter. McAuliffe and Jack Skelly were former co-workers in a Brooklyn cooperage.

New Orleans was a city of unimaginable contrasts. A visitor circa 1840 would have been startled to see free people of color "in purple and fine linen [walking past] slaves in rags and chains," to borrow a line from an oft-cited poem by one Colonel Creecy. The city it most closely resembled, despite a stark dissimilarity in race relations, was San Francisco. Both cities were famously decadent, and the top elected officials, by and large, were men of a similar stripe. When the Carnival of Champions came about, the city's mayor was John Fitzpatrick. This was the same John Fitzpatrick who had refereed the bare-knuckle fight between John L. Sullivan and Jake Kilrain, a match staged on the estate of a lumber baron in a hamlet on the outskirts of Hattiesburg, Mississippi. Sullivan and Kilrain fought with a bounty on their heads, the governor of Mississippi offering a $1,500 reward for their capture if they flouted the state's anti-prizefighting law. The master of ceremonies for the fights at the Olympic Club was former New Orleans mayor Joseph Guillotte.

Tom O'Rourke was reportedly skittish about taking George Dixon to New Orleans, worried that a Black man wouldn't get a square deal in the Crescent City. But if he could get his fighter to the arena unscathed, it was a low-risk, high-reward opportunity. A survey of 102 fistic experts (mostly active and retired prizefighters, sportswriters, ring officials, and bookmakers) found an 89–13 skew in favor of Dixon with 26 of the respondents forecasting that he would stop Skelly inside 10 rounds, and the odds were concordant.[18] Besides, O'Rourke would be going there with or without Dixon. A fight as big as Sullivan vs. Corbett had the trappings of a national convention or industrial trade show in that it was a gathering of fellow travelers in an environment conducive to forging business deals. The bigger the fight, the bigger the powwow.

The line between amateur and professional was muddled. Jack Skelly's signature win was a 10th-round stoppage of a man named McTiernan. Because no money ostensibly changed hands—Skelly's reward was a gold watch—it did not peel away his amateur status. He incurred only one loss before being thrust against Dixon, that coming in a bout with Johnny Gorman at a Brooklyn roller rink. According to a report in the *Brooklyn Eagle*, Skelly hammered Gorman around the ring in the final round, and the spectators were aghast when the referee's decision went against him.[19]

George Dixon arrived in New Orleans on August 11, three weeks before the fight, for "meet and greets" with civic leaders and newspaper writers. When he arrived at the train depot, there were reportedly 1,600 members of the city's Black community on hand to cheer his arrival. With first-class hotels off-limits to men of his race, the Olympic Club had arranged for him to stay in the home of J. Madison Vance. A force in politics—he spoke at the 1896 and 1900 National Republican Conventions, seconding the nomination of William McKinley—Vance was the city's most prominent Black attorney.[20]

Dixon trained for the fight in Biloxi, Mississippi, a seaside community where the topography mirrored Coney Island and where many wealthy New Orleanians kept summer homes. In Biloxi, Dixon was purportedly visited by hundreds of admirers every day who stood around for hours watching him exercise. Jack Skelly shared training quarters with McAuliffe in nearby Bay St. Louis.

The Olympic Club was founded in 1893 by a group of young professionals. It was situated on Royal Street just east of the French Quarter in the neighborhood known as Faubourg Washington and now called Bywater. The four-story clubhouse housed a natatorium, a shooting range, a bowling alley, and other accoutrements. There were more than a thousand books in the library, which received daily newspapers from major cities across the country.[21]

Chapter 3. George Dixon: Champion of Three Continents

For the Dixon–Skelly fight, the club set aside a separate section in the balcony for Black attendees, 700 seats in all, roughly 15 percent of the arena's capacity. Those remanded there reportedly filed in meekly as two white policemen stood guard over them. But they did not bridle their enthusiasm as Dixon put on another masterful performance. The fight, contested at 118 pounds with five-ounce gloves, was one-sided from the opening gong. It ended in the eighth round when Dixon put Skelly down for the 10-count with a blistering combination. The punches landed so fast that it was impossible to determine which one was the knockout blow. During the bout, said a florid ringside scribe, Skelly's nose "swelled as big as a corncob" and he developed a welt over his eye "the size of a California egg plum."[22]

The directors of the Olympic Club took a lot of heat for allowing an interracial match to be staged on their premises, and the manner in which the bout played out heightened the opprobrium. The upshot was an informal ban on interracial boxing matches in Louisiana that was codified into law in 1956 (and overturned by the U.S. Supreme Court three years later). Jack Skelly continued his pro career with mixed success. In retirement he worked as a sportswriter for a paper in Yonkers, New York; managed and trained former heavyweight champion Jess Willard; worked hundreds of fights as a referee; and served on the New York State Athletic Commission. George Dixon's career hadn't yet reached the halfway point, but his travels would never again take him into the Deep South.[23]

Chapter 4

Coney Island: Sodom by the Sea

Coney Island, a formerly barren stretch of marshland separated from the main body of Brooklyn by a narrow inlet, evolved in the 1880s into America's most famous seaside resort. The thrill rides in the amusement park gave Coney Island its postcard physiognomy, but for many visitors the attraction was a walk on the wild side. "In the main," said a travel writer for the *San Francisco Chronicle* in 1883, "vice is the ruling spirit there."[1]

Three racetracks emerged in Coney Island between 1879 and 1886, and on the biggest days of the summer racing season, the resort was flooded with horseplayers. One of these tracks was built in the area called Gravesend, which was the most notorious section of the island. It was the headquarters of John Y. McKane, a building contractor who dominated the economic life of the area by virtue of holding a variety of elected positions simultaneously, including chief of police and town supervisor, the latter of which gave him the authority to approve or disapprove applications for building permits. McKane, born in Ireland, was a mass of contradictions. He allowed prostitution and gambling to thrive but was also the superintendent of the Sunday School at the Sheepshead Bay Methodist Church and the lead tenor of its choir. McKane was able to consolidate his power so effectively because until May of 1894, when it was annexed by Brooklyn, Coney Island was a self-governing township, a law unto itself.

McKane was related by marriage to Paul Bauer, who owned a hotel and adjacent concert hall in the district called West Brighton. When Bauer entered a sanitarium in 1887, McKane took over his business affairs. In 1892, he leased the concert hall to the Coney Island Athletic Club, an organization formed by a consortium of Brooklyn politicians for the primary purpose of prizefighting.[2]

The Coney Island Athletic Club was incorporated on March 3, 1892.

Chapter 4. Coney Island: Sodom by the Sea

The club's first boxing event was held in May of that year. Billy Plimmer opposed Tommy Kelly, the Harlem Spider, in a fight-to-the-finish with four-ounce gloves. Plimmer, from Birmingham, England, strengthened his claim to the world bantamweight title with a 10th-round stoppage. The Spider was knocked down five times in all and was covered with blood when the bout was halted.[3]

Another Englishman, Fred Johnson, was in the opposite corner when George Dixon appeared before the Coney Island Athletic Club on Monday, June 27, 1892. When the match was signed, the agreed-upon date was Saturday, June 18, when the fight would have ridden the coattails of the Suburban Handicap at Sheepshead Bay, one of the biggest events of the Coney Island racing season. However, Tom O'Rourke had second thoughts, worrying that the fight would extend past midnight into a Sunday, which would have increased the odds of police interference, and he succeeded in getting the date pushed back.[4]

A 26-year-old Londoner, Johnson had claimed the nine-stone championship of England the previous year, defeating one James "Jumper" Howe, who was well-beaten when his seconds entered the ring in the 10th round, forcing a disqualification. In England, he was best known for his rivalry with Bill Baxter, whom he had fought at least 10 times, mostly in quasi-amateur tournaments. "If faithful training and hard work count for anything," said a story in a Buffalo paper, "Fred Johnson, the featherweight pugilist of England should be in excellent form.... A more conscientious and earnest worker has seldom or never been seen."[5] That was hardly a ringing endorsement.

When Johnson arrived in New York on May 18, a reporter on the reception committee offered this description: "He stands 5 feet 4 inches tall, has a strong neck, firmly set jaw, handsome teeth and good legs.... He is of dark complexion and his features suggest the Hebrew." The muscular development of his shoulders, noted the reporter, was a concern as it "may make him a little bound up in movement."[6]

Johnson's seconds brought a large number of white towels with them that they strung across the top strand of rope in his corner. It looked as if the family washing had been set out to dry. As for the fight, it was a virtual walkover for the Bostonian. The defensive-minded Englishman lasted into the 14th round, when Dixon knocked him out with a straight right to the jaw. The force of the blow caused Dixon to land on top of Johnson as he fell, with the result that Johnson hit his head hard on the platform. It was a typical Coney Island crowd, said the *Brooklyn Daily Eagle*, with the $5 seats filled with "bartenders, waiters, shouters, and fakirs" and the $10 seats thick with politicians and race track men. John L. Sullivan and James J. Corbett, who would shortly begin preparations for their showdown in New Orleans, were in attendance, John L. "having imbibed a moderate amount of enthusiasm."[7]

Dixon's next bout at Coney Island, which followed his match with Jack Skelly (discussed in the previous chapter) and a lengthy vaudeville tour, came against George Siddons on March 20, 1893. Siddons' claim to fame was his two marathon fights with George "Kid" Lavigne, the first held in a barn on the outskirts of Saginaw, Michigan, Lavigne's hometown, and the second, eight weeks later, at a roadhouse in nearby Grand Rapids. The first meeting reportedly lasted five hours and eight minutes, the longest prizefight to date, and the second went 55 rounds before it was stopped by the police.

Tom O'Rourke accepted this bout for Dixon with three days notice after Siddons' original opponent, Jack Skelly, took ill with what was suspected to be malaria. Dixon was then finishing an engagement at Miner's Eighth Avenue Theater, an iconic burlesque house in New York's notorious Bowery, and O'Rourke did not regard Siddons as an opponent for whom Dixon needed a conventional training camp. The bout was scheduled for 12 rounds with an agreement that the match would be scored a draw if Siddons was still standing at the final bell.

Siddons fought a survivors' fight, constantly on the retreat, and the contest proved to be a stinker. The only round that was fairly entertaining was the 12th, but by then half the crowd had left. After the bout, Siddons expressed interest in a rematch. "In the event of such a battle," said a correspondent for the *Boston Globe*, "spectators would do well to bring their lunches and their hammocks with them."[8]

Twelve days after this match, on April 1, 1893, Dixon was presented with the *Police Gazette* world featherweight championship belt during a ceremony at Miner's theater. He continued to work the theater circuit until August, when he returned to Coney Island and regained whatever luster he had lost in the Siddons fight with a smashing third round knockout of Eddie Pierce.

Pierce, like Jack Skelly before him, was a Brooklyn man who had made his mark as an amateur. As a pro, he had fought only twice, knocking out his first opponent before going 42 rounds to a draw with George Siddons. He had developed a strong local following in the amateur ranks, which portended a good turnout despite his flimsy credentials at the professional level.

The fight was barely a minute old when it became apparent, much

Chapter 4. Coney Island: Sodom by the Sea

to the chagrin of the paying customers, that Eddie Pierce was out of his league. Dixon ramped up his attack in the third, raining blows on his overmatched opponent with lightning speed. Pierce had his hands at his side, too dazed to protect himself, when Dixon ended the contest with a sweeping right hand to the jaw that "toppled Pierce like a ten pen, completely knocked out." According to a correspondent for the *Milwaukee Daily Sentinel*, Pierce, who received a thunderous ovation when he entered the ring, was out for nearly 10 minutes before he regained his faculties.[9]

After back-to-back cakewalks, Dixon was likely overconfident when he took on Billy Plimmer 15 days later in a four-round match at Madison Square Garden. The Dixon–Plimmer contest was the featured attraction of a six-bout card that drew a turn-away crowd to the ornate entertainment palace that had opened three years earlier, replacing the first Madison Square Garden, which had no roof. The referee for Dixon–Plimmer was Steve O'Donnell, a 27-year-old boxer from Australia who would go on to fight some of the top heavyweights of his era.

Underestimating Plimmer would prove costly. He posed a far greater threat than the other Englishmen that Dixon had fought, namely Nunc Wallace and Fred Johnson. In his last appearance in a New York ring, Plimmer beat Joe McGrath to a pulp in eight one-sided rounds before the Coney Island Athletic Club. McGrath, a Dubliner billed as the 110-pound champion of Ireland, had his face "literally pounded into a jelly."[10]

In a fight without a dull moment, Plimmer, much to everyone's surprise, actually out-quicked Dixon. Referee O'Donnell awarded the bout to him, a popular decision as the crowd was solidly in Plimmer's corner. But not everyone agreed with the ref's verdict. There were a few dissenters among the ringside press.[11]

Heading into this match, Dixon had suffered only one loss. That came very early in his career in Boston against a man named George Wright. In that bout, Dixon was disqualified after only two rounds for hitting Wright after the bell. According to the *Boston Globe*, Wright had the look of man who wanted to quit before the infraction occurred. He left the ring before the start of round three and had to be summoned back to have his hand raised.[12] It was a fluke loss. The same could not be said of his setback to Billy Plimmer, but the fact that it came in a four-round fight lightened the blemish.

Inevitably, there was talk that Dixon may have peaked. He was only 23 years old, but he already had a lot of mileage on him. Prior to his bout with Eddie Pierce, it was written that he had fought "all comers" in 450 fights on vaudeville tours. But it was far too early to write off the gladiator that a few writers were now calling Little Chocolate, a nickname that would achieve wide currency and stick to him into eternity.

Solly Smith, Dixon's next opponent, was born in Los Angeles, where he had his early fights and won recognition as the West Coast featherweight champion. He went on to claim the world featherweight title with a fourth-round stoppage of Johnny Griffin in Roby, Indiana, a town just over the Illinois line (it would be annexed by Hammond) that was the playground of gamblers who had been run out of Chicago. Smith's claim was specious—George Dixon had a far more legitimate claim to that title—but with no over-arching government body, promoters were free to package any event as a title fight, a situation not much different than what prevails today.

Solly Smith, half–Irish and half–Mexican, wasn't a bona fide title-holder, not yet anyway, but he was a rough customer who wasn't opposed to bending the rules to come out on top. With broad shoulders and muscular arms, he looked more like a middleweight than a featherweight. The pre-fight hype was greater than for any of George Dixon's previous fights. "Smith," said the *Brooklyn Eagle*, "is accounted the strongest lad of his weight and inches that ever stepped over a rope."[13]

It rained hard on the day of the fight, September 25, 1893, depressing attendance, but the turnout was the largest in the brief history of the Coney Island Athletic Club. Attendants with large palm leaves whisked the blue cigar smoke up to the rafters as best they could, and the betting, with Dixon the favorite, was feverish. "Nearly every one who

Solly Smith, ca. 1897.

Chapter 4. Coney Island: Sodom by the Sea

claims to be a genuine sport was there ... [from] the heavy bettors and bookmakers, down to the mixed-ale scrappers and tinhorn gamblers of the Bowery. Then, too, were bankers, brokers, lawyers, doctors and merchants ranged around the roped platform; every one of them with a strange glitter in his eyes that betokened a lingering, longing hope that blood might be spilled and slugology exhibited to its fullest degree," wrote the reporter for the *New York Sun*.[14]

Both fighters came out blazing; the "slugology" was intense. Smith was knocked down three times in the third stanza when Dixon had him almost out, but the Californian fought his way back into the fight and battled Dixon on even terms in round six. The next round, however, proved his undoing. Dixon battered him to the canvas twice more, and Smith was in no condition to continue when the referee waved the fight off with a mere 18 seconds remaining in the round. But Smith certainly got in his licks before Little Chocolate broke him down. At the conclusion, Dixon's left eye was closed, he was bleeding from the mouth, and his nose "resembled a piece of raw beef."[15]

* * *

Coney Island wasn't legally part of Brooklyn until 1894, but it was Brooklyn's next-door-neighbor, and that put it in the crosshairs of those that were discomfited by its unsavory reputation. The sea gave Brooklyn its tone, but nationally its image was shaped by its informal motto as the City of Churches, a badge that was a source of pride for many of the locals.

Brooklyn was home to Henry Ward Beecher, America's first great celebrity preacher; his sermons ran in dozens of major newspapers and, when bundled into anthologies, out-sold popular fiction. A spellbinding orator, Beecher served as the pastor of Brooklyn's Plymouth Congregational Church from 1847 until his death in 1887. Thomas De Witt Talmage, who arrived in Brooklyn somewhat later than Beecher, became almost as well-known. During his tenure at Brooklyn's Central Presbyterian Church, Talmage became a nationally known reformer, a thorn in the hide of professional gamblers, racetrack owners, prizefight promoters, and other "purveyors of vice."

The row between the reform element and Coney Island prizefight organizers reached a fever pitch in the fall of 1893 when the *New York Times* marshaled the clergy to serve as the wedge in a crusade to prevent the fight between James J. Corbett and Charlie Mitchell from taking place at Coney Island. Corbett would be making the first defense of the world heavyweight title he won from John L. Sullivan. The *Times* then took a keen interest in goings-on in Brooklyn, where several members of upper management kept homes.

Mitchell, a brassy 31-year-old Englishman of Irish ancestry who had toured extensively in the United States, developing a following on both sides of the pond, returned to the U.S. on September 20, 1893, to finalize arrangements. Three days later, at the elegant Hoffman House on Broadway, the favorite rendezvous of Tammany chieftains and of Democratic politicians from out-of-state in New York for business or pleasure, he affixed his signature to the Articles of Agreement. It specified that he would meet Corbett, who was out of town and would sign several days later, on or about December 18 at the Coney Island Athletic Club in a "scientific contest for points" (standard verbiage) to be contested "over 20 rounds or more." The club was represented by its matchmaker, R.V. Newton, whose day job was that of a justice of the peace.

The *Times* launched its crusade the very next day in a front-page story, beginning with a broadside against Newton: "At Coney he is understood to have studied law for an undefined period in somebody's office, but the record of his practice, except at one kind of bar, seems to have been lost or mislaid. Prior to the organization of the Coney Island Athletic Club, he was interested in the ownership and backing of race horses."[16]

The Brooklyn clergymen embraced the crusade with great enthusiasm. A representative sample:

> The Rev. Dr. George Van Alstyne, pastor of the Sands Memorial Methodist Episcopal Church—"Is there anything more disgraceful, or that more fully sets at defiance every humane and Christian sentiment and feeling than a cold-blooded prize fight? If there is, I have not yet discovered it.... Shame on our morals, our Christianity, our laws, our chosen guardians of the peace and well-being of society, that a prize fight should be tolerated anywhere in the Nation, much less that it should be countenanced within ten miles of Brooklyn, the 'city of Churches.'"[17]
>
> The Rev. R.R. Meredith, D.D., pastor of the Tompkins Avenue Congregational Church—"This proposed international fight at Coney Island is an outrage without precedent, and should not be allowed. When I heard of these things taking place in New Orleans, I did not think much of it, as I considered it only another evidence of the moral decay in Louisiana. But I never dreamed that the scoundrels would bring their brutal pastime [here]."[18]
>
> The Rev. Nathan Hubbell, D.D., pastor of the Wesley Methodist Episcopal Church—"Picture to yourself those men standing there covered with blood,

Chapter 4. Coney Island: Sodom by the Sea

pounding each other, surrounded in the meanwhile by thousands of thieves, thugs, dishonest and criminal officials, gamblers, perhaps murderers ... while thousands of voices, laden with the odor of gin and reeking with profane utterances, urge them to give each other a 'knock out' blow."[19]

On October 18, the *Times* published excerpts from 18 anti-prizefighting sermons delivered by Brooklyn clergymen over the previous three Sundays. The Rev. Dr. Lyman Abbott, who had succeeded Henry Ward Beecher at Plymouth Church, could have been speaking for the consortium when he expressed this sentiment: "If we are going to permit these things right in the shadow of our homes, with the aid and connivance of public officials, let us bring over here the bull fights of Spain; the brutal sports of the Middle and Dark ages; the gladiatorial contests of pagan times and everything that bestiality and brutishness can suggest."[20]

Much of the paper's vitriol was directed at John Courtney.

Formerly the head of Brooklyn's volunteer fire department and now the sheriff of King's County, Courtney not only countenanced the fights sponsored by the Coney Island Athletic Club, but he acknowledged that he brought his two young boys along with him to watch the fights that were held there. They attended the Dixon–Smith slugfest, and Courtney acknowledged his sons would be going to see Corbett vs. Mitchell as well.[21]

Courtney was beholden to Hugh McLaughlin, the informal boss of Brooklyn's Democratic machine. (The two families were close; one of Courtney's sons married one of McLaughlin's daughters.) McLaughlin blundered when he defended the proposed Corbett–Mitchell fight by saying it would be no more brutal than the sparring matches at the YMCA. That was throwing coals on the fire, provoking the organization into petitioning the governor to stop the fight in a letter-writing campaign that drew thousands of signatures. The *Times* published McLaughlin's rationalization under the headline "Mc'Laughlin's Base Calumny."[22]

The *New York Times* and its allies would win this battle. The directors of the Coney Island Athletic Club gave up in the face of these broadsides and pulled the plug. When Corbett vs. Mitchell came to fruition, it was in a ring pitched on a sand dune on a beach in Jacksonville, Florida, where local organizers successfully pulled it off in the face of strenuous opposition from state legislators in conservative Tallahassee. Looking back, former *Times* city editor William H. Muldoon (no relation to the famous conditioner of the same name) considered it a great victory for righteousness: "[The fight] would have drawn to Coney Island the scum of Manhattan and resulted in an exhibition of brutality likely to prove demoralizing to the youth of Brooklyn."[23]

The paper's high moral tone did nothing to enhance circulation. The *New York Times* was bleeding money when it was sold to Adolph Ochs in 1896. (Ochs' heirs continue to run the paper today.) Moreover, it was a short-lived triumph although it did have the effect of ending fights-to-a-finish at New York's licensed athletic clubs. The Coney Island Athletic Club ceased operations, but within two years of losing the Corbett–Mitchell fight, a new club, the Seaside Athletic Club, was staging fights inside the same building, overcoming the opposition of Brooklyn's new mayor, Charles Schieren, who was shackled by a decision handed down by the State Supreme Court.

The first Seaside Athletic Club show, staged on August 1, 1894, pitted Eddie Pierce against Mike Leonard in a 10-round featherweight bout. That was a soft opening, an appetizer, as it were, for a more compelling match 26 days later, a contest between Jack McAuliffe and Young Griffo, the latter of whom would figure prominently in the pugilistic career of George Dixon.

Chapter 5

Young Griffo and the Kentucky Rosebud

In Manhattan's Tenderloin, which had a high concentration of Black residents and where nearly every saloon had a sports ticker, news of George Dixon's victory over Solly Smith inspired scenes of jubilation. In a block on West Thirtieth Street inhabited almost completely by Blacks, men whooped it up in the street amidst shouts of "Dixon! Dixon!" and tenement dwellers opened their windows to add their voices to the cacophony.[1]

Dixon the boxer was famous, but not much was known about Dixon the man, beyond the fact that he was unassuming, a code word for "not uppity." A syndicated story that ran in dozens of papers in March and April of 1894 was the first fleshing out of him in the white press. The story confirmed the scuttlebutt that Dixon was married to a white woman and portrayed him as a man with a mellow disposition and a scholarly bent. Of his spouse, known as Kitty, it was said, "She is not only a dutiful wife, but she is also intelligent and thrifty, and it is to her shrewdness and craftiness that this well-to-do prizefighter is indebted for their snug little fortune." Dixon's home in Malden, Massachusetts, was filled with "rare works of art and bric-a-brac, and books of which he is very fond. For Dixon is not illiterate, as many suppose. On the contrary, he is possessed of a large amount of intelligence, and is very fond of reading. His favorite author is Charles Dickens, whom he regards as a genius. With his book and his cigar, he whiles away his time when he is not training."[2]

Nine days after this puff piece appeared, Dixon appeared at a benefit show in Philadelphia's Industrial Hall. The March 22, 1894, event, with boxing and wrestling exhibitions interspersed with band music and political speeches, was held to raise money for the textile workers mired in a protracted strike against the bosses of the city's Kensington mills, the world's leading producer of carpets and rugs. Dixon was matched against a local man, 41-year-old Walter Edgerton, who was known as the Kentucky Rosebud. Edgerton was identified as the champion of Lombard Street, tantamount to identifying him as the best Black fighter in Philadelphia. (The eastern end of Lombard Street, the city's main east-west thoroughfare, intersected one of the oldest free Black neighborhoods in the U.S.). He and Dixon were meeting for the fifth time. Their previous meetings were in four-round exhibitions held on Philadelphia vaudeville stages.

Near the end of the second round, the Kentucky Rosebud knocked Dixon unconscious with a right-hand swing to the jaw. Dixon didn't open his eyes for two minutes, and approximately five minutes elapsed before he came to his senses. He then pleased the crowd by fighting another round.[3]

Tom O'Rourke didn't appear too steamed-up by this turn of events. Dixon had caught a cold in Boston and was running a fever when he arrived in Philadelphia. According to O'Rourke, he had taken a large quantity of quinine before he entered the ring, and this made him dizzy. O'Rourke further asserted that Dixon had the Kentucky Rosebud groggy at the conclusion of the tussle, an assertion that the Rosebud vigorously denied.[4]

Edgerton attempted to parlay his fluke knockout of Dixon into a lucrative rematch. Arrangements were made for a 20-round contest at Boston on June 29, 1894. Edgerton's backer established a training camp for him in Atlantic City, but then Edgerton inexplicably backed out of the fight. Tom O'Rourke had reserved a large entertainment hall and didn't want to lose the date. Young Griffo was available and O'Rourke plugged him in.

Although he was a notorious barfly, Griffo posed a far greater threat than the Kentucky Rosebud.

Among the many top-shelf boxers minted at Larry Foley's academy, only Peter Jackson, the heavyweight, arrived in the U.S. more highly-touted than Albert Griffiths, the fighter who bore the ring name Young Griffo. It would be written of Griffo that his hand-eye coordination was such that he could catch a fly between his thumb and forefinger and release it unharmed. He bobbed and weaved so adroitly that it was near-impossible to hit him above the neck even when he was standing still. Griffo was Willie Pep before there was Willie Pep, with the added facet of a more unsparing mean streak. A favorite tactic was to rub the heel of his glove across an opponent's face as he was coming out of a clinch.

Chapter 5. Young Griffo and the Kentucky Rosebud

Griffo arrived in San Francisco on June 8, 1893, and immediately lit out for Chicago. There was a lot going on in the Windy City, which was teeming with visitors to the World's Fair. In Chicago, where he had his first six U.S. fights, Griffo was tossed right into the deep end of the pool, pitched against such top-tier glove men as Solly Smith, Johnny Van Heest, and Kid Lavigne. He never lost, but all of these fights were scored as draws as was customary in Cook County when both men were standing at the final bell.

Dixon vs. Griffo was a homecoming fight for Dixon. Aside from a few vaudeville engagements, he hadn't appeared in Boston in more than four years, and his last fight in the Hub (against Cal McCarthy) was a private affair. Dixon–Griffo was a sellout with an estimated 5,000 fans shoe-horned into the auditorium and thousands more stranded outside. Some managed to break through a side door and see the fight without paying, but attendants quickly sealed the passageway.

Dixon's fight with Solly Smith had been a vicious affair; a Pier-6 donnybrook as writers of a later generation might have described it. The Dixon–Griffo fight took a different tack. "It was a contest that was marked by marvelous cleverness on both sides and was wholly devoid of brutality and slugging," said the writer for the *Boston Globe*. Dixon was the aggressor and threw many more punches, but few of those punches landed cleanly, and the referee declared the match a draw as he was obligated to do unless the bout was conspicuously one-sided.[5]

Dixon and Griffo renewed acquaintances seven months later before the Seaside Athletic Club. The big concert hall was now controlled by the estate of Coney Island "czar" John Y. McKane, who now resided in Sing Sing, having been sentenced to six years at hard labor for a laundry list of offenses that pushed the envelope too far when his goons assaulted investigators sent to Coney Island to look into fraudulent election returns. Griffo had fought there recently, a 10-round engagement with Jack McAuliffe, who was deemed the winner, a verdict widely derided as a bum decision by a referee who lacked the courage to vote against the hometown fighter and thereby smudge his unblemished record.

A month prior to the rematch, there was an ugly incident at Philadelphia's Lyceum Theater where Dixon was appearing with his vaudeville troupe. Griffo jumped on the stage and hot words were exchanged. After the show, Griffo and Tom O'Rourke had a row at a nearby saloon. According to the *Washington Times*, Griffo told O'Rourke that he was "only fit to manage niggers anyhow, whereupon the Australian was

Clash of the Little Giants

An artist's rendition of the January 19, 1895, fight between George Dixon and Young Griffo at the Seaside Athletic Club, Coney Island.

staggered by a vigorous blow in the face." Mutual friends interceded to stop the fracas from escalating into a full-blown brawl.[6]

Dixon–Griffo II, on January 19, 1895, was a near-replica of their first meeting with the exception that it went five rounds longer. At the end of the contest, ruled a draw, Dixon had a few marks but Griffo hardly a scratch. Tom O'Rourke reputedly bet heavy on Dixon with betting commissioners in Chicago and elsewhere, fueling talk that the fix was in. To the contrary, said the *Philadelphia Times*, the fight "was not only as square as a die, but also the grandest exhibition of fistic skill, perhaps, ever seen in America."[7]

The two Dixon–Griffo fights were fought at catch-weight. Dixon's featherweight title wasn't at risk. The weights for the second meeting were announced at 126 for Dixon and 129 for Griffo, but the Australian, who had the thicker torso, looked much heavier.

Dixon–Griffo II would be the last of George Dixon's five fights at Coney Island. A bout on May 27, 1895, between welterweight title claimants Tommy Ryan and Mysterious Billy Smith, raised such a stink that the Seaside Athletic Club, under threat of impeachment, chose not to renew its lease. (The police stopped the fight in the 11th round with Ryan out on his feet, but then after a recess of roughly two-and-a-half minutes, allowed the match to continue. Ryan regained his senses and gained the upper hand, and Smith was in a helpless condition when the police intervened again and this time for keeps in Round 18. The referee called it a draw, but that hardly appeased the Smith contingent. "It was as cold-blooded a piece of business as I ever saw," said influential Boston scribe Ben "Rob Roy" Benton.)[8]

* * *

Dixon and Young Griffo would meet up again before the year was out, but not before Dixon had two more fights in Boston.

His July 31, 1895, match with Tommy Connolly, a local man, was a farce. The inexperienced Connolly was knocked down in the fourth round by a phantom punch and disqualified when his second entered the ring as the referee was completing his count. His match four weeks later with Johnny Griffin was a more attractive pairing. Griffin, known as the Braintree Lad in reference to the Boston-area city of his birth, surprised the "knowing ones" by lasting the full 25 rounds. Three days before the fight, Dixon suffered a severe attack of the cramps, and O'Rourke came close to calling the fight off.[9]

The final chapter of the Dixon–Griffo trilogy played out at the New Manhattan Athletic Club, a new organization whose palatial abode at Forty-Fifth Street and Madison Avenue was the most impressive of any athletic club in the city. It was a 10-round fight that went the distance and thereby ended in a draw as the terms of engagement prohibited the referee from naming a winner if both were still standing at the final bell. He would have likely called it a draw regardless. Although Griffo was hog fat—a reporter guessed that he was the heavier man by 25 pounds—he had enough stamina to make a good showing in a 10-round fight. "It was a marvelous exhibition of skill and science," said the correspondent for the *San Francisco Call*. "Dixon was the harder hitter but the Australian's marvelous guard more than equalized matters."[10]

Dixon offered to go another five rounds if the referee would consent to name a winner, but Griffo's handlers nixed the idea.[11]

Chapter 6

Eastern Precincts and a Wild Goose Chase

Five-and-a-half weeks after his final match with Young Griffo, Dixon was back at the New Manhattan AC for a 10-round match with Frank Erne. They met on December 5, 1895. They were originally scheduled to fight in June of that year for the Seaside Athletic Club, but that date was lost when the club was dissolved.

Born in Switzerland, Erne had grown up in Buffalo. Not quite 21 years old, he hadn't yet matured into a major talent, but his two most recent fights—back-to-back knockouts of Jack Skelly—served notice that he bore watching. Both encounters were lively back-and-forth skirmishes until Erne turned out the lights, leaving Skelly splattered on the canvas.

The only betting was on whether Erne would last the distance and those betting "will not go" laid odds of 3 and 4 to 1. But Erne wildly exceeded expectations, and the fight was ruled a draw, a decision that met with general satisfaction although the Buffalo contingent felt cheated.[1]

Dixon's next assignment found him back at Madison Square Garden. Twenty-nine months had elapsed since his lone previous appearance at "The Garden" where Billy Plimmer sullied his record. Another Englishman, Thomas "Pedlar" Palmer, would test Dixon on this occasion in a six-round contest, the featured attraction of a nine-bout card.

Pedlar Palmer grew up in a circus family. He reportedly first laced on the gloves at the age of five to join his brother in a novelty act. He had his first documented pro fight at the age of 15 and had nine fights at the National Sporting Club while still in his teens. He won the British 102-pound title with a 17th-round stoppage of Walter Croot and claimed the world 112-pound title with a 14th-round stoppage of the aforementioned Plimmer, a triumph that became his calling card when he set forth from London to introduce himself to U.S. boxing enthusiasts. He

Chapter 6. Eastern Precincts and a Wild Goose Chase

was 20 years old and looked younger, but his ring IQ was said to be off the charts. The nickname that he would acquire, "Box o' Tricks," captured his canniness.

Dixon had trouble landing a punch on Palmer during the first three rounds, but he came on strong in the last three and was the fresher man at the finish. The verdict was a draw, a decision widely accepted as fair. Palmer, who had been in the U.S. less than a week, would return to England the very next day but would return in 1899 for a fight of far greater magnitude.

Within a few days of this fight, Dixon, O'Rourke, and Joe Walcott were off to El Paso, where Dixon was booked to fight veteran Jerry Marshall, a Black Australian, during Dan Stuart's Grand Fistic Carnival, an event originally conceived as a five-day affair in Dallas culminating in a world heavyweight title fight between James J. Corbett and Bob Fitzsimmons.

Stuart, a big gambler with investments in poolrooms (horse betting parlors) and in racetrack bookmaking—he was half-owner of the so-called Big Store at Saratoga—underestimated the clout of the Dallas Ministerial Association. Bit by bit, his grand spectacle unraveled, and what he was left with after Corbett bailed out was a fight between Fitzsimmons and Peter Maher that played out before a few dozen paid customers on a patch of ground on the Mexican side of the Rio Grande across from the lonely little town of Langtry, Texas, a fueling stop for the Southern Pacific Railroad. All of the supporting bouts were canceled. For Team Dixon, the trip to El Paso was a wild goose chase.

Pedlar Palmer, England's "Box-o-Tricks," shown here in 1899.

The aborted fight found a home in Boston.

On March 17, 1896, Dixon "simply chopped Marshall to pieces," making him quit after seven rounds of a bout slated for 15. The Australian came in at 126, three pounds above the agreed-upon weight, and would claim that he boiled off nine pounds in a Turkish bath to reach 126 which left him too weak to make a competitive showing.[2]

Three weeks later, on June 16, Dixon met old foe Martin Flaherty in a 20-pound match in Boston. This proved to be a dull fight. Each round was a near-carbon of the round that preceded it. Dixon was a solid favorite, but a rumor that he had broken up with Tom O'Rourke discouraged many from betting on him. The rumor was false, but O'Rourke had pressing business in New York, and for the first time since he latched hold of Dixon, he wasn't in Dixon's corner. Four local boxers of no great repute, three of whom were Black, accompanied Dixon into the ring.[3]

The fight was declared a draw. In the estimation of *Boston Post* sporting editor George V. Touhey, the result did not indicate that Dixon had regressed but rather that Flaherty had improved tremendously since their first encounter five years earlier.[4] This would prove to be Dixon's last fight of consequence in his home state. Three days after the fight, a law prohibiting prizefighting (soon overturned) went into effect in Massachusetts. This was consistent with the tenor of the times. Earlier that year, on February 8, 1896, President Grover Cleveland signed into law a bill that made prizefighting a felony in Washington, D.C., and other U.S. territories: Oklahoma, New Mexico, and Arizona.[5]

Chapter 7

The Horton Law and the Broadway Athletic Club

There's an old saying that when one window of opportunity closes, another will open. As boxing was being driven out of Massachusetts and elsewhere, New York became more welcoming. In 1896, the state legislature passed the Horton Law, which permitted fights up to 25 rounds "by a domestic incorporated athletic association in a building leased by it for athletic purposes only for at least one year."[1] There was some confusion about whether non-members of the club would be allowed to attend the fights, but a judge ruled "yes" so long as the club purchased a separate boxing license. The courts would rule that the Horton Law superseded municipal anti-prizefighting ordinances, with the result that prizefighting returned to places where it had been forced out, most notably Coney Island. At some of the early Horton Law fights, the combatants were arrested for "slugging," but the cases were thrown out of court, and the police, by and large, stopped interfering.

The Horton Law sprung from an unlikely source. The sponsor was Assemblyman George S. Horton who resided in Wolcott, a town on the shore of Lake Ontario near Rochester, and represented rural Wayne County. A reporter described him as a quiet sort of man with a farming background who regularly attended church and who, prior to entering politics, "to my knowledge never saw anything more exciting than a country baseball game."[2]

The invisible hand behind the Horton Law was New York State Senator (and future U.S. Congressman) Timothy D. Sullivan. Mr. Big in the Bowery, Big Tim Sullivan made a fortune in kickbacks from shady businessmen in his vice-rich district, money that he shrewdly invested in various enterprises, notably a national chain of vaudeville houses. He was said to be the major stakeholder in what became the two leading boxing clubs in New York City, the Broadway Athletic Club and the Lenox Athletic Club, both of which opened with Tom O'Rourke as the manager and matchmaker. Of the two, the Broadway A.C. would play a larger role in the sporting life of the city. Situated in lower Manhattan near Washington Square, it was a club in name only. "It leases and occupies the building for no other purposes than [slugging matches]," said the *New York Times*, "and it is practically unoccupied except when one of these exhibitions is going on."³

The Horton boxing bill was passed into law very quietly; there was hardly a mention of it in the papers until the law took effect. The law had a short shelf life, but during its existence, New York City became the epicenter of the boxing universe, harboring a great profusion of internationally important fights, and George Dixon would be right in the thick of it.

Big Tim Sullivan, the King of the Bowery and the invisible hand behind the Horton Law. Big Tim was at the height of his power in 1896 (detail from image at the Library of Congress).

The law took effect on September 1, 1896. Twenty-five days later, Dixon had the first of what would be six consecutive fights at the Broadway Athletic Club. In the opposite corner was lanky Tommy White, a boxer whose unassuming appearance and refined tastes belied his ruggedness.⁴ A remnant of the bare-knuckle era—his first documented fight lasted three hours and 36 minutes—White was a protégé of Harry Gilmore, whose Chicago boxing academy produced a steady stream of boxers who would make their mark in the professional ranks.

White gave Dixon all that he could handle. The Chicago lad's defense was air-tight, and although he never hurt Dixon, he drew blood from the champion's mouth and nose. At the conclusion, both of Dixon's eyes were nearly closed. But Dixon was the aggressor, and referee Sam C. Austin, the sporting editor of the *Police Gazette*, called it a draw. At the final bell, the crowd stood and accorded the fighters a long ovation.

Chapter 7. The Horton Law and the Broadway Athletic Club

The show's maiden offering was a big success. When the boxers entered the ring, "the building was packed from pit to dome, and the aisles were jammed with late comers who couldn't find seats." Several thousand people without tickets congregated outside.[5]

The fight left the impression that Dixon was on the downgrade, a feeling that would be reinforced two months later when Dixon met Frank Erne for the second time, this time in a match slated for 20 rounds, double the distance of the first meeting. What transpired was a fast-paced, exciting fight that went the distance and produced a new champion. At the finish, Dixon had two deep gashes under his left eye, the first of which appeared in round four. While the decision was popular—a large contingent from Buffalo went wild when the decision was announced—some people yet thought that Dixon was entitled to a draw. Many old-time fight fans were of the opinion that a title shouldn't change hands unless the challenger was demonstrably superior and felt that Frank Erne's showing didn't quite measure up.[6]

The fight cried out for a third meeting and Erne would accommodate him, but not before Dixon had two intervening bouts. His opponents were Torpedo Billy Murphy and Jack Downey.

Torpedo Billy Murphy, born in Auckland, New Zealand, was recognized as the featherweight champion of the Antipodes when he made his U.S. debut in 1889 at San Francisco, and the history books would credit him with being the first Kiwi to win a world boxing title after he conquered Ike Weir, the Belfast Spider, in a fierce fight before the California Athletic Club in January of 1990. But the peripatetic Murphy, who then resided in Cincinnati, was now 33 years old, ancient for a man in his weight class, and proved to be no match for Dixon who collapsed him in the sixth round with a punch to the pit of the stomach.[7] The fight with Downey, a Brooklyn man who had fought Frank Erne on even terms in three fights consuming 30 rounds, was a bitter struggle. Dixon was more marked-up at the finish—both of his eyes were nearly closed—but the 20 round bout went into the books as yet another draw, Dixon's third in his last five starts.[8]

Little Chocolate was no longer a gem of consistency. He was finding it harder to string together strong performances back-to-back. But Dixon–Erne III attracted a lot of buzz, arguably more buzz than any of his previous fights. Erne was the first man to beat Dixon in a fight that lasted more than four rounds. Dixon would be dressing in an unfamiliar role, that of the would-be avenger. There was talk of taking the match to Carson City, where it would be hitched to the Corbett–Fitzsimmons megafight and fashioned into a fight-to-the-finish, but O'Rourke nixed the idea, reportedly sore at promoter Dan Stuart who had failed to reimburse him for the expenses he incurred from the futile expedition to El Paso.[9]

Dixon–Erne III was slated for 25 rounds at 122 pounds. At the weigh-in, Erne came in 8¼ pounds overweight. O'Rourke wanted to call the fight off, but Dixon overruled him. As a concession, Erne's manager Jim Kennedy agreed to forfeit $500 in the event that his man won. Because of the weight discrepancy, all bets made prior to the weigh-in were declared off. Bets consummated after the weigh-in were mostly at even-money.[10]

The fight went the full distance without a drop of blood being shed. Erne came on late but by then he needed a knockout to win; the decision in Dixon's favor was a foregone conclusion. "Dixon never looked better in his life, and his work in the ring was worthy of his very best days," said a syndicated sportswriter.[11] That was over-stating matters, but what was undeniable was that Little Chocolate was once again the featherweight title-holder.

Dixon completed his run of six straight Broadway A.C. appearances with a non-title, 20-round match with Johnny Griffin, the Braintree Lad. Griffin had lasted the distance when they first met and once again succeeded in staying the route. A glutton for punishment, the Braintree Lad absorbed at least a dozen punches that would have put an ordinary man out, in the estimation of the stringer for the *New York Times*.[12] Then it was back to Boston for Little Chocolate for some R & R and then more vaudeville engagements interrupted by a lengthy stay out west. There he and Joe Walcott shared training quarters in the town of Alameda in preparation for assignments across the bay in San Francisco. His opponent in the first of these engagements was a local man, Dal Hawkins.

Chapter 8

Highs and Lows on Opposite Coasts

Six years had elapsed since Dixon's previous appearance in San Francisco, when he ran roughshod over the Australian champion Abe Willis. During the interim there had been a ring fatality that had the effect of bringing about a dry spell; a self-imposed moratorium by local organizers was standard procedure following a ring death. The ill-fated prizefighter was William "Swede" Miller, who succumbed to his injuries the morning following his bout with Dal Hawkins at the California Athletic Club on February 24, 1893. Hawkins would go on to knock Martin Flaherty out cold in a match hitched to the Corbett–Fitzsimmons fight at Carson City, collapsing Flaherty with a left hook before the match was a minute old, cementing Hawkins' reputation as one of the sport's hardest punchers.

The tragic Hawkins–Miller fight put an end to fights-to-a-finish in the Golden State and halted major promotions, but the sport came back with a flourish with shows now staged with legal impunity in public auditoriums. The Dixon–Hawkins fight, held on July 23, 1897, was potted at Mechanics Pavilion, the city's premier entertainment and convention hall, a building that took up an entire city block.

Had the fight been a mere 10-rounder, Dixon would have almost assuredly won the decision, but Hawkins fought him on even terms over the second half of the fight and the referee called it a draw. What was surprising was that neither man was able to score a knockdown. The feeling among old-time fight fans, said the *San Francisco Examiner*, was that Dixon had trailed off considerably since the Willis fight: "He's as cunning at defensive work as he was then, but he does not fight as fast by any means, and his blows are not as stinging as they used to be.... [However] if Hawkins had defeated him, Dixon's record would still be sufficient to proclaim him the greatest fighter that ever lived."[1]

Dixon concluded his San Francisco Bay area sojourn on October 4,

1897, with a bout against old foe Solly Smith. They met at Woodward's Pavilion, a large entertainment hall on the grounds of an amusement park in the city's Mission District.

Smith had improved tremendously since their first meeting, as reflected in his most recent showing, a seventh-round stoppage of the normally durable Johnny Griffin. In Dixon–Smith II, set for 20 rounds, Smith proved to be more adept at in-fighting, and his punches to the stomach weakened Dixon, who slowed down as the fight wore on. There was no dissent when referee George Green, who was younger than both combatants, raised Solly Smith's hand in triumph.

"George Dixon has seen his best days," stated the story in the next day's *San Francisco Call* under a headline that read, "Solly Smith is now the featherweight champion." According to various sources, Dixon received only $1,100 as the loser's end of the purse; Smith got $5,850 plus whatever gratuities that came his way from those that bet on him.[2]

It was plain that Dixon needed a long rest. He spent part of January and almost all of February at West Baden Springs, Indiana, before returning to the ring on March 30, 1898, for a match with former (and future) rival Tommy White. In its heyday, West Baden in French Lick township, roughly 65 miles from Louisville, was as well-known as Saratoga and Hot Springs, Arkansas. The water that bubbled out of the mineral springs was renowned for its medicinal properties. The luxurious West Baden Hotel had a handball court, and the hills outside were considered ideal for roadwork. And like Saratoga and Hot Springs, it catered to the sporting crowd. One of the features of the hotel was a copious and well-appointed poolroom where results were wired in from all the major tracks.[3]

Dixon and Tommy White had met in Syracuse, New York. While White was hardly a pushover, his reputation had taken a tumble since their first encounter. A trip to London in November of the previous year had resulted in a loss to Ben Jordan, and in his most recent fight, at Athens, Pennsylvania, he suffered a shocking setback on points to a plumber from Racine, Wisconsin, a near-novice who competed under the name Young Mahoney. As in their first meeting, White would extend Dixon the full 20 rounds, but he wasn't quite as competitive, and the fight was dull. The verdict, yet another draw, did nothing to refurbish Dixon's reputation, but the bout was useful exercise for Dixon, allowing him to shake off the rust and show that his stamina wasn't irretrievably diminished.[4]

Another Chicagoan, Eddie Santry, served as Dixon's next opponent.

Chapter 8. Highs and Lows on Opposite Coasts

They met at the new Lenox A.C., which had taken over a former ice palace in uptown Manhattan at 107th Street and Lexington Avenue. The building wasn't as well-situated as the Broadway A.C. but could accommodate a larger crowd. Tom O'Rourke had moved his tack there for the time being.

Eddie Santry had only one loss on his record, that coming against intra-city rival Tommy White. All of his previous fights had been in or near Chicago, save for one excursion to Toronto. Predictably, he extended Dixon the full 20 rounds. It was a clean and scientific fight according to press reports. "Although he did not show his former wonderful speed, [Dixon] out-pointed his rival in aggressiveness and in hard hitting," said a correspondent for a Brooklyn paper.[5] The referee concurred, naming Dixon the winner.

Ben Jordan, the featherweight champion of England, was an interested observer. He had crossed the ocean with the intent of meeting Dixon, and the match was sealed the very next day. There was a hole in matchmaker O'Rourke's schedule owing to a cancellation, and he slid Dixon vs. Jordan into the vacancy. It was set down for July 1, 1898, giving Dixon only 25 days to prepare for what would be a 25-round fight.

Jordan was reportedly the son of a minister who disowned him when he entered the prize ring.[6] He was said to be undefeated in 40 fights. His two most recent wins were over American opponents at the National Sporting Club. Spike Sullivan, a top-shelf lightweight from Boston, happened to be in London and caught both fights. He offered this scouting report: "Ben Jordan is a wonder.... He is not so very clever, but he is strong. He hurts every time he lands."[7]

When Dixon and Jordan entered the ring, the building was unbearably warm. Ringside attendants waved palm leaves to make the conditions less oppressive. Yet, although the Englishman was as strong as advertised, Dixon never wilted to the point where he could no longer keep his hands moving.

A reporter characterized Ben Jordan's performance as phlegmatic. He went about his business in a workmanlike fashion, never showing any signs of discomfort. Dixon suffered a cut over his left eye in the third round and a cut over his right eye in the 10th. At the conclusion, when the referee raised Jordan's hand, Dixon accepted the verdict stoically. As he left the ring, the crowd stood and clapped, a token of respect for the vanquished warrior who had seemingly reached the end of the trail.

Dixon's hardest blows, said a reporter, "amounted to no more than rain on a window pane." His wrinkled face showed the effects of too many ring battles and perhaps something more. There were rumors that Dixon had developed an affection for champagne and other liquid intoxicants. John Barleycorn, some said, was accelerating his erosion.[8]

George Dixon was a cat with nine lives. There would come a day when it would be foolish of him to take one more fight, but that day wasn't there yet. A six-round exhibition with a local man in Fall River, Massachusetts, and a six-round workout with Joe Bernstein in Philadelphia, where neither man tried for a knockout, prefaced a return engagement at the Lenox AC, where he was pitted against Dave Sullivan. By an odd set of circumstances, the match afforded Dixon an opportunity to regain his featherweight title.

Dave Sullivan, an Irishman by birth, was a fellow Bostonian. In September of 1898 he challenged Solly Smith, who had wrested the title away from Dixon in San Francisco. In the second round, Smith broke his left arm. After three more rounds, with Smith's arm dangling uselessly at his side, the referee saw no reason to let the fight continue and awarded the fight to Sullivan who, in a sense, became the featherweight champion of the world by default. (In England, they recognized Ben Jordan.)

Dixon vs. Sullivan, on November 11, 1898, attracted an SRO crowd. Sullivan and his older brother Spike Sullivan, who competed in the division above him, had large followings and the attendees included a large group of Sullivan boosters who arrived on a special train from the Hub. The sum of their wagers knocked the odds down to where Sullivan closed a slight favorite.

Their mood went from bright to gloomy. At no point in the contest did Sullivan have the upper hand. In the 10th frame, Dixon wobbled Sullivan with a hard right and then pushed him to the floor. At this juncture, Spike Sullivan, Dave's chief second, jumped over the ropes shouting that the round was up. When he realized his mistake—20 seconds remained—he quickly retreated, but then rushed into the ring again, forcing the referee to declare Dixon the winner by disqualification.[9]

Little Chocolate was a title-holder once again. Dave Sullivan's reign as the world featherweight champion had lasted only 46 days.

The advance publicity for the fight said that the winner would meet Ben Jordan in a unification fight, but instead, Dixon's second reign as featherweight champion began with a defense against veteran Oscar

Chapter 8. Highs and Lows on Opposite Coasts

Gardner. They met at the Lenox A.C. on November 29, 1898, a mere 18 days after Dixon regained his title.

Most of Gardner's early fights were in Omaha, earning him the sobriquet Omaha Kid, although he was actually from Minneapolis. A peripatetic fighter—have gloves, will travel—he roamed the country with his scrapbook, picking up a new manager at each new stop. When he got to New York, Paddy Sullivan, the brother of Big Tim Sullivan, took charge of his affairs. The Omaha Kid was a big puncher, inviting comparisons to Dal Hawkins, and like Hawkins, he had killed a man in the ring.[10]

Gardner had an awkward style that puzzled Dixon. Although George did most of the leading, he had difficulty landing a clean punch. But neither man was damaged in the fast-paced, 25-round fight, and at the end, the referee sided with the champion. The decision was assailed as an out-and-out robbery by some ringside reports, but other accounts were more measured. If the ref had called it a draw, said Nat Fleischer, everyone would have been satisfied.[11]

Whatever the integrity of the verdict, George Dixon remained the featherweight champion in the eyes of most of the world. He would take this laurel with him into the final year of the century, a year that would further cement his status as an all-time great. However, a relative newcomer was turning heads, and the new kid on the block would prove to be every bit as good as advertised.

Chapter 9

Terry McGovern: The South Brooklyn Comet

"Don't look back because someone may be gaining on you," said the great Negro League pitcher Satchel Paige. Terry McGovern, fully 10 years younger than George Dixon, was a work in progress, lacking Dixon's unsurpassed ring IQ. However, he had burst out of the amateur ranks like a comet and was gaining ground fast. His crowd-pleasing style—he was a swarmer with a bottomless well of vitality—enhanced his aura.

Terry McGovern, christened John Terrence McGovern, was born in Johnstown, Pennsylvania, in 1880, nine years before the great flood. He moved with his parents to Brooklyn when he was six months old. When Terry was in his early teens, his father died. With two younger brothers at home, Terry assumed the role of the family breadwinner until his mother remarried, taking the surname of her new spouse, Joseph Kenny, a saloonkeeper. Terry sold newspapers on horsecar trolleys, "hopping on and off in the most daring manner," and then found steady work as an apprentice shipping clerk in a lumberyard where his immediate supervisor was a man named Charles Maywood.[1]

Maywood, who had an amateur boxing background, showed young Terry how to box and eventually became his lead trainer. Before turning pro, McGovern made his mark on the local amateur scene. In one of the tournaments, he disposed of three opponents in one evening, and in another he defeated five boys in two nights.[2]

Terry McGovern's Brooklyn

At the start of the Civil War, Brooklyn was America's third largest city. It was the fourth largest city—trailing New York, Chicago, and Philadelphia—when it was submerged into the modern city of New

Chapter 9. Terry McGovern: The South Brooklyn Comet

York along with the counties of Bronx, Queens, and Richmond (Staten Island) in 1898.

A key development in the growth of Brooklyn was the building of the Gowanus Canal, which made the city a more important international seaport. When the dredging started in 1860, Gowanus Creek was famed for its enormous oysters. They disappeared as the waterway became polluted. In 1887, said a story in the Brooklyn Eagle, "All South Brooklyn mourns and weeps and will not be comforted because of this canal, which is becoming more pestiferous every year."[3] By then the Gowanus had become the informal sewage system of the growing city.

The fame of Protestant clergymen like Henry Ward Beecher and Thomas De Witt Talmage gave Brooklyn, the City of Churches, the appearance of being a largely WASPish enclave, but this wasn't so. By 1860, roughly half the population was foreign-born, roughly half of whom were Irish. The Brooklyn that resembled a Colonial-era New England town existed only in memory.

Many of the Irish immigrants who settled in Brooklyn brought with them from the old country an abiding interest in prizefighting. "It is to the everlasting honor of the Irishman that he takes so naturally to fistic combat," pontificated Chicago boxing writer Howard Carr, an ex-prizefighter better known as Kid Howard. "While other peoples seek to slice the enemy with swords or blow their heads off with shells, the Irishman, if left to follow his natural bent, is quite content with giving his foe a black eye, or, at worst, a cauliflower ear."[4]

Bare-knuckle bruiser Jim Dunn and transitional figures Nonpareil Jack Dempsey and Jack McAuliffe put Brooklyn on the pugilistic map. All were born in Ireland. Dunn parlayed his fistic prowess into a cushy job as Brooklyn's deputy collector of assessments and taxes, an appointment that caused a bit of a scandal.[5] Brooklyn Jimmy Carroll, another prominent scrapper (called "Brooklyn Jimmy" to distinguish him from an English bare-knuckle fighter with the same name), used his ring earnings to open a roadhouse in Coney Island, a combination boxing gym and saloon that became a favorite watering hole for the sporting crowd.

During much of its existence, the Brooklyn Navy Yard, founded in 1801, was Brooklyn's largest employer. During Terry McGovern's day, the Yard's longtime foreman was Hugh McLaughlin, whom everyone called "Boss." Born in Brooklyn in 1827, the son of Irish immigrants, McLaughlin's position put more patronage at his disposal than any elected official, and he used his influence to become the chief engineer of Brooklyn's Democratic machine, an unofficial post he would hold for nearly four decades. A story about him in 1888 noted that as a young man, McLaughlin was handy with his fists: "The fondness for boxing, which he entertained in his youthful days still clings to him, and an orderly athletic entertainment in which first class pugilists appear, generally attracts him to a seat well up front."[6]

As was true in Boston, the Irish were over-represented among the founders and members of athletic clubs. In February of 1893, according to a survey by the *Brooklyn Daily Eagle*, there were 10 bona fide athletic clubs in Brooklyn (presumably clubs with a well-appointed gymnasium and a well-rounded curriculum that included both indoor and outdoor sports). However, the popularity of boxing had given rise to fly-by-night clubs that did nothing but put on a boxing show, the profits of which went into the pockets of men who would "scatter [the proceeds] on the race track or in the pool rooms." Boxing shows in Brooklyn were becoming more numerous than toads after a shower, said the author of the survey.[7] Indeed, during the late 1890s, fight fans in the City of Churches could usually choose between three professional boxing cards on a Saturday night without leaving the borough.

Terry McGovern in a standard boxing pose, ca. 1898.

Terry McGovern grew up approximately two miles south of the Navy Yard in South Brooklyn in the neighborhood that came to be called Park Slope. South Brooklyn became a misnomer when the city annexed the land south of it, a wide swath that ran all the way to Coney Island, but it remained South Brooklyn as a point of reference long after it made no sense geographically speaking. Park Slope has become

Chapter 9. Terry McGovern: The South Brooklyn Comet

gentrified with home prices now well beyond the means of the average one-income family, but in McGovern's day, it was a hardscrabble neighborhood heavily populated by Irish immigrants, many of whom found work on the waterfront.

Although the men were mostly low wage earners, the residents had a strong sense of community that wasn't lost when Brooklyn was folded into Greater New York, an action that met with stern opposition (a non-binding referendum on whether to accept consolidation passed by only 227 votes out of 129,211). Indeed, it would be written that all of Brooklyn, despite ethnic and religious divisions, had an esprit-de-corps that remained tight until the Dodgers baseball team left the borough following the 1957 season.

Be that as it may, Terry McGovern came to achieve a level of idolatry in Brooklyn greater than any other homegrown athlete, before or after. The scenes in South Brooklyn after he won some of his biggest fights were scenes of great jubilation.

* * *

McGovern's first professional fight didn't go well. Paired against a fellow novice named Johnny Snee, he was disqualified in the fourth round. Details are vague, but it would be written that the bout was a messy "rough and tumble" affair that was waved off after a "palpable tangle."[8] The match was held on March 3, 1897, at South Brooklyn's Greenwood Athletic Club, an entity established by railroad workers. The Greenwood AC would be Terry's steady landing-place when he was just starting out. He had eight more fights there over the next six months. All of these bouts were scheduled for 10 rounds.

In McGovern's sixth pro fight, he was matched against Tommy Sullivan, another boy from South Brooklyn. Sullivan came from Red Hook, a neighborhood teeming with sailors and longshoremen, and at age 16 was a year younger than Terry. This would be a fierce fight. At the end, the referee could not decide between them and called the fight a draw.

One would have surmised that Terry's upside was limited if he could not defeat a boy from his own backyard, but history would show that Sullivan was no small potatoes. He would go on to have a long and decorated career. To distinguish him from a raft of other Sullivans, newsmen came to identify him as Brooklyn Tommy Sullivan.

McGovern met Tommy Sullivan on June 19, 1997, and would have nine more fights before the year was out, including a match against one Jack Doyle that was stopped in the seventh round by the police to prevent Terry from dishing out more punishment. The referee awarded the fight to McGovern, a superfluous gesture, and modern record-keepers would label it a "TKO." Terry accepted this fight when Doyle's opponent failed to show. McGovern was ready to go although he had fought the previous week.

During his early fighting days in Boston, George Dixon had a great intra-city rival in Hank Brennan. Similarly, Terry McGovern developed a keen rivalry with a local man before acquiring a national reputation. McGovern's adversary, George Monroe, born George Joseph Cooney, the son of a blacksmith, appeared headed to a career as a jockey. By age 11, he was so adept as a horseback rider that he gave an exhibition during a Brooklyn appearance of "Buffalo Bill's Wild West Show."[9] He and McGovern first tangled on May 13, 1898, at a skating rink in Yonkers, a town along the Hudson River abutting the Bronx. They battled 20 rounds to a draw. According to news reports, it was a see-saw fight. McGovern was superior during the first half of the fight, Monroe had the best of it in rounds 13–16, McGovern regained the upper hand in Round 17, and Monroe finished with a flourish to salvage a draw. "Science was displayed at every point of the battle and the blows were delivered with a nicety and evenness that drew forth much applause," said the *Brooklyn Times Union*.[10]

The next month, McGovern and Monroe locked horns in Coney Island in a match slated for 25 rounds.

McGovern was much stronger than in the first meeting. He was comfortably ahead after eight rounds when he purposely slowed things down to conserve his energy. He picked up the pace again in Round 12 and after 15 stanzas, ringside bookmakers were laying three to one that Monroe wouldn't last two more rounds. But he got a second wind and lasted into the 24th before he was all in. McGovern closed the show with a smash to the jaw that left Monroe on the seat of his pants, too weary to rise.[11]

McGovern–Monroe III, staged on August 4 at the Greenwood A.C., was anticlimactic. In round seven, Monroe struck McGovern coming out of a clinch after the referee had called "break," and the ref awarded the bout to Terry on a foul. Prior to the stoppage, it was noted that McGovern had landed the more telling blows.

The crowd thought the referee over-reacted, and George Monroe's manager and chief second, Sam H. Harris, persuaded him that he had been too hasty to wave it off. The referee agreed to vacate his decision if McGovern agreed to continue the fray, but by then Terry was back in his dressing room and in no mood to renew hostilities. He had fought 13

Chapter 9. Terry McGovern: The South Brooklyn Comet

days earlier, had taken the Monroe fight on short notice as a favor to the club's managers, and had another fight booked in sixteen days.[12]

Thirty-eight days after McGovern–Monroe III, on September 11, 1898, McGovern married the former Grace Smalley. About this time, he also acquired a new manager, the aforementioned Sam H. Harris. Terrible Terry, as sportswriters were starting to call him, was only 18 years old, and the world was his oyster.

Sam H. Harris, who was only 26 years old when he took on Terry McGovern, was quite the go-getter. Born poor on Manhattan's Lower East Side, he went on to have an illustrious career on Broadway, producing or co-producing 130 shows including many of Broadway's biggest hits. Many of his early efforts were collaborations with George M. Cohan, the astoundingly prolific playwright, songwriter, and actor. As Harris became more involved in the theater, he entrusted the day-to-day affairs of Terrible Terry to Joe Humphreys. Best remembered as New York's top ring announcer during the effervescent 1920s, Humphreys was omnipresent. Boxing aficionados were a tight-knit fraternity, socially active, and rare was the banquet in or around Gotham at which Humphreys wasn't at the podium serving as the toastmaster.

Then, as now, a boxer, no matter how talented, had scant chance of going all the way to the top without a well-connected manager. Sam Harris was a different breed of cat than Tom O'Rourke—his shoes were not firmly planted in the pugilistic subculture—but like O'Rourke, he was a hard negotiator who instinctively knew how to "move" a fighter. In the early years of the 20th century, Harris was briefly the president of the politically powerful Hesper Club. The club was named for the first racehorse owned by Tammany bigwig Big Tim Sullivan, a horse that returned a hefty price when it won the Myrtle Stakes at Gravesend on June 11, 1900.[13]

Harris kept McGovern busy while ratcheting up his level of opposition, and McGovern concomitantly ratcheted up his game. His three fights with Tim Callahan, a very good featherweight from Philadelphia, were illustrative.

McGovern first fought Callahan on July 23, 1898, between his second and third fights with George Monroe. In this bout, McGovern had trouble closing the distance on Callahan, who had the longer reach and repeatedly found a home for his jab. Callahan fell to the canvas during the eighth round, and Terry punched him while he was down, drawing a stern rebuke from the referee. In Round 11, another infraction of this nature resulted in McGovern getting disqualified.

They met again the next month in a 20-round affair that was fairly ruled a draw. In their third and final meeting, it was all McGovern, who scored a brutal 10th-round knockout. After knocking Callahan down with a punch to the pit of the stomach, Terry sank him for keeps with a right/left combination. Callahan was unconscious for 10 minutes.[14] The Philadelphian entered the match unbeaten in his last 24 and wouldn't be stopped again until very late in his career. That the third meeting ended so conclusively bore witness that McGovern was improving in leaps and bounds.

McGovern's third meeting with Callahan came after a bout with Harry Forbes and preceded a match with Austin Rice. They too were considered strong opponents who would provide Terry with a good barometer of where he stood in terms of career development.

Harry Forbes, whose younger brother Clarence was a featherweight of note, had come to New York two months earlier after having his first 20 pro fights in Chicago. He would go on to become the first man to defeat future Hall of Famer Abe Attell. But he was no match for McGovern; Terrible Terry softened him up with a hard punch to the midsection in the 15th round and then ended matters with a swing to jaw. Forbes' strategy going in was to beat McGovern at his own game, crowding him, and this was ill-advised. "Terry is at his best when close to his opponent," noted a ringside reporter.[15]

At age 26, Austin Rice was already something of a grizzled veteran. Ten of his previous bouts lasted 20 rounds. He came from New London, Connecticut, and would earn the sobriquet Connecticut Iron Man. At the time of his death in 1921, it was widely reported that he had never been knocked out. Terry wasn't able to knock him out, but gave him such a severe beating that his corner tossed in the sponge after 14 rounds. But there was an anxious moment for McGovern's backers. In Round 11, Terry got careless and left his jaw exposed. Rice smashed him to the canvas, but McGovern recovered and quickly regained the upper hand.[16]

The bouts with Forbes and Rice, both scheduled for 25 rounds, were held at the new Pelican Club in the Bay Ridge neighborhood of Brooklyn. The proprietor was Johnny Reagan, a former bare-knuckle fighter of considerable repute. The fight with Rice was held on New Year's Eve. Terrible Terry closed the year with a bang, and the year 1899 would bring fireworks that boomed louder.

CHAPTER 10

1899: The Year of the Deluge

Novice boxing historians are invariably astounded at how active the old-timers were, relative to their modern-day counterparts. Joe Gans once defended his lightweight title in Fort Erie, Canada, and then fought a 10-round fight the very next day in Lancaster, Pennsylvania, more than 300 miles away. The sport was especially bustling in 1899, the last full year of Horton Law Boxing in New York. Terry McGovern had 18 fights that year, George Dixon "only" 10. One of McGovern's opponents, Billy Barrett, crammed 17 fights into his 1899 slate, answering the bell for a staggering 258 rounds.

The year 1899 was especially good to McGovern, who gathered in the world bantamweight title with a spectacular performance that captured the imagination of fight fans on both sides of the Atlantic, but Little Chocolate was first out of the box. On January 17, he met the Black Australian boxer Young Pluto at the Lenox Athletic Club. Pluto, christened William Dudley Brown, was born in 1871 in the South African seaport city of Port Elizabeth, or in St. John, New Brunswick, Canada (reports differ). He reportedly stowed away on a clipper ship bound for Sydney and found his way to Foley's Hall. He later settled in Melbourne, where he found work as a hot walker for a racing stable. Before coming to the U.S., he resided briefly in the Australian gold mining boomtowns of Coolgardie and Kalgoorlie and in Dawson City, Alaska, during the Klondike gold rush. His claim to fame was a series of draws with Young Griffo in Melbourne, one of which lasted 70 rounds. His bout with Dixon would mark his U.S. debut.

Young Pluto, said a story in the *Brooklyn Citizen*, was as quick as lightning and a terrific finisher. But the scrawny Australian was no match for George Dixon, who had all the best of it before sinking him in the 10th round with a left hook to the stomach. Pluto "was treated to a greater variety of punches than he ever had any idea were in existence," said a ringside reporter.[1]

Dixon was out of action for the next four months during which he paid another visit to West Baden to drink the water and soak in the mineral baths. As Dixon was resting, Tom O'Rourke worked on making a match for him in England that never materialized—the target was Pedlar Palmer—and Terry McGovern, with whom Dixon was on a collision course, kept busy, storming up the bantamweight ladder with decisive wins over well-known opponents.

McGovern's first match of 1899 came on January 30 when he opposed Casper Leon at the Greenwood AC. Born Gaspare Leoni in Palermo, Sicily, and raised in Lower Manhattan, Leon was one of the few Italian boxers in this era who did not bury his ethnicity behind an Irish or ethnically nebulous ring name, and reporters took to dubbing him the Sicilian Swordfish. He was coming off a draw with the great Jimmy Barry in a bout billed for the world paperweight (110 pounds) title, and Barry's recent retirement imbued this contest with the trappings of a title fight, although it was fought at 115 pounds. "The bantam-weight championship of America has long been in dispute," said the *Brooklyn Times-Union*, "but [when McGovern and Leon meet] the question will be practically settled."[2]

McGovern's recent bouts at the Greenwood A.C. had drawn SRO crowds, and this match was no exception, reportedly drawing the largest turnout in the history of the club. And Terry rewarded the locals with a smashing knockout. He had the Sicilian almost out in the 11th round and finished the job in the 12th, terminating the fight with a short left to the point of the jaw. "Leon dropped like a log," said the *Brooklyn Eagle* reporter. It took several minutes before he regained all his faculties.[3]

McGovern's performance drew raves from *Denver Post* sports editor Otto Floto, a nationally recognized authority on boxing. "At last, after years of waiting, a bona fide successor to George Dixon is in sight," said Floto.[4]

Terry McGovern was getting too big for Brooklyn. Purses were larger on the other side of the famous bridge. His next major engagement after his match with Casper Leon was fought at the Lenox A.C. His opponent was Patsy Haley.

The aggressor from the opening bell, McGovern knocked Haley down half a dozen times. Saved by the bell in rounds 15 and 17, Haley went down for good in the 18th and had to be carried to his corner. "It was one of the battles to which others will be compared for years," said the *New York Journal* scribe. "From the first feint to the last deadening

Chapter 10. 1899: The Year of the Deluge

punch there was not a dull spot." The story ran under the headline "Greatest Fight in Years Seen at the Lenox Athletic Club," a declaration that was a bit over the top.[5] Patsy Haley, who fought out of Buffalo, went on to become one of New York's top referees.

Planting the McGovern–Haley match at the Lenox A.C.—Manhattan's largest boxing arena—was a mistake. Haley had a spotty record, and the turnout was disappointing. But it was also a mistake to put McGovern's next fight at the Broadway A.C. as the arena was too small to accommodate everyone who wanted to see it.

Joe Bernstein, the original "Pride of the Ghetto," ca. 1898.

Terry's opponent, Joe Bernstein, the original "Pride of the Ghetto," had a big following among his *landsmen* in the Yiddish-speaking community on the Lower East Side. At the start of their 25-round fight, there was no room left for standees.

"The way the money was bet on the outcome seemed to astonish the old-timers," said the reporter for the *Brooklyn Citizen*. McGovern's backers offered 2-to-1, and these odds were "grabbed up by the East Side jewelry dealers and pawnbrokers."[6]

The reporter guessed that many of Bernstein's backers returned home flat broke. McGovern's nose started leaking in the opening round, but he never wavered and was the aggressor throughout in a bout devoid of knockdowns but entertaining in spurts and exceedingly entertaining in the final round. While many of the rounds were close, the *New York Sun* reporter was of the opinion that there were only two rounds in which Bernstein clearly had the best of it.[7] They would meet twice more in matches where McGovern was more dominant, but Joe Bernstein would have the distinction of being the only man to extend Terrible Terry McGovern the distance in a 25-round fight.

Clash of the Little Giants

* * *

George Dixon returned to the ring on May 15 in Buffalo where he met Kid Broad in a fight slated for 20 rounds. Broad, who fought out of Cleveland, was born William Thomas in Liskeard, Cornwall, England, leading some reporters to dub him the Little Cornishman, an allusion to Bob Fitzsimmons. Billed as the newsboy champion of Ohio when he was just starting out, Broad wasn't in Dixon's league but was very strong for his weight. His specialty was in-fighting.

Dixon elected to fight Broad at his own game, crowding him rather than sharp-shooting him from a distance. The strategy worked but only in the sense that he got the decision; his effort won him no new fans. "Dixon was not the Dixon of old, by a great margin," said the *Buffalo Courier*. "He was still very fast on his feet, and he threw big blows in quickly, but that old-time dash and cyclonic force were sadly missing." The match redounded well to Kid Broad as he ended the fight without a scratch, and many thought he was entitled to a draw.[8]

Little Chocolate had no time to relax. He was back in the ring 18 days later for a match with Joe Bernstein at the Broadway A.C. O'Rourke was over-working him, it was plain, but Dixon wasn't inclined to have him slow down as his money was disappearing as fast as he made it. Dixon was a plunger, a man who bet big at the track, said an 1898 story in a Kentucky paper, but the money that went into the pockets of bookmakers was less than what he dribbled away in handouts and loans that he likely knew would never be repaid. Dixon could not resist helping out a friend in need, although some of those friends were not so needy; they just knew that Little Chocolate had trouble saying "no" to a supplicant, especially when he was drinking.[9]

Dixon vs. Bernstein, which played out before a packed a house, was in many ways a carbon of Bernstein's fight with Terry McGovern five weeks earlier. Dixon forced the action and proved conclusively that he was the superior ring general, but the rugged Bernstein was still standing after 25 hard rounds. There were some hisses mingled among the cheers when the referee gave the fight to Dixon, but the malcontents were thought to be those who wagered on Bernstein and were hoping against hope that the referee would salvage their bets by calling it a draw.[10]

Dixon's title defense against Tommy White in Denver was set for July 11. Dixon took a zigzag route that included a stopover in Louisville. His match there with Sam Bolen, although ostensibly a title fight, stands as one of the more curious episodes of his career.

Chapter 10. 1899: The Year of the Deluge

Dixon and his team arrived in the Derby City on the morning of the fight, having taken a red eye train from Chicago. With them was Parson Davies, who would serve as Dixon's timekeeper for his match with Bolen at the Music Hall that evening. It isn't known if Bolen was on the same train, but he and Dixon were close friends. In fact, Bolen had frequently worked Dixon's corner, assisting Tom O'Rourke.

The fight, held on the eve of the Fourth of July, was a blowout. Dixon knocked Bolen down once in the second stanza and four more times in the third, after which the referee decided that no purpose would be served by letting the contest go another round. "Dixon was like a cyclone, one of those pent-up tornadoes which, when it finds itself turned loose, sweeps all before it," said the *Louisville Courier-Journal*. "No feather-weight in the world could have whipped Dixon last night."[11]

In boxing, it isn't unusual for good friends to meet up inside the ropes and fight like mortal enemies; it happens all the time. However, looking back, the Dixon–Bolen fight had a bad odor about it. O'Rourke certainly wasn't going to put his cash cow in tough with a far more lucrative match coming up in only eight days. Sam Bolen, who had an eight-pound weight advantage (129–121) was on his feet when the gong sounded to end the third frame. Most referees would not have pulled the trigger as quick.

Tommy White had given Dixon a tough battle when they met three years earlier in New York. The rematch, in common with the first meeting, went the full 20 rounds. Dixon forged ahead in the 13th and was named the winner by referee Bat Masterson, the fabled western lawman who was then managing a burlesque house in Denver and was the president of the organization that sponsored the prizefight.

"It was the greatest fistic battle ever seen in this part of the West," read the front-page story in the *Boston Globe*, but one would not have gleaned this from the wire-service story which said that Tommy White didn't make a concerted effort to win, "his purpose being to avoid a knockout and stay the limit."[12]

* * *

Meanwhile, back in New York, Terry McGovern's career was progressing nicely, and his fans were starting to talk about a showdown with George Dixon. That talk subsided when it became known that Sam Harris was working on a match almost as enticing, a bout between Terrible Terry and Pedlar Palmer. To secure it, McGovern couldn't afford a slip-up, and he didn't let that happen. Building on his win over Joe

Bernstein, he scored knockouts over Sammy Kelly (KO 5), Billy Barrett (KO 10), and Johnnie Ritchie (KO 3). The Kelly and Barrett fights were at the Broadway A.C., the Ritchie fight in Tuckahoe, New York.

Tuckahoe was a little village in Westchester County, 16 miles from midtown Manhattan and 22 minutes by train from Manhattan's Grand Central depot. The athletic club that hosted the McGovern–Ritchie fight was a new organization that had acquired an undeveloped parcel of land that was situated a stone's throw from Tuckahoe's new railroad station, a parcel ideal for a little outdoor stadium. The driving forces behind the club were Billy Gray, a music publisher, and William Molloy, the sheriff of Westchester County.[13]

Holding a big fight in an open-air arena in this part of the country was a novelty. It smacked of the bare-knuckle days except that those fights were hush-hush affairs. But the time was ripe as new money was infusing into boxing from the infant medium of motion pictures. A prizefight film had better clarity if filmed in natural sunlight.

Johnnie Ritchie, a barber in St. Louis when he left the amateur ranks, wasn't looked upon as a major roadblock for McGovern. He made a credible showing for two rounds, but Terry knocked him out in the third, knocking him groggy with a right hand and then knocking him unconscious with a left to the jaw before he had time to gather his senses. The bout, held on July 1, 1899, was designed as a test case of sorts, a soft opening to expose any things that needed fixing before the spanking new arena welcomed the McGovern–Palmer crowd. One thing that needed fixing was better security. When Ritchie hit the canvas, McGovern's supporters in the bleachers swarmed the ring, knocking over everything in their path, and danced about cheering "like wild men."[14]

The McGovern–Palmer Fight

Three-and-a-half years had elapsed since Pedlar Palmer's 6-round match with George Dixon at Madison Square Garden, his lone previous fight in America. He had proved to be Dixon's equal that night, and upon returning to England, he enhanced his reputation with five successful defenses of his bantamweight title, a division with no firm ceiling, fluctuating between 112 and 118 pounds. In the U.K., even casual boxing fans were familiar with "Box o' Tricks," the fighter who was said to be as agile as a cat. Fighting him was like fighting two men at once.

All of Palmer's title defenses were made at the National Sporting

Chapter 10. 1899: The Year of the Deluge

Club, an exclusive men's club housed in a building in London's fashionable Covent Garden district that was formerly a Victorian music hall. Founded in 1891, the club, with its intimate boxing theater, was patronized by men of noble pedigree and the crème-de-la-crème of London's entrepreneurial class. They watched the fights in formal evening attire while adhering to a strict code of decorum that prohibited shouting. The Queensberry rules weren't invented here but were firmly applied here (with a few minor adjustments), a big step toward universal acceptance. The NSC was the precursor of the British Boxing Board of Control.

The day-to-day affairs of the club were in the hands of A.F. "Peggy" Bettinson. A former English amateur lightweight champion, Bettinson would take a pecuniary interest in Pedlar Palmer, becoming his manager. Whenever a Bettinson fighter was matched against a U.S. fighter, Aaron P. "Doc" Ordway, the U.S. representative of the National Sporting Club, was involved in the arrangements. A chemist who maintained homes in Needham, Massachusetts, and New York City, Ordway published a short-lived sporting weekly and would grow rich manufacturing and selling worthless patent medicines under the Dr. Kaufmann brand.

When Team Palmer—Palmer, Bettinson, and Palmer's trainer Sam Blakelock—arrived in New York from London, a 16-piece brass band was waiting at the pier to greet them. Terry McGovern was in the welcoming committee and for publicity purposes rode with Palmer in the carriage that transported the Englishman to his quarters at the Vanderbilt Hotel where a sumptuous banquet was held in his honor. A reporter noted that when Palmer came down the gangplank, he looked bigger and stronger than when he fought Dixon. Arrangements had been made for him to train at Saratoga where the weather was cooler than in the city and the climate more similar to what Palmer was accustomed to in England.[15]

The fight was set for September 11. This was a Monday, which meant that the racetracks would be dark. Unfortunately for the promoters, it rained, and the fight had to be pushed back a day, hurting attendance as it now went head-to-head with the opening day of the autumn meet at the Gravesend track in Coney Island. Racetrack workers and racetrack denizens, by and large, were big fight fans.

Estimates of the crowd ranged from 8,000 to 12,000. While this wouldn't be considered a large crowd by modern day standards, it was a splendid turnout for the era and made more notable by the famous people in the gathering. Among them were British grocery chain magnate

Sir Thomas Lipton, the famous yacht racer whose name would be immortalized in a popular brand of tea. Lipton had reserved a ringside box for his party, as had the great plunderer Richard "Boss" Croker, the former Grand Sachem of Tammany Hall who had spent most of the year in England, where he had established an annex of his thoroughbred racing stable.[16]

At the back of the arena, which was enclosed by a wooden fence that gave it the appearance of a stockade, there were two little two-story cottages that looked down upon the gently-sloped expanse to where the ring was pitched. These served as dressing rooms. Terry McGovern's wife watched the fight unfold from the window in the upper floor of his cottage. She was accompanied by Mrs. Sam Harris, two of her lady friends, little Joseph (the McGoverns' two-month-old baby boy), and the baby's nanny. It would have created a scandal if the ladies were seated near the ring, as it was taboo for a woman to attend a prizefight.

It was common for boxers and their seconds to sport insignias on their ring gear that represented their national origin, and this practice was considered almost obligatory in fights between boxers from different countries. Although the Revolutionary War was old history, there was still a trace of hard feelings between the two nations, and the McGovern–Palmer fight pandered to it. Sam H. Harris had a better appreciation for showmanship than Thomas O'Rourke, and McGovern's big fights had more bells and whistles than those of George Dixon.

Pedlar Palmer appeared first. Someone in his cottage signaled the band to strike up "God Save the Queen," and the anthem accompanied him as he made his walk to the ring behind a man holding aloft the British flag. After Palmer climbed through the ropes, the band struck up "The Star-Spangled Banner," McGovern's cue to begin his ring walk. Twelve-year-old Phil McGovern, the younger of Terry's two younger brothers, led the way, carrying the American flag. The fellow at the back of Terry's procession waved the green flag of Ireland with its golden harp. When McGovern slipped through the ropes, the cheer was deafening.

McGovern was favored. The private wager between Sam Harris and Peggy Bettinson—Harris wagered $1500 laying 6 to 5—established the opening line, but inside the arena the betting was lopsided in favor of Terrible Terry, the odds lengthening to 10/7 and 5/3 as the bout drew closer to its mid-afternoon starting time. The famous bandleader John Philip Sousa was no greenhorn when it came to getting the best of it. He reportedly risked $300 on McGovern to win $275.[17]

Chapter 10. 1899: The Year of the Deluge

Scheduled for 25 rounds at 116 pounds, the fight had a purse of $10,000, 75 percent to the winner. Both fighters were to share in the proceeds from the fight film—the picture-taking machine, a bulky contraption covered with tar paper, was identified as a "Sportograph"—but their shares were not identified. The boxers were gloved in the ring under the watchful eye of referee George Siler, and then they went at it in what would be one of the most anti-climactic fights in the history of the prize ring.

After all that pre-fight hoopla, it took only two minutes and 32 seconds for Terrible Terry to send the "Box o' Tricks" off to dreamland, and that included a 12-second halt in the action when the mallet slipped out of the timekeeper's hands, and he accidentally rang the bell. (The timekeeper, Johnny Pollock, was multi-tasking, keeping time while also taking notes for his ringside report in the *New York Evening World*.)[18]

Before the bout was 90 seconds old, McGovern had put Palmer on the canvas, depositing him there with a right-left combination. He beat the count but looked woozy, and McGovern moved in for the kill. But he was over-anxious, and Palmer was able to dodge his punches until he succeeded in tying him up. But as soon as the referee pried them apart, McGovern resumed his attack, snapping Palmer's head back with a left to the jaw that sent him staggering toward the ropes and then putting him down for the count with a straight right hand to the point of the jaw. The story of the battle was front page news in dozens of newspapers. "America Forever: Knocks Out England in One Round," read the headline above the story in the *Los Angeles Times*.[19]

McGovern was mobbed as he left the ring. Prior to the opening bell, he had been presented with a large horseshoe-shaped floral arrangement from his friends at the Greenwood Athletic Club. As his handlers were bringing it back to his dressing room, it was denuded of all its flowers by souvenir hunters. Back in Brooklyn, the scene was even more tumultuous.

According to the *Brooklyn Daily Eagle*, fireworks were set off as McGovern alighted from the streetcar, holding his baby in his arms with his wife at his side. With much difficulty, the police cleared a path to his residence. The McGoverns then resided at 605 5th Avenue in an apartment above a saloon that Terry had recently purchased. Downstairs, the saloon was mobbed, and so much money was going across the bar, said the paper, that it seemed as if everyone in the neighborhood had won something.[20]

* * *

Clash of the Little Giants

The scene in Tuckahoe at the McGovern–Palmer fight, September 12, 1899.

George Dixon closed out his 1899 campaign with five engagements, three of which were featherweight title fights at the Broadway A.C. The first of these was with Eddie Santry. It was their third meeting and second in 28 days, as Dixon had made a hasty stop-over in Chicago while returning from Denver to meet Santry in a six-round go at a vaudeville theater. Dixon–Santry III was originally announced for 25 rounds at 122 pounds, but O'Rourke abbreviated the contest to a 20-rounder and re-set the weight at 125.

Dixon had out-pointed Santry when they fought in June of the previous year. Their second clash, on Santry's turf in Chicago, was ruled a draw. And this final meeting, on July 11, also ended in a draw, a fair verdict according to most news reports.

Dixon's left eye started swelling in round two and started bleeding two rounds later. According to the correspondent for the *Boston Globe*, the injury was the result of a pre-existing condition, the eye having been bruised two days earlier when Dixon sparred with Sam Bolen for a motion picture company in a kinetoscope studio.[21] But the wellspring likely ran deeper. More and more, the tissue above Dixon's left eye was tearing open. It had become a regular occurrence.

Dixon's last two fights of 1899 were in November spaced 19 days

Chapter 10. 1899: The Year of the Deluge

apart. On November 2 he met Will Curley, who came from Newcastle, England, a great fight town with many of the boxers and most ardent fans drawn from the nearby mining villages. Little was known about Curley (who was actually very good), and the entire lot of British boxers had suffered a loss of esteem as a result of Pedlar Palmer's feeble showing in Tuckahoe. However, with the big heavyweight fight between James J. Jeffries and Tom Sharkey going off the next day in Coney Island, Gotham was swarming with fight fans, and Dixon vs. Curley played to a full house.

The fight was slated for 25 rounds and went the distance with the referee scoring it for Dixon, who landed fewer punches but pressed the action and landed the more effective blows. Curley was saved by the bell in Round 12 when Dixon put him down hard with a right-left combination, but the Englishman shook off the cobwebs and stayed the course. Dixon had a five-week training camp, sharing quarters with Tom Sharkey in Staten Island, and in the estimation of one reporter he entered the ring looking in better condition than he had looked in years.[22]

Little Chocolate had suffered little if any loss in stamina, but it was becoming increasingly hard for him to show well in back-to-back fights. He out-pointed Eddie Lenny in his last outing of 1899, but Lenny performed better than expected in the 25-round fight—up in the cheap seats the prevailing opinion was that he earned a draw—and Dixon's decline was a common thread in the post-fight reports.[23] Born Edward Setaro in Philadelphia to Italian immigrants, Lenny would be credited in some quarters with being the first Italian-American to fight for a world title (a distinction also applied to Casper Leon). He and Dixon would hook up again.

* * *

The fight between Little Chocolate and Terrible Terry had already been signed when George Dixon squared off against Eddie Lenny. And it wasn't as if Terry McGovern was made to wait in the weeds until he and Dixon locked horns. He stayed busy after his sensational knockout of Pedlar Palmer, keeping his name in the news with a series of quick knockouts, "marinating" their forthcoming showdown.

Seventeen days after knocking off Palmer, Terry appeared at Philadelphia's Industrial Hall for a match with Fred Snyder, a local man. They had fought the previous February in what was a stay-busy fight for Terry between his engagements with Casper Leon and Patsy Haley. That was a "no-decision" fight in accordance with the local ordinance, but the ringside reporters were all in accord that McGovern was superior.

Clash of the Little Giants

The rematch, which lasted less than two full rounds, was a messy affair. Snyder did nothing but clinch when he was not visiting the canvas to inspect the resin in the words of a snarky reporter who wrote that some of his trips were impelled by the force of his own blows. The spectators did not like what they were seeing, and sensing trouble, the police interceded and stopped the bout.[24]

Ten days later, on October 9, McGovern made his first appearance in Chicago, where he opposed Billy Rotchford, a local man, at Tattersalls. A barn-like structure on Chicago's near South Side, erected in 1891 by British interests for the purpose of thoroughbred horse auctions, Tattersalls was the Windy City's premier venue for boxing and political rallies, and down the road would become the setting for Terry McGovern's most controversial fight. The matchmaker was Lou Houseman, the sporting editor of the *Chicago Inter Ocean*.

Terry McGovern "is a unique specimen of the fighting brigade. Gifted by nature with muscles of steel, abnormal strength and hitting power, there probably was never a more dangerous fighting machine launched into the fistic arena since the days of Tom Figg," read the unsigned *Inter Ocean* story published on the morning of Terry's fight with Billy Rotchford. Regarding Rotchford, it was said that he was a terrific hitter with either hand and a glutton for punishment. "[Rotchford] knows every turn of the pugilistic game from A to Z, and is, besides, a ring general of considerable ability. It will be East and against West, the local favorite against the national favorite, two of the best boxers in the world in their class, battling to the bitter end for fame and many dollars."[25]

Asked how he planned to fight McGovern, Rotchford said that he would feel him out for two rounds and proceed from there. That battle plan invited a horse laugh after Terry blew right through him. Rotchford was on the deck four times and his face was a bloody mess when the fight was stopped after only 135 seconds.

McGovern returned to Tattersalls the following month and fought two men on the same night. He took on Patsy Haley and Turkey Point Billy Smith in the third and final bouts of a five-bout card. The odd promotion drew a big gate, a testament to Terry's magnetism. "The rush of the crowd at the doors resembled a football scrimmage at its hottest," said the *Inter Ocean* in a story that was re-printed in the *Brooklyn Citizen*. "Re-enforced by sturdy, broad-shouldered Pinkerton men, the doorkeepers fought valiantly to stem the torrent."[26]

Terry stopped the timorous Smith in round three after disposing

Chapter 10. 1899: The Year of the Deluge

of Haley in the opening stanza. This was the same Patsy Haley who was considered a world class fighter and who had extended Terry into the 18th round when they met earlier that year in New York. After the bout, Haley declared that McGovern had improved "500 percent" since their first encounter.[27]

McGovern was then touring with a theatrical troupe, the "cherry" for his spectacular knockout of Pedlar Palmer. On December 18, while on his way back to New York for a rematch with Harry Forbes, he fought another doubleheader in Cincinnati, appearing in the second and final bouts of a four-bout card. He knocked out a fellow named Charlie Mason in the second round and eliminated Freckles O'Brien even faster. Freckles chose to stay down after being knocked off his pins with a left to the jaw in the opening frame. Both of McGovern's victims looked frightened when they entered the ring.[28]

Terrible Terry was on quite a roll. When he fought Harry Forbes in October of the previous year, Forbes lasted into the 15th round. In the rematch, Terry dispatched Forbes in the second frame. After visiting the canvas—put there with a right to the jaw—Forbes came up swinging, fighting fire with fire, and was knocked out in short order. His seconds tossed in the towel when McGovern felled him with a vicious uppercut, a superfluous motion as Forbes would not have beaten the count.[29]

Five days later, McGovern was feted at a gala in Brooklyn attended by 150 invited guests. The highlight of the evening was the presentation of the *Police Gazette* belt, emblematic of his standing as the world bantamweight champion. For an American prizefighter, there was no ornament more prized than the diamond-studded *Police Gazette* belt.

The private discussions of the invited guests undoubtedly centered on McGovern's date with George Dixon, coming up in nine days. Handicapping the match went beyond analyzing the relative skills and current form of the two combatants; the merits of their respective teams was also a relevant consideration. Terrible Terry McGovern was the young gunslinger taking on the established pro and his 27-year-old manager, Sam H. Harris, was in the same role vis-à-vis Dixon's man, Tom O'Rourke, who was more well-versed in all the artifices that would give a fighter an edge.

Chapter 11

Tom O'Rourke and the Other Guy

"[George] Dixon looks up to [Tom] O'Rourke the same as a dutiful son would to a good, kind father," said a writer for a Philadelphia paper. That white-supremacist, paternalistic sludge, so characteristic of the times, teaches us nothing about Tom O'Rourke, but it's hard to rebut Nat Fleischer's assertion that O'Rourke's ability as a manager was on par with that of the great George Dixon as a fighter.[1] (This isn't meant to suggest that O'Rourke gave every fighter he promoted a square deal; there is plenty of anecdotal evidence to the contrary.)

Thomas O'Rourke was born on May 13, 1856, in Boston. As a youth he was an outstanding oarsman and reputedly a good amateur boxer. He worked in the construction trades as a plasterer before acquiring a saloon in Charlestown, a heavily Irish community that was annexed by the city of Boston in 1874. He fixed up the back room with pulleys and punching bags. For a time, he was a city alderman. The Irish saloonkeeper-politician was a well-established personality in Boston and many other large cities.[2]

An early sighting of O'Rourke came on July 21, 1887, when he seconded Charlestown featherweight Johnny Havlin, "The Pride of Donegal Square," in Havlin's match with Ike Weir, the Belfast Spider. Contested with skin-tight gloves, the match was held in a clearing in a forest near Providence, Rhode Island, with the ring illuminated by lanterns. The bout, which started shortly after 9 p.m., lasted four hours and seven minutes and was so brutal that even old-time ring-goers turned away in disgust, drowning the sight of it "with copious amounts of corn juice." The correspondent for the *Boston Globe* declared that the fight, which was stopped after 61 rounds and ruled a draw, "will be forever memorable in the history of ring contests in this country."[3]

Havlin went on to become the *Police Gazette's* American Featherweight Champion, a diadem he acquired on March 1, 1888, when

Chapter 11. Tom O'Rourke and the Other Guy

he stopped Johnny Farrell in the seventh round in the ballroom of a "quiet resort" just over the Massachusetts line in Connecticut. By then, O'Rourke had become Havlin's manager.

Havlin met his Waterloo on November 27 of that year when he was stopped in the 25th round by Tommy Warren in San Francisco before the members of the California Athletic Club. Havlin, who reportedly spent most of the afternoon on the day of the fight in a Turkish bath to boil off weight, lost a considerable amount of blood during the battle and by some accounts was knocked down 10 times in the last two rounds alone before getting hit by the punch that put him down for the 10-count. The *San Francisco Examiner*, noting that O'Rourke used a pen knife to reduce the swelling around Havlin's eyes between rounds, took O'Rourke to task for allowing the fight to go on as long as it did.[4] But Havlin did not begrudge O'Rourke's callousness, if that is the right word. After he quit fighting, he stayed in O'Rourke's employ as a trainer and occasionally assisted O'Rourke in Dixon's corner.

O'Rourke reportedly lost a big bet on Havlin but may have benefited in the long run as it taught him a valuable lesson about the importance of conditioning. Damon Runyon, noting that O'Rourke's fighters never ballooned up in weight between engagements, anointed him one of the greatest conditioners the sport has ever known.[5]

When O'Rourke latched hold of Dixon, George hadn't yet engaged in a fight-to-a-finish, the true measure of a legitimate prizefight in the eyes of the old guard. Indeed, he hadn't completely left the ranks of preliminary boys. Before O'Rourke came along, Dixon basically trained himself. "His training consisted of a short walk before going to work in the morning and dumb bell exercises at the dinner hour," said the *Boston Globe*.[6]

It would be written that O'Rourke was a millionaire by his mid–30s but that he lost virtually all of it in the Panic of 1893. The million-dollar figure is a bit of a stretch, but it's easy to visualize O'Rourke going broke as he was by nature a gambling man and thus prone to wild swings in the state of his personal finances. He carried himself like a high-roller with his fingers encrusted with diamond rings and a roll of big bills secured by a money clip in his hip pocket. A man who spoke his mind and had a hot temper, he grew stout as he grew older. The widely syndicated columnist O.O. McIntyre wrote that O'Rourke "was pot-bellied, short-legged and toed-in, a human gargoyle always impeccably attired even to the flower in his lapel."[7]

O'Rourke's initial attempts to penetrate the lucrative New York market ended disastrously. There was the Dixon–McCarthy fiasco in Long

Clash of the Little Giants

Top row[MOU1], from left: Sam H. Harris, Joe Humphries, Johnny O'Connor, Charley Miner, and Tom O'Rourke. Middle row, from left to right: Terry McGovern, Johnny White, and George Dixon. Bottom row, from left: McGovern's trainer Charley Maywood and McGovern's frequent sparring partner Danny Dougherty in 1900.

Island City touched upon earlier and a replica of it in 1896 when O'Rourke attempted to plant a fight there between Frank Slavin, the Sydney Cornstalk, and Peter Maher. Enemies of Mayor Paddy Gleason once again succeeded in shutting it down. Arrest warrants were issued for O'Rourke and the two fighters, and they were detained in the police station until midnight to prevent the fight from going forward.[8] O'Rourke succeeded in reconstructing the fight and put it in Madison Square Garden, but that necessitated reducing the duration of the fight from 20 to six rounds, and he lost money. Between these two misadventures, O'Rourke promoted a seven-fight card at New York's Academy of Music that was continually interrupted by the police, with the result that several of the fights had to be cut short. An interesting aspect of this promotion is that the fights were held in an octagonal ring with no posts, an O'Rourke invention that he had patented.[9] In many ways, the man was ahead of his time.

To avoid further hassles, O'Rourke needed stronger political connections and no one had more "juice" in Gotham than Big Tim Sullivan. Merely to be seen on the street in the company of Big Tim "established that man's credit and reputation solidly with the lower political world in

Chapter 11. Tom O'Rourke and the Other Guy

New York," observed muckraking journalist George Kibbe Turner in a story for *McClure's* magazine.[10]

Sullivan was the invisible hand behind the truce that brought about the O'Rourke/Considine/Brady boxing trust. Considine was George Considine, a well-known sporting man with an interest in prizefighters and racetracks and the brother of John Considine, Sen. Sullivan's partner in a national chain of vaudeville theaters. Brady was Billy Brady, more formally William A. Brady, the former actor who managed heavyweight champions James J. Corbett and James J. Jeffries before making his mark as a Broadway theatrical producer on par with Sam H. Harris. Brady was the prime mover behind the resurrection of the old Coney Island Athletic Club.

With the three major New York fight venues—the Broadway, the Lenox, and the Coney Island—at their disposal, the trio had a stranglehold on the big fights. "No boxer who values his future will cross them, because when New York is closed to a boxer, he might as well be in Kalamazoo," said a correspondent for a Buffalo paper.[11]

O'Rourke would be forever identified with George Dixon and Joe Walcott. This was inevitable as the two Black Bostonians were all-time greats, and their careers took flight with O'Rourke at their side. But O'Rourke had dealings with dozens of boxers during a career that lasted nearly five full decades. Most of these others were Caucasian and most were ready-made, or nearly so, when Tom took hold of them. "O'Rourke was a great man with fighters already developed, but he never brought out any green timber," asserted one of his critics.[12]

Tom wasn't immune to the White Hope virus that swept boxing after Jack Johnson seized the world heavyweight title. One of the sorriest episodes during Johnson's title reign was O'Rourke's White Hope tournament, a one-day affair in 1911 that drew 11 largely unknown contestants and served only to prove that none of the hopefuls would have stood a snowball's chance against Johnson. But while this promotion fizzled on several fronts, O'Rourke's most lucrative promotions didn't involve George Dixon but, rather, a white man, Tom Sharkey. "There's boxing and then there's heavyweight boxing," goes an old saying, and the Sharkey dossier is a vivid example.

Sharkey

Tom Sharkey had his early fights in Honolulu while serving in the U.S. Navy and came to the fore in San Francisco. O'Rourke induced the barrel-chested sailor man to come east following his May 1898 match with James J. Jeffries, a 20-round bout that saw Sharkey lose a narrow decision. Jeffries subsequently wrested the heavyweight title from Bob Fitzsimmons.

According to a 1905 story, Sharkey was a principal in four of the top eight highest-grossing fights in New York during the Horton Law years. His opponents, in chronological order, were James J. Corbett, Kid McCoy, James J. Jeffries, and Bob Fitzsimmons.[13]

Of the four, the rematch with Jeffries was the lollapalooza. Staged at Coney Island on November 3, 1899, the contest wasn't as historically important as the Sullivan–Corbett match of 1892, but it raked in far more dough. According to the *New York Times*, the gate receipts could not have been less than $70,000 (approximately $2.7 million in 2022 dollars). The *Times*, a thorn in the side of prizefight promoters just a few years earlier, devoted an entire page to the event including an extensive round-by-round report and a list of notables in attendance that consumed four paragraphs, 73 names in all.[14]

New York fight-goers who felt cheated when the McGovern–Palmer fight ended in the opening round certainly got their money's worth with Sharkey–Jeffries. "The battle was probably the fiercest that the American fight-going public ever witnessed," said the *Times*. This was a hackneyed testimonial, but the fight was truly a fight for the ages.

Sharkey would have undoubtedly got the nod if the bout had been limited to 20 rounds, but Jeffries, who outweighed the Sailor 210–185, was the stronger man in rounds 21–25 and retained his title on the say-so of referee George Siler. Both men were badly punished, notably Sharkey who fought the last two rounds with two broken ribs. This was the first heavyweight title fight filmed under artificial light. The savagery, as recounted in all the newspapers, was the best advertisement for the film, magnifying the post-fight revenue, but had its downside as it heightened the pressure to repeal the Horton Law.[15]

Sharkey and O'Rourke never got along. For months after the big fight, they exchanged insults in the press. Sharkey wanted out, but O'Rourke had an ironclad contract that kept Sharkey noosed to him until September of 1900. Sharkey's last fight under O'Rourke's management was his match with Fitzsimmons, who knocked him out in the second round.

* * *

O'Rourke used his earnings as a prizefight promoter to become a hotel man, leasing the Delavan at Broadway and West 40th Street,

Chapter 11. Tom O'Rourke and the Other Guy

Inside the Broadway Athletic Club, ca. 1899. Note the advertisement for Tom O'Rourke's Delavan Hotel.

which he took over in the fall of 1899. The hotel's rathskeller was a popular gathering place as it was equipped with a ticker that brought in the results from all the major tracks. The Delavan and George Considine's Metropole, situated three blocks away, became known as the favorite haunts of the sporting crowd, places where many large bets were sealed. Bat Masterson resided at the Delavan with his wife during his first four years in New York.[16] The fabled Western lawman had transitioned into a newspaper columnist, covering mostly boxing for the *Morning Telegraph*, a tabloid devoted primarily to sports and theatrical news.

The repeal of the ultra-liberal Horton Law (discussed in Chapter 12) compelled O'Rourke to seek out greener pastures. In 1901, he acquired a parcel of land in East Port Chester, Connecticut, just over the New York state line, on which he planned to build a golf course spangled with a large clubhouse suited to serve as a boxing arena. A spur of the New York, New Haven, and Hartford Railroad would lead directly into the building. His partners in the venture were Richard Howell, the managing editor of the *Bridgeport Herald* and its sister paper in Waterbury, and Jacob Rubenstein, better known as Jack Rose, the latter of whom would acquire notoriety as a murder-for-hire go-between.[17] (Rose hired the gunmen that assassinated Herman Rosenthal in 1912.

The proprietor of a small, late-night gambling casino, Rosenthal died in a hail of bullets on the sidewalk in front of the Metropole Hotel. Rose arranged the hit on behalf of New York City Police Lieutenant Charles H. Becker, for whom Rose was a graft collector. The sensational murder sent Becker and the four gunmen to Sing Sing where they died in the electric chair. Rose was granted immunity for his testimony.)

Newspaper editor Howell was an important man in Connecticut politics, but public sentiment in Port Chester was strongly opposed to the scheme and the antagonists were able to muster enough support in the state legislature to force O'Rourke and his partners to abandon the project.[18]

O'Rourke's next scheme was somewhat less ambitious but no less audacious. In 1906, he founded the Tuxedo Club in Kensington, Pennsylvania. In Kensington, a hamlet 10 miles from Philadelphia, fights would be scheduled for up to 20 rounds, 14 rounds longer than what were then allowed in Philadelphia. O'Rourke's partner in this venture was Philadelphia newspaperman William "Billy" Rocap, a former amateur boxer of considerable repute who would go on the become the first chairman of the Pennsylvania Boxing Commission, an agency created in 1923.

Once again O'Rourke had miscalculated. For his second show, slated for May 29, 1906, he matched the new heavyweight champion Tommy Burns (successor to James J. Jeffries who had retired, vacating the title) against Bob Fitzsimmons. At age 43, former multi-division champion Fitzsimmons was rather long in the tooth but still had a strong following.

As had happened to him previously in Long Island City, O'Rourke had the rug pulled out from under him at the 11th hour. The Governor of Pennsylvania sent a battalion of heavily armed state troopers from their barracks in Reading to stop the fight. An attempt to stave off the insurrection failed. O'Rourke's Tuxedo Club died a quick death, and the Burns–Fitzsimmons fight never did come together.[19]

By then, O'Rourke no longer had his hotel. He had sold his interest in the property to business partners Parson Davies and James J. Corbett. In an effort to boost his sagging finances, he turned to the sport of wrestling, taking on Joe Rogers, a 270-pound Iowa farm boy billed as the American Apollo. O'Rourke dreamed of luring James J. Jeffries out of retirement and pitting him against Rogers in a freak fight that he felt certain would go over big with fans of both sports. But this proved to be nothing more than a pipe dream. O'Rourke was running cold, and history would show that as a promoter, his best days were behind him. His steady meal ticket George Dixon was long gone, and losing the other guy placed more strain on his finances.

Joe Walcott, O'Rourke's Other Guy

"Tom O'Rourke writes to a friend that he has a new fighter who is likely to astonish the world," read a story that appeared in the *Kansas City World* in October of 1892.[20] O'Rourke's new fighter was Joe Walcott, and yes, he was truly astonishing.

When this story appeared, Walcott had only one pro fight under his belt, that a 4-rounder at a theater in Philadelphia where he was appearing with George Dixon's vaudeville troupe. But O'Rourke thought so highly of his barrel-chested phenom that he was already angling for a match between Walcott and George Dawson, the welterweight champion of Australia.[21]

Before turning pro, Joe Walcott won laurels as a boxer and wrestler on the New England amateur circuit. An early mention of him in the *Boston Post* described him thusly: "Joe is a lump of muscle and brawn. He is only about five feet tall and weighs about one hundred and thirty-six when he is ready for a scrap. Joe is as strong as a bull and hard as adamant. He has very broad shoulders and very largely developed arms. He is very quick and can dodge and skip about as if he were rubber." The story noted that he was about to turn pro and that Tom O'Rourke would handle his affairs.[22]

Walcott was a shade over five feet tall, ostensibly five-foot-one-and-a-half. His arms were not only muscular but conspicuously long for a man of his height. His dark complexion coupled with his freakish appearance was a spur to racist sports cartoonists who painted him as a stereotypical Sambo in panels that simultaneously celebrated his fistic exploits. Nat Fleischer championed the cause of good Black fighters stonewalled by discrimination, but Fleischer wasn't free of the scurrilous rhetoric that was so prevalent in his day. "His build was that of a chimpanzee," wrote Fleischer, who added that the "bullet head" that sat deep on his short neck had the texture of the hardest wood. In Fleischer's opinion, Walcott's rock-hard skull was one of his chief assets, as many boxers ruined their hands hitting on it.[23]

Joe Walcott was born on March 13, 1873 (some sources say April 7, 1872), in Demerara, British Guiana, the second oldest of 13 children.

Nat Fleischer would write that he shipped to Boston from Barbados as a cabin boy on a schooner, and that before he became a full-time prizefighter, he worked as a kitchen helper and an elevator operator in a Boston hotel. Walcott didn't talk much about his background (likely because reporters never bothered to ask) other than to correct the misconception that he was born in Barbados after promoters started billing him as the Barbados Demon.

Walcott appeared on the August 22, 1893, card at Madison Square Garden that featured George Dixon vs. Billy Plimmer and stole the show, flattening Jack Hall in 25 seconds (including the 10 seconds that Hall lay prone on the canvas). It was the U.S. debut for the well-touted Hall, a veteran of many fights-to-a-finish in Australia where he previously held that nation's 138-pound title. Wearing "a smile as broad as the Atlantic Ocean," Walcott did a little victory dance before vaulting over the ropes and leaving the ring.[24]

Another Australian, Melbourne's Tom Tracey, was the victim in Walcott's next notable fight. Tracey stood a head taller than Walcott and was thought to be too clever for him, but the Barbados Demon wore him down and ultimately stopped him in the 16th round. According to some accounts, the Articles of Agreement specified a 10-round fight to be decided on scientific points, but a superseding private arrangement transformed it into a fight-to-the-finish, much to the satisfaction of the crowd.[25] This fight, held at Boston's Music Hall under the auspices of that city's Cribb Club, would appear as a title fight in some early record books, but it wasn't labeled as such in the local papers.

The first "official" world title fight for Walcott was his

Joe Walcott, the "Barbados Demon," ca. 1894.

Chapter 11. Tom O'Rourke and the Other Guy

March 1, 1895, bout at the Music Hall with Mysterious Billy Smith. They fought 15 rounds to a draw before the largest crowd ever assembled for a prizefight in this building. "Looking down from the stage where the ring was pitched, the scene disclosed a sea of intellectual faces; doctors, lawyers, merchants, college professors, artists, actors, politicians... the so-called vicious element being in the minority," said the ringside reporter for the *Boston Globe*, who chastised the referee for calling it a draw, saying that Walcott clearly had the best of it.[26] (Mysterious Billy Smith, although a supremely talented fighter, would be best known as a serial rule-bender, some say the dirtiest fighter of his era. This bout would be the first of their six meetings. Walcott won the last three to finish 3–1–2 in their series.)

Later that year, on December 2, 1895, Walcott fought Kid Lavigne at Maspeth, Queens County, Long Island. At the end of the 15-round fight, which would be ranked among the most brutal of all time, Lavigne was badly punished but still standing. The Articles of Agreement specified that Walcott had to knock out Lavigne to be considered the winner, so this match went into the books as a loss for Barbados Joe. Forced to scale down to 133 pounds, Walcott, now a full-fledged welterweight, faded in the late rounds.

Walcott would appear in 12 title fights in all, the last two after shattering his right hand when his new toy, a revolver, discharged as he was displaying it to friends at a Boston dance hall, the bullet passing through his hand and killing a man sitting across from him. (Walcott was indicted for manslaughter, but a grand jury found that the killing was accidental, and the charge was dropped.) The injury kept the Barbados Demon out of action for sixteen months.[27]

Walcott would come to be best remembered for winning fights against much bigger men; he was the sport's consummate giant killer.

His signature win was a seventh-round stoppage of Joe Choynski, the same Joe Choynski who fought a 20-round draw with James J. Corbett and would go on to KO up-and-comer Jack Johnson. Walcott knocked Choynski down five times in the opening round and kept up a steady assault until the referee halted the massacre.

Choynski, a super middleweight by today's taxonomy, had a 16-pound weight advantage. By Walcott's standards, this wasn't an especially large deficit. The following year he scored a 20-round decision over George Gardner. According to the *San Francisco Call*, the crowd laughed when the fighters were brought to center ring to get their instructions from the referee. Gardner, who would come to be recognized as the second man to hold the light heavyweight title (the division was born in 1903), was the taller man by 11 inches. More striking yet was Walcott's 1902 match with Fred Russell in Chicago. Russell was merely a journeyman, but he stood six-foot-three and out-weighed Joe by approximately 80 pounds. Walcott knocked him down in the opening round with a punch that connected when both of Joe's feet were off the ground and then bullied him around the ring for the remainder of the six-round contest.[28]

Walcott and George Dixon were the greatest of friends, but Walcott chafed at toiling in Dixon's shadow. Unlike Dixon, he found himself on the wrong end of quite a few dubious decisions, an indication that O'Rourke wasn't using all of his pull to protect him. Moreover, Joe fought several fights that were decried as fakes, a common thread among Black fighters who were routinely underpaid relative to their less talented Caucasian brethren, a disincentive to fight full-bore as that would be reckless. In this manner too was Walcott different from Dixon, as Little Chocolate's reputation as a square shooter was impeccable.

The relationship between O'Rourke and George Dixon wasn't always hunky-dory. There were periods of mutual dislike. But their rifts were quickly patched up, and on balance their longstanding relationship was harmonious (so long as Dixon commanded hefty purses). However, O'Rourke and Joe Walcott were constantly at loggerheads, and their relationship ruptured well before Joe's marketability had dried up. "Walcott was one of the hardest men to manage I ever had," O'Rourke told a reporter in 1903. "He did not want to train, but was so strong that it did not make much difference... He could take an amount of punishment that would have sent a white man to the hospital for repairs."[29]

When O'Rourke and Barbados Joe were feuding, the mainstream press was inclined to take O'Rourke's side. In their eyes, Walcott was an ingrate and moreover, behaving stupidly, cutting off his nose to spite his face. An article in the *Waterbury Evening Democrat* implied that it wasn't wise to make an enemy of a man like O'Rourke who rubbed elbows with a number of hard-boiled characters: "Somewhere in New York there is an extremely black and squat negro who, if the truth were known, probably is in mortal terror of his life.... If Walcott has broken with O'Rourke, one of the wonders of the ring has happened, because until now O'Rourke has dominated him completely. When Walcott loses O'Rourke, he loses a man who made a fighter of him."[30]

After Walcott left him, O'Rourke found a new "colored wonder" in the form of Larry Temple. O'Rourke moved in on him after Temple

Chapter 11. Tom O'Rourke and the Other Guy

blew away Pittsburgh knockout artist Eddie Kennedy on a Christmas Day 1901 card in Cincinnati. Temple, a New Yorker and not quite 20 years old, was described in one newspaper story as a human battering ram, the same words that had previously been used to describe Barbados Joe Walcott.

O'Rourke brought Temple to Boston in December of 1903 to fight Walcott in a bout slated for 15 rounds. Temple was still green—he had never gone past 10 rounds—and was a decided underdog to Barbados Joe who hadn't yet messed up his right hand and wasn't yet seen as a fighter on the downgrade. But the bad blood between O'Rourke and Walcott was useful in promoting the fight, and a crowd of 3,000 braved a severe winter storm to see it.

Temple made a good showing but wasn't ready to topple a fighter as formidable as Barbados Joe Walcott, who outpointed him handily. (Temple and Walcott would fight twice more. Their second meeting, a 10-round scrap in Baltimore, was ruled a draw, and their final meeting, staged in Boston, resulted in Temple winning by knockout. By then, Walcott was conspicuously shopworn, and Temple was no longer with Tom O'Rourke.)[31]

CHAPTER 12

Dixon vs. McGovern: The Championship Fight

George Dixon began his training in West Baden Springs and completed it in Lakewood, New Jersey, a resort community for the rich and famous located 70 miles from New York City. He spent the night before the fight in a suite at the Delavan. Terry McGovern returned to his regular training camp in Fleetwood, a township in Westchester County just north of the Bronx. In Fleetwood, McGovern did his running in a park that previously had housed a harness racing track.

McGovern opened the favorite at odds of 10/6. The price fluctuated between 10/8 and 2/1 in the final days of betting.

It was easy to build a case for Terrible Terry, or more precisely a case against George Dixon. Little Chocolate was only 29 years old, but he had seemingly been around forever, and he had a lot of wear and tear. Off and on beginning with his four-round fight with Billy Plimmer in 1893, reporters had written that he had passed his peak. He hadn't knocked a man unconscious with a single punch since KOing Billy Pierce earlier in 1893, and counting his vaudeville fights, he had fought several hundred bouts in the interim. They say that a boxer's legs go first, but with Dixon, it was the force of his punches.

It was easy to visualize McGovern winning on cuts. Dixon had emerged from several fights with a bad cut over his left eye. McGovern didn't drink, smoke, or chew, whereas Dixon's affection for alcoholic beverages had become an open secret; his frequent visits to West Baden Springs were increasingly seen as impelled by a need to dry out. And Terrible Terry was in much better form. He had stopped 13 straight opponents, 11 in the first three rounds, and this in an era when a long string of knockouts was far less common than in modern times. A popular wager was on the "under" as to whether Little Chocolate would make it past the 10th round. It was an "even money" proposition. Tom O'Rourke reportedly covered many of these bets.[1]

Chapter 12. Dixon vs. McGovern: The Championship Fight

In a fight of this magnitude, it was common for some reporters to seek out the opinions of experts in the medical field. By 1900, the pseudo-science of phrenology had largely fallen out of favor, but there were yet occasional references to it in the sporting press. Born in Vienna and first popularized in Britain, phrenology rested on the principal that propensities and capabilities of individuals are founded on the physiology of the brain and can be identified by examining the conformation of the skull.

There were two versions of a pre-fight story that appeared in the papers, stories identical in nearly every little detail save for the identity of the consultant(s) cited by the author. Both stories informed their readers that McGovern was seen as the smart pick based on his "superior dynamic force [manifested] in the length of his jaw from the opening of the ear to the tip of the chin, the thin athletic cheeks and the roundness of the back of his head, the most trustworthy sign of muscular energy and determination."[2] These words were attributed to the famous Professor Fowler and also to a panel of New York phrenologists, the phantom panelists presumably pressed into service when it came to the attention of the author that Orson Fowler, the greatest popularizer of phrenology in the United States, had been dead for more than 12 years! (Little Chocolate wasn't going to get the best of it in a phrenological battle with a white man. Practitioners assumed that different races were at different stages of evolutionary development, and that the Caucasian race was the most advanced.)

But while Terrible Terry was the consensus, Dixon certainly had his backers. McGovern's victories had come with such consummate ease that one couldn't really get a line on him. Terry was a terror, but he was still a pup, not quite 20 years old. Some thought that Dixon would take the upstart to school, giving him a harsh lesson in the finer points of the sweet science. Having Tom O'Rourke in his corner was considered a plus. Moreover, it was noted that the odds were out of whack from a historical standpoint. In memory, no reigning champion had ever dressed as such a conspicuous underdog.

Those inclined toward Dixon felt that way more firmly when Dixon announced that, win or lose, this would be his final fight.[3] Like all professional boxers, Dixon always went into a fight proclaiming that he was in the best shape of his life. This time, no one questioned his sincerity. He was a proud warrior, a man protective of his legacy, and it made sense that he would leave no stone unturned in his quest to exit the sport on a winning note. He had entered the ring as high as 128 pounds, but had no difficulty meeting the 118-pound weight requirement for this bout. Both he and McGovern tipped the scales at 116½ at the weigh-in, which was conducted at 3:00 p.m. on the day of the fight.

Around the country, people gathered outside newspaper offices where telegraphic reports of the fight were posted on bulletin boards. Some enterprising theater owners leased a Western Union wire so that reports could be interjected into the evening's bill of fare. The play *The Great Train Robbery* was playing at the Bijou in Pittsburgh. Updates were read between acts, and advertisements promised that if the fight went the full distance, the theater would remain open until the referee gave his decision.[4] In New York, the street in front of the entrance to the Broadway Arena was choked with people unable or unwilling to meet the price demanded by scalpers who were getting more than four times face value for some choice seats. Some of those that found themselves stranded out in the cold were out-of-town sportswriters who had been

McGovern (left) and Dixon face off in a promotional photograph prior to their 1900 rematch.

Chapter 12. Dixon vs. McGovern: The Championship Fight

led to believe that there was a seat inside the building with their name on it.⁵

The Fight

In the history books, Terry McGovern would be limbed as a fighter who burst out of his corner like a caged animal at the sound of the opening bell. Against Dixon, he reined in this impulse. From the onset, he concentrated on Dixon's body. In the clinches, he banged away at Dixon's ribs with his free arm. The intent was to wear him down while smothering his attack. But Dixon had good success whenever he was able to open up distance between them. In round two and again in round three, he staggered McGovern with a left to the jaw. The third round was clearly all Dixon, and ringside bookmakers were now dealing odds of even money, notwithstanding the fact that a big lump had developed under Little Chocolate's left eye.

McGovern did a lot better in round four. Dixon slowed down, and when he returned to his corner at the conclusion of the round, he had a worried look on his face. The fifth stanza was pretty much a carbon. During one segment, Dixon rushed in, shooting a left to McGovern's face, but Terry countered with a hard left to the jaw and then, as they fell into a clinch, he rammed Dixon's kidneys with three sharp uppercuts. Dixon's left side and his back over his kidneys developed a pinkish tint.

Rounds six and seven were big rounds for McGovern. In round six, Terry staggered Dixon with a right to the jaw and then staggered him again with the same punch. Dixon remained upright only because his back was against the ropes. In the following round, one of Terry's punches appeared to break Dixon's nose. It bled profusely. At the bell, Little Chocolate looked exhausted. The spring in his legs was gone, and he staggered back to his corner.

Round eight was Dixon's worst nightmare. McGovern battered him all over the ring, knocking him down at least six times. (Some reports said eight.) After each of the first two knockdowns, Terry helped Dixon to his feet. Dixon's final trip to the mat was the result of a fusillade of punches ending with a punch to the ribs as he pitched face first to the canvas. He rose on unsteady legs but looked as if he could be knocked over by a feather, and O'Rourke, with just a few seconds remaining in the round, mercifully threw in the sponge.⁶

Seconds later, Joe Walcott bounded into the ring. Fearing that he was a catalyst for mayhem, a police sergeant bounded in after him and collared him, followed by two of his fellow officers. But Joe wasn't of a mind to cause any trouble. Weeping openly, he convinced the bluecoats that all he wanted to do was console his best friend and congratulate the victor, and they let him go. Barbados Joe was not completely sober in the estimation of a reporter, who wrote that the officers' uniforms were in danger of being stained by his copious tears.[7]

Talking to reporters after the bout, both spoke kindly of the other. "I have been fighting for fourteen years and have met men in the lightweight class ten pounds heavier than McGovern was tonight, but not one of them could land a blow as hard as those he sent in. He is a wonderful fighter and fairly won the championship. He has my best wishes," said Dixon.

"I have at last beaten the greatest fighter of them all and the featherweight championship is mine," said McGovern. "I have beaten some good men and taken some heavy punches, but the hardest fighter and as game a man as I ever met in the ring is George Dixon."[8]

The press almost to a man pronounced the fight a stirring battle and applauded Dixon for his gallant effort. "Battle Will Live in History as One of Remarkable Courage on the Part of a Ring Veteran Who Met His Match in the Youth and Vigor of an Opponent in the Very Last Bout of an Extraordinary Career of Success," read a sub-headline on the front page of the next day's *Boston Globe*.[9] However, one of the attendees saw things differently. Benjamin Odell, Jr., the chairman of the New York Republican Committee, thought the fight was a fake and that the audience had been humbugged. "It was all cut and dried by those who had fixed the betting," he said. "I was disgusted. The [Horton] law must be repealed at once." Odell's wild allegation, which made all the papers, was dismissed by a Buffalo reporter as the blather of a lunatic.[10] (Odell went on to become the Governor of New York, succeeding Theodore Roosevelt.)

In the bare-knuckle days in England, fight fans were constantly holding benefits for their favorite bruisers. A popular fighter would be feted with a testimonial dinner after a hard loss. The money collected for him would assuage the financial hurt of coming up empty in an era where winner-take-all was the norm. The tradition carried over to the United States, continuing into the day when fight managers negotiated terms that assured that the loser would walk away with something, perhaps even the larger share of the spoils. Forty-three days after the fight, a benefit for George Dixon was held at the Broadway Arena.

Chapter 12. Dixon vs. McGovern: The Championship Fight

A big turnout was expected. Dixon was always the first to volunteer his services for a benefit and never took a cent, said a Buffalo writer. Moreover, Dixon would always pay his way at the door, even if he was on the program.[11]

Now it was time to reciprocate, and the boxing community responded in spades; it was a lavish affair. James J. Corbett, Tom Sharkey, Joe Gans, and Joe Choynski, among other pugilistic notables, engaged in a playful sparring exhibition with a foil. Terry McGovern sparred three rounds with Dixon after presenting Dixon with a $500 check. All told, Little Chocolate raked in $8,000.[12]

George Dixon had won more championship battles than any fighter that ever lived to that point in history, but the outpouring of affection for him said as much about Dixon the man as about Dixon the prizefighter. "[He] has never been a coward; he has never been a trickster; nor a schemer.... He has not added a stain to the sport's escutcheon, nor has he done a public act in connection with it that he need feel ashamed of," said a writer, adding that honoring him was a way of showing people that admirers of pugilism appreciate traits such as honesty, generosity, and modesty and encourage the fostering of these traits among young people.[13] He might have added that Dixon was abstemious, at least on the surface. "[He] never gave outward evidence of being a spendthrift."[14]

In retirement, Dixon would be a saloonkeeper. Tom O'Rourke had set him up in an establishment in Lower Manhattan. Situated at 511 Sixth Avenue, the place was prophetically named the White Elephant. If the business was slow to turn a profit, said the *Boston Globe*, Dixon had a host of friends ready to prop him up financially.[15]

CHAPTER 13

Terry McGovern: High Times and a Shocking Reversal

The Dixon–McGovern fight came at a momentous time in the history of prizefighting in New York. Five days earlier, on January 4, 1900, Governor Theodore Roosevelt dropped a bombshell on the Empire State boxing community when he came out in favor of abolishing the Horton Law in his annual address to the legislature. "When any sport is carried on primarily for money—it is in danger of losing much that is valuable and of acquiring some exceedingly undesirable characteristics," said Roosevelt. "In the case of prize-fighting, not only do all the objections which apply to other professional sports apply in aggravated form, but in addition the exhibition has a very demoralizing and brutalizing effect.... Moreover, the evils are greatly aggravated by the fact that the fight is the occasion for unlimited betting and gambling."[1]

Although Gov. Roosevelt was cozy with the man spearheading the effort to repeal the Horton Law, Rochester assemblyman Merton E. Lewis, a future New York State attorney general, and although he had previously indicated that he favored repeal, the fight mob yet did not see this coming. To the contrary, they assumed that Roosevelt, who had boxed while a student at Harvard, advancing to the finals of an intramural tournament in his junior year, was "one of theirs." In November of 1896, while serving as the president of the New York City Board of Police Commissioners, Roosevelt had attended a fight between Peter Maher and Joe Choynski at the Broadway Athletic Club. What had been a relatively tame fight turned violent in the sixth frame when Maher knocked Choynski unconscious with a right-hand swing to the jaw. Asked his opinion, Roosevelt said he thought the contest was a "grand struggle" and "I could find nothing brutal in it." He would later assert that he had suffered a worse knockout, not once but twice, when he fell

Chapter 13. Terry McGovern: High Times and a Shocking Reversal

off his horse in a polo match and that when he recovered, he was as good as new.[2]

The backlash was loud. A common argument heard in defense of prizefighting was that the sport had come a long way since prizefights attracted the dregs of society. "When one stops to consider the class of spectators who witness the big bouts ... one can see that the best element of the public is attracted and delights in boxing," said James J. Corbett.[3]

Life-threatening and fatal injuries were occurring with greater and greater frequency on the football field, a fact not lost on the proponents of prizefighting, who argued that boxing was being unfairly singled-out. As for betting, John L. Sullivan asserted that it couldn't be stopped and that more money was bet on the annual Harvard–Yale boat race and on Ivy League football games "than on any boxing contest that ever happened," which may well have been true. John L. had an interesting twist on matters when he laid part of the blame for this unexpected development at the feet of sports cartoonists whose newspaper drawings made it seem as if every bout was a brutal slugfest.[4]

As would be true to a far greater extent several years later when reformers succeeded in shutting down the racetracks, those with a vested interest in the continuation of things as they were bemoaned the loss of jobs. Boxers and their managers were merely the tip of the iceberg. Referees, timekeepers, announcers, seconds, ticket speculators, and those that placed bets for the big sports would also be out of work, noted a writer for a Connecticut paper.[5] Killing prizefighting would kill off the special editions that tabloid papers cranked out in conjunction with big fights, meaning less money for newsboys. Because the stereotypical newsboy had spent his formative years in an orphanage, newsboys were sympathetic characters.

There was still a chance that the anti-prizefighting bill could die on the vine. It had to be approved by both houses of the legislature before being signed into law by the governor, and if it advanced that far, there was still an outside chance that Roosevelt could be persuaded to change his opinion. Thus, it was business as usual until it became obvious that the repeal of the Horton Law was inevitable, and then it would be more business than usual as organizers scrambled to get in one last lick before the door was closed.

* * *

After his fast knockout of Pedlar Palmer, Terry McGovern capitalized on his growing fame by appearing on the stage of Brooklyn's

Star Theater. He sparred with George Monroe in an exhibition that was awkwardly book-ended by sketch comedy acts. But Sam Harris had bigger plans for him. The week after defeating George Dixon, Harris rolled McGovern into the cast of "Gay Morning Glories," a variety show with comedians, singers, acrobats, a cakewalk dancing duo, and a large chorus line. Terry's contribution was a three-round exhibition of sparring and a short, animated talk telling how he conquered the great George Dixon. A bit later, the film of the fight, and a fake version of it, began circulating in vaudeville houses.

McGovern capitalized on his fame in other ways too. The Shrewesbury Publishing Company of Chicago released *How to Box to Win*, a book that was part autobiography and part instructional manual. McGovern was listed as the co-author along with James J. Corbett; Dr. Gardner J. Smith, a physical fitness expert; and the Keeley brothers, Gus and Arthur, vaudevillians whose act was punctuated by a bag punching routine. The actual author, however, was the astoundingly prolific hack journalist Albert Payson Terhune, who had ghostwritten Jim Corbett's biography among many others.[6] McGovern also received royalties (likely only a smidgen) from *My Sweet Camilla*, a love song that he ostensibly wrote, penning both the score and lyrics. (The song "was no more written by McGovern than I wrote the Bible," snorted the sporting editor of the *Buffalo Enquirer*, who wrote under the pen name Hotspur.)[7]

Periodically Sam Harris would arrange a fight for McGovern while Terry was out touring on the road. On January 29, a mere 20 days after his fight with Dixon, Terry put the unheralded Jack Ward to sleep in the opening round of a fight at an ice rink in Baltimore. Three days later he was in Chicago where he stopped Eddie Santry in the fifth round at Tattersalls. According to an article in the *Baltimore Sun*, McGovern vs. Santry was the greatest boxing show ever held in the Windy City: "Special trains were run from nearby towns and fully 15,000 persons jammed and pushed through the building."[8] Then it was back to the Broadway A.C. where Terry celebrated his 20th birthday with a third-round stoppage of Oscar Gardner, the Omaha Kid.

Gardner had given George Dixon a world of trouble—the verdict favoring Dixon was controversial—and Gardner's fame grew larger when he conquered Solly Smith, stopping the former title-holder in the seventh round in a bout billed for the American featherweight title. But his recent efforts had been spotty amid reports that he had been pushed into fights by an "injudicious" manager before he had fully recovered from a bout of malarial fever.[9]

Chapter 13. Terry McGovern: High Times and a Shocking Reversal

McGovern was such a heavy favorite that virtually the only betting was on whether the Omaha Kid would last 10 rounds. He didn't come close, but he gave McGovern's backers an anxious moment in the first round when he knocked Terry down with a left hook to the jaw. McGovern was up in a jiff, grabbing hold of Gardner's leg as he pulled himself upright. It was the first time that Terry had ever been rattled according to some news reports, and McGovern made him pay, bombarding Gardner with "a torrent of fistic abuse" before the fight was stopped at the 19-second mark of the third stanza.[10]

Six days later, Terry KOed Eddie Lenny in the second round in Philadelphia, and then it was back

A 1900 poster displayed wherever McGovern appeared during his association with the play, ca. 1899.

to Tattersalls where Tommy White lasted the distance in a six-round contest, ending McGovern's skein of 19 victories by way of stoppage.

Old war horse Tommy Warren and Philadelphia journeyman Ellwood McCloskey were next on McGovern's docket. Neither offered much of a challenge, especially Warren, who had fought only once in the previous eight years, his career having been interrupted by a stay in a Texas prison for manslaughter and employment with the Army transport service in Manila during the Spanish-American War. Once recognized as the best man in his weight class on the Pacific Coast, Warren was a shell of the fighter that conquered Jack Havlin in 1888, and McGovern needed only one round to dismiss him in a bout that was such a gross mismatch that management hurriedly patched together an extra bout to appease the crowd.[11]

Clash of the Little Giants

These "stay busy fights" prefaced a second meeting between Terrible Terry and Tommy White. The rematch was staged before the Seaside Athletic Club in Coney Island on June 12, 1900.

In their first meeting, McGovern was clearly dominant, but White came on strong in the final round, leaving the impression that he would have prevailed if the fight had been scheduled across a longer route. But in the rematch Terry took him apart. The bout was delayed for half an hour when the lights in the arena went out, and another lighting failure in the first round interrupted the action. When the lights came back on, "Terry waltzed into White like a Nebraska tornado," said the well-known boxing scribe J.B. "Macon" McCormick, and he never took his foot off the pedal. White was knocked down eight times in all in less than three full rounds and sprained his ankle on his final trip to the canvas, terminating the fight.[12]

Eleven days later, Terry was back in Chicago. In the opposite corner was none other than George Dixon, whose retirement was short-lived. McGovern had defeated Dixon so thoroughly in their first encounter that the rematch (discussed in the next chapter) wasn't an especially big news story and played to a lot of empty seats. Suffice it to say that Little Chocolate was beyond the point where he was capable of arresting McGovern's momentum.

For some months it had been speculated that Terry would be moving up to the lightweight division. It wasn't because he was outgrowing the featherweight class but because he was considered so far above the featherweight pack that he had run out of viable opponents. The most appealing fight for him was a match with Frank Erne.

Erne had boxed George Dixon on fairly even terms in three bouts consuming 45 rounds. He then went on to wrest the world lightweight title from George Lavigne, out-pointing the Saginaw Kid in a 20-round contest, and solidified his hold on the title with a 12th-round stoppage of Joe Gans, who gave in after suffering a terrible gash over his left eye. The incision likely resulted from an accidental clash of heads, but Erne was coming on strong before the pivotal moment.[13]

When McGovern and Frank Erne met at Madison Square Garden on July 16, 1900, Erne's title wasn't at stake. The match was made for 128 pounds, a "catchweight." Moreover, the bout was a 10-rounder and the Articles of Agreement specified that Terry would get the larger share of the purse if the fight went the limit. These were ill-advised concessions on the part of Erne's management, but Erne stood to receive a nice payout no matter how the bout turned out.

Chapter 13. Terry McGovern: High Times and a Shocking Reversal

The fight didn't last very long, but while it lasted it was wildly entertaining. George Siler, who was not given to hyperbole, wrote that it was undoubtedly the fastest three rounds of fighting ever witnessed in the East.[14] Erne rocked McGovern repeatedly with his stiff left jab, but he couldn't keep Terry from boring in. In round three, a left-right combination sent the blood spurting from Erne's nose, and McGovern knocked him down twice, the second time with a flurry climaxed by a punch behind the ear that left Erne in such bad shape that his seconds threw in the sponge.

The fight was held on one of the warmest days of the year in New York, and the arena was unbearably warm. Venders selling palm leaf fans did a landslide business, increasing the price as the supply began to run out. But the weather did not hurt attendance. The gate receipts were said to be the largest for a one-night event in the 10-year history of the building. McGovern, who was entitled to 75 percent of half the box office take, cleared $27,187.50 (approximately $920,000 in 2022 dollars).[15]

In Brooklyn, there was the usual scene whenever Terrible Terry vanquished an opponent thought to represent a significant threat. Several thousand people, including hundreds of barefoot boys, gathered outside the main office of the *Daily Eagle* to follow the action. When the final bulletin was posted, there was "delirious excitement." It took a considerable time before policemen and railroad inspectors were able to clear the streetcar tracks.[16]

Frank Erne, ca. 1899.

Terry no longer rushed home to Brooklyn after a fight. He hid out in a Manhattan hotel rather than face the crushing horde of liquored-up well-wishers waiting to press the flesh.

McGovern wouldn't fight again until November, but he stayed busy in the interval. On August 18, 1900, he made his debut as a thespian at the Trocadero in Philadelphia where he played the role of the hero in *The Bowery After Dark*.

A boilerplate melodrama, the play was in its second season. When Terry signed on, a replication of his fight with Frank Erne was melded into the script. A synopsis: A knave intercepts and destroys love letters sent from a soldier fighting in the Spanish-American War to his girlfriend and convinces her that the soldier, the love of her life, has stopped communicating with her because he has died in combat. The miscreant, who has gambling debts, wants to marry her himself to gain access to her money. A bootblack overhears the ne'er-do-well bragging about his scheme, exposes it, and gives the scoundrel a good thrashing. McGovern played the bootblack, a variation on the raggedy but honest-to-a-fault newsboy, a stock character in the melodrama genre. Actors in supporting roles played stereotypical Bowery characters. For a time, Terry McGovern's wife played the role of Nell the Bowery waif, the bootblack's girlfriend. Like her husband, she had no previous acting experience. The play would undergo numerous revisions during McGovern's association with it.

Notable boxers had previously appeared in stage plays. Peter Jackson, the esteemed Australian boxer, played the title role in *Uncle Tom's Cabin*. John L. Sullivan toured the United States and Australia in *Honest Hearts and Willing Hands*, a play in which he played a poor blacksmith threatened with eviction from his home. Terrible Terry wasn't an actor on the level of James J. Corbett, who could hold his own with classically trained stage actors, but Terry was far better than John L. Sullivan and could comfortably handle a bigger role in a play. And the play, although not written with him in mind, was in concert with his ring persona as it had few dull moments. *The Bowery After Dark* doesn't flow, said a reviewer, "but jerks along like a bunch of firecrackers."[17]

McGovern would appear in two other melodramas: *The Road to Ruin*, described as the story of a badger game with comedy trimmings, and *For Fame and Fortune*. The former was a revival. During its long run, several other boxers took on the role that Terry played. *For Fame and Fortune* was a dramatization of McGovern's life story with Terry playing himself. The highlight was a reproduction of his fight with Pedlar Palmer. According to his ghost-written 1900 biography, when McGovern was on the road with a theatrical company, he ran eight to 10 miles each morning and skipped rope for an hour after his final performance.

Chapter 13. Terry McGovern: High Times and a Shocking Reversal

McGovern returned to the ring in Louisville where he defended his world featherweight title against old foe Joe Bernstein. The rugged Jewish battler was the only man to take Terry the limit in a long fight, lasting the full 25 rounds in their previous engagement, but Terry had no fear of him and arrived in Louisville with only one day to get ready after fulfilling a theater engagement in Indianapolis.

In a pre-fight story in the *Louisville Courier-Journal*, McGovern, not yet 21 years old, was called "the greatest pugilist the world has ever known," and, against Bernstein, he did nothing to corrode that exalted opinion, scoring five knockdowns before George Siler stopped the match in the seventh round. Bernstein's best moment came in round five when he feigned grogginess, and Terry took the bait, but after being jolted with a hard punch to the face, McGovern quickly re-established his dominance.[18]

McGovern closed out his 1900 campaign with two bouts in Chicago. Kid Broad made things warm for him on November 13, but Broad wilted after suffering a badly cut lip, and Terry pummeled him all over the ring in the final stanza. His December 13 match with Joe Gans, his seventh and ultimately final appearance at Tattersalls, would go down as one of the most infamous fights in boxing history.

Joe Gans, a Black Baltimorean, would come to be recognized as one of the all-time greats, arguably the best lightweight ever, although partisans of Benny Leonard and Roberto Duran might choose to differ. When he fought Terry McGovern, he was 26 years old and hadn't yet achieved the renown that would come to him, but he was considered the cream of the lightweights, and those in the know could see that he was special. The man who would acquire the cognomen "Old Master" was unbeaten in 14 fights since losing to Frank Erne, winning the last 10 inside the distance.

Terry McGovern's win over Erne was tainted because Erne, a natural lightweight, was forced to come in at 128 pounds and slimming down diminished his vigor. Joe Gans wasn't similarly hampered. He was allowed to weigh in at 133 for McGovern, the generally accepted benchmark for a lightweight. However, the terms of agreement specified that he would be relegated to taking the short end of the purse if he wasn't able to stop Terry inside six rounds.

George Siler didn't make a prediction—as the fight's referee, that wouldn't have been kosher—but he reminded his readers that McGovern had a lot working against him: weight, height, reach, experience, and ring generalship. Joe Gans vs. Terry McGovern, wrote Siler, was the most important fight in Chicago fight history.[19]

Fights of this magnitude invariably elicited rumors of skullduggery, but in this instance, the scent of corruption was especially strong. There were several suspicious fights in New York in the final days of the Horton Law, putting the sport under a more sensitive microscope, and the odd betting gave credence to the scuttlebutt that Gans would take a dive. When the fight was announced, the odds of McGovern scoring a knockout were 5/2 (plus-250 in modern U.S. gambling lingo).

Joe Gans, shown here ca. 1907, rebounded from his baleful showing against Terry McGovern and went on to be recognized as one of the all-time greats.

This was quickly bet down to 2/1 and then to "even money" on the eve of the bout with no buy-back. Members of the African American community were caught up the wave, putting their coin on the white boy. This phenomenon wasn't limited to Chicago. Bet-takers in other parts of the country were also inundated with "unnatural money."[20]

When the fight played out as it did, there was a great outpouring of outrage. Fighting off his back foot, Gans threw very few punches, none with bad intentions, during the brief encounter. McGovern knocked him down twice in the opening round, the second knockdown coming as the bell sounded, and then put him down twice more in the second and ultimately final stanza. Terry's final punch put Gans on his back, but he rolled over and was counted out while taking a knee.

Gans would claim that he had trouble breathing after absorbing a hard body punch early in the fight, and his manager Al Herford claimed that Gans had been bothered by a stomach ailment. However, in the court of public opinion, Gans' feeble effort marked him a willing pawn in a betting coup. Siler, the third man in the ring, felt that way too. "If Gans was really trying," he said, "[then] I don't know much about the

Chapter 13. Terry McGovern: High Times and a Shocking Reversal

game."[21] The stigma wore off Joe Gans as his career progressed, and it was generally conceded that Terry McGovern wasn't aware that the fix was in, if it was indeed a hippodrome (i.e., a fake).

It would be written that the Gans–McGovern fiasco killed professional boxing in Chicago. This wasn't true. Boxing continued, but on a much smaller scale. There were 106 professional boxing shows in Chicago in 1900, only 46 the following year, and these were low-budget promotions. Mayor Carter Harrison, Jr., was so infuriated by the Gans–McGovern fight and the backlash to it that he issued a manifesto stating there would be no more boxing shows at Tattersalls while he was in office.[22] McGovern vs. Gans was the last fight ever at Tattersalls, which was converted to a warehouse before being torn down in 1910.

The clampdown in Chicago and strictures elsewhere accelerated the sport's westward drift. In San Francisco, a new entity, the Twentieth Century Athletic Club, was established by Jim Kennedy in partnership with local investors Jim Coffroth and Jack Gleason. A man of some importance in New York boxing circles, Kennedy, in common with Tom O'Rourke and other promoters, fled the Big Apple following the repeal of the Horton Law.

Kennedy's first offering in his new stomping grounds came on June 28, 1901, with a fight between George "Elbows" McFadden, a New Yorker, and Dal Hawkins, which McFadden won on a foul. Terry McGovern made his West Coast debut for Kennedy the following month against Oscar Gardner, the first of two consecutive appearances for Terry at Mechanics' Pavilion.

McGovern made short work of Gardner when they met the previous year. "After the first round it was merely an exhibition of bag punching, and the bag was the once redoubtable Omaha Kid," summarized the reporter for the *New York Journal*.[23] But Kennedy's PR people had a ready-made hook to sell the rematch. The punch that put McGovern on the deck in the opening stanza became more explosive in the re-telling, and it would be written that McGovern was the beneficiary of a long count. "Oscar and disinterested parties say it was a clear case of highway robbery," wrote George Siler in the *Chicago Tribune*. "After Terry had regained his feet, he was several blocks up queer street and [that's when referee Charley White] stepped between the boys and entertained Gardner regarding the rules until Terry had fully recovered."[24]

McGovern–Gardner II lasted one round longer than the original, but was no less one-sided. The Omaha Kid was saved by the bell after being knocked completely out of the ring in round three, but that merely postponed the inevitable. He "took a beating such as must have churned his insides and rattled every tooth in his head," said a reporter for the *San Francisco Call*, which ran three post-fight stories side-by-side under a banner that read "M'Govern, The Prize-Fighter Is Still, 'Terry, The Terrible.'"[25] One of the stories carried the byline of the bout's referee, Harry Corbett, an unexpected pick to work the fight as he didn't have a great deal of experience. The older brother of Jim Corbett, Harry Corbett ran the largest poolroom in the city. He was an important cog in the San Francisco boxing machinery; weigh-ins for important fights were customarily held in Harry's betting establishment.

McGovern's next opponent, Aurelio Herrera, came from Bakersfield, a wooly city in California's San Joaquin Valley that was then teeming with roughnecks and roustabouts drawn there by the discovery of vast oil deposits in the nearby foothills. He was managed by Frank Carillo, who owned Bakersfield's Standard Theater, a combination burlesque house and gambling casino. A man who was always seen with a pistol strapped to his hip, Carillo purportedly employed Herrera as a poker dealer before Herrera the prizefighter fell right into his lap.[26]

Herrera would be stamped by a boxing writer of a later era as the hardest hitter for his weight and inches that ever breathed. His fight with Terry McGovern was refashioned into a corker in which McGovern came back from the brink of defeat. Herrera was a fierce hitter, that was certainly true, but newspaper accounts of the fight tell a different story than the fanciful 1927 re-telling of it by hack journalist Hype Igoe.[27]

The author of the front-page, post-fight story in the *Humboldt (CA) Times* speculated that McGovern, who stopped Herrera in the fifth, may have "carried" Herrera to let it go past four rounds for betting purposes.[28] That the fight was a mismatch wasn't entirely unexpected. Herrera was undefeated and had a slew of fast knockouts to his credit, but all of his victims were novices or men of little repute. His best wins would come later in his career.

When McGovern returned to Brooklyn, he was feted by the club that he established as a hobby, the Terry McGovern Athletic and Social Club. At the banquet, he was gifted an expensive gold-headed ebony cane with his name inscribed on it. He stayed mostly at home over the next few months, keeping a low profile, but made the news in July of 1901 when, after a lunch engagement in the city, he and Joe Humphreys joined a band of protestors at Madison Square Park rallying against the introduction of pay chairs in New York's public parks. Terry occupied one of the designated chairs, refused to pay the 5-cent tariff, and dared

Chapter 13. Terry McGovern: High Times and a Shocking Reversal

the attendants to try to evict him. When they realized who he was, they backed off, as the police, whose sympathies were with the protestors, looked on bemusedly. When McGovern and Humphreys left the park, they were joined by a great throng of cheering fans who accompanied the pair as they walked to the streetcar stop several blocks away.[29] (The pay chairs had a short life; they were kicked out of the parks when a judge sided with a taxpayer who balked at having to pay for the privilege of sitting in the shade and sued to have them removed.)

In truth, despite his dominating performance, McGovern did not look all that sharp against Aurelio Herrera. His punches were often wide. But there was yet the perception that Terry had evolved into an even more formidable fighter since his first meeting with George Dixon. Bat Masterson, a recognized authority on pugilism, saw Terry McGovern in the flesh for the first time when he fought Dixon for the second time and was impressed. "From what I heard about him," said Masterson, "I supposed that he relied altogether on his strength and hitting powers to bring home the money. But I think differently now. He's a clever fighter in every sense of the word, quick on his feet, hits straight, doesn't swing wildly, and is a capable judge of distance."[30] When Terry consented to risk his belt against Young Corbett II, it figured to be another cakewalk.

Young Corbett II, whose ring name paid homage to his trainer Johnny Corbett but who was sometimes disingenuously packaged as Jim Corbett's nephew, was born William Rothwell in Denver. He had won a 10-round decision over comebacking George Dixon in his most recent fight, but Dixon was considered damaged goods, and the word from Denver was that Corbett II had been a tad fortunate to get the nod, finishing the fight with his face bathed in blood. Eight months younger than young McGovern, he had earlier lost to Billy Rotchford despite an eight-pound weight advantage, had been stopped by Benny Yanger, and had fought almost exclusively in his home state, venturing only as far east as Des Moines. "As far as cleverness is concerned there are probably fifty men at his weight who could make Corbett look like an amateur," ventured Lou Houseman.[31]

McGovern vs. Corbett appeared headed to Butte, Montana. A predominantly Irish Catholic industrial city with the personality of a Wild West boomtown, Butte had a flourishing club scene, but its remote location in copper mining country was a drawback when trying to land a nationally important fight. Butte ultimately fell out of the running, and the match would be planted at Connecticut's Hartford Coliseum, where it materialized on a snowy Thanksgiving afternoon. The consensus of opinion was that the fight wouldn't last long, and that proved to be true, but not in the manner expected. In a massive upset, Corbett knocked out Terrible Terry in the second round.

Terrible Terry and Young Corbett II fought hammer and tongs from the opening bell. Both fighters were on the canvas in the second round, first McGovern who came up swinging like a wildcat after being sent down by a left hook. He returned the favor with a right hook and then staggered Corbett before a rattling exchange in which Corbett put Terry on the deck again with a right to the jaw. McGovern struggled to get upright, but was unable to beat the "10" count.

New York Evening World sports editor Robert Edgren, who covered thousands of prizefights, would write that the first round of the battle was the most furious three minutes of boxing that he had ever seen.[32] Edgren was not above over-dramatizing old fights when he re-visited them years later, but other eye-witness accounts of the battle bear witness that it was a jaw-dropper. Looking back 25 years, syndicated sportswriter Joe Williams wrote that no featherweight fight, before or since, matched it for savagery and drama.[33]

When Young Corbett returned home to Denver, several thousand people were at the depot to welcome the new featherweight champion, and he was paraded through the streets in a carriage drawn by six white horses.[34] Terry McGovern's homecoming was quiet. Those in the special train that brought the New York contingent back to the city, recalled Edgren, were as somber as if they had attended a funeral.

Chapter 14

George Dixon's Second Act: A Career on the Skids

On the morning after his walloping by Terry McGovern, George Dixon released a statement reiterating that he had fought his last fight. "It was a case of once too often," he said. "I am through with the fight game forever," before borrowing a leaf from John L. Sullivan's concession speech in New Orleans and saying that if he had to lose, he was glad that he lost to a fellow American.[1]

Dixon's retirement lasted barely five months. On May 5, 1900, this story appeared on the news wire: "George Dixon has decided to sell his saloon on Sixth Avenue and re-enter the ring. Although Dixon has been doing a rushing trade he thinks it is far better to put on the gloves than to stand in front of the bar and greet thirsty customers. About two weeks ago Dixon deserted the place and did not show for several days … now the place is for sale."[2] Saloon-keeping was the occupation most closely identified with ex-boxers. In merry old England, the cradle of pugilism, famous bare-knuckle bruisers invariably became publicans. But the occupation was all wrong for Dixon, who had developed a drinking problem and was a magnet for moochers. Why did Tom O'Rourke allow it, nay encourage it?

The re-boot of Dixon's boxing career started off on the wrong foot when he showed none of his old form in a six-round contest with Tim Callahan in Philadelphia. For his second comeback fight, O'Rourke picked a less daunting opponent, Benny Yanger. This was a crossroads fight for Little Chocolate; a rematch with Terry McGovern hung in the balance.

Born in New York and raised in Chicago, Yanger, born Frank Angone, was unbeaten and had already acquired two prized scalps in Harry Forbes and Young Corbett II, but he was only 18 years old and had been a pro for only a year. He had an interesting nickname, Tipton Slasher, a nickname formerly bestowed on William Perry, a celebrated

British bare-knuckle battler of an earlier era. The nickname was chosen for him by his 21-year-old manager John Hertz, whose name would be immortalized in the rental car company that he founded.

Dixon managed only a draw against Yanger in a six-round match at Tattersalls but showed well enough to salvage the rematch with McGovern.

McGovern–Dixon II, on June 23, 1900, piggy-backed the American Derby held at nearby Washington Park, one of America's most prestigious horse races. With the Windy City flooded with sporting men, Tattersalls' management anticipated a sellout, but the fight actually drew poorly, an indication of how far George Dixon had fallen in public esteem. The six-round fight was in many ways a carbon of the first six rounds of their first meeting. Dixon had some good moments, but McGovern ultimately proved too strong for him. Dixon was holding on for dear life as the final seconds ran out.[3]

Things went from bad to worse for Little Chocolate when he was forced to quit after six frames with a fractured arm in his next fight, a match with Brooklyn Tommy Sullivan at Coney Island. He returned to fight a 20-round draw with Harry Lyons in Baltimore, looking good in spurts, but there was talk that Lyons had pulled his punches.[4] This was his first fight without Tom O'Rourke, who had washed his hands of him, declaring to all who would listen that George was no longer fit to fight.

Dixon's fights with Callahan, Yanger, Sullivan, and Lyons had a common thread. In each instance, Dixon's opponent had the "home field advantage." Little Chocolate had crossed the divide to where, more often than not, securing a payday meant venturing into hostile territory and taking on a man who had acquired a fervent local following. In modern fight lingo, he was now the "B" side. His bout with Young Corbett II in Denver—his sixth comeback fight—was another example.

By all accounts, Dixon would have been accorded the winner if the match had been fought at a neutral site. Young Corbett II was the aggressor, but Little Chocolate had little difficulty dodging his punches and, according to one account, punished the Denverite severely.[5] But it was Corbett's hand that was raised at the conclusion of the 10-round go, and with that victory in his pocket, the Denverite was able to negotiate a life-changing bout with Terry McGovern.

When Dixon went to collect his purse, he received a rude surprise. O'Rourke had filed an attachment, claiming that Dixon owed him $300 and that he had a signed note to prove it.[6] The legal motion stranded

Chapter 14. George Dixon's Second Act: A Career on the Skids

Dixon in the Colorado city until he was able to work out a compromise with his ex-manager, but if a prizefighter were to suddenly find himself stranded, he could do a lot worse than Denver. At the turn of the century, Denver had a robust boxing scene, and there were opportunities galore for itinerant boxers in the nearby mountain towns that were booming with unmarried men making good money working for the mining companies or seeking their fortune digging in the gold and silver fields.

Abe Attell, boxing's "Little Hebrew," ca. 1901.

Five days after fighting Corbett, Little Chocolate opposed an 18-year-old featherweight who would go on to accomplish great things. Born in San Francisco to Polish immigrants, one of 12 children, Abe Attell, dubbed the Little Hebrew, was exceedingly clever and advanced beyond his years. They fought to a 10-round draw in Denver, went 20 rounds with the same result 20 days later at an opera house in Cripple Creek, and met for a third time later that year in St. Louis.

The Denver fight, on August 23, 1901, was tame. There was talk that the teenage upstart "carried" Dixon so as not to spoil interest in the rematch. That would not have been out of character for Abe Attell. The middle fight in Cripple Creek was reportedly also a snoozer (details are murky), and their third encounter, a 15-round affair, was also devoid of fireworks. The prevailing sentiment among the attendees and the local sportswriters was that Little Chocolate had a shade the best of it, but George Siler awarded the match to Attell.[7]

The West End Athletic Club, which promoted Dixon–Attell III, hastily arranged a fourth bout between them, but the St. Louis authorities thwarted it, saying that the law allowed only sparring exhibitions.[8] This was another bad break for Dixon, who could have used the money. (The edict was soon rescinded, and for several years thereafter the West

End Club, where Abe Attell became a regular attraction, was an important entity on the national boxing scene.)

Unable to secure another match with Attell, George drifted back East and landed a fight with Austin Rice, the Connecticut Iron Man, in Rice's hometown of New London. Dixon faded over the second half of the 20-round match, or perked up after a sluggish start—newspaper reports differ—but regardless, the decision went against him.

Austin Rice was a veteran of many ring wars. Joe Tipman, Dixon's next opponent, was just a pup. Born and raised in Baltimore, Tipman was only 18 years old. Before joining the professional ranks, he was literally plucked off the street where he had a streetcorner newspaper pitch to serve as Terry McGovern's foil during a performance of *The Road to Ruin* at Baltimore's Holliday Street Theater. Tipman knocked McGovern down, prematurely bringing down the curtain. It made all the local papers, and within days he was persuaded to turn pro.

Dixon and Joe Tipman met in Baltimore on January 17, 1902. Little Chocolate outclassed his young adversary through the first 19 frames but Tipman, who looked to be about 20 pounds heavier, battered George around the ring in the final stanza and received a draw.[9] The very next week, in the very same ring, Dixon was knocked out in the ninth round by Harry Lenny, the Philadelphia lad who had lasted 25 rounds with him in 1899. Knocked down by a flurry of punches, Dixon hit his head hard on the padded floor and stayed down as the referee tolled the 10-count. He wasn't unconscious, but his gait was unsteady as he returned to his corner. Prior to the knockout, George never landed a meaningful punch.[10]

The rematch with Lenny was Dixon's 13th fight since resuming his career and he had yet to have his hand raised in triumph. Twenty-six months had elapsed since he had last experienced the sweet taste of victory.

The drought ended on February 13, 1902, when Dixon was awarded the decision over Charles Tucker in a 20-round contest at a dance hall in New Britain, Connecticut. Although Dixon was well past his prime, Tucker, 19 years old and relatively new to the game, was in over his head. But things returned to normal in Dixon's next start when he met Danny Dougherty in Philadelphia.

Dougherty had toured extensively with Terry McGovern, helped McGovern prepare for many of his big fights, and appeared in the chief supporting bout on several shows that McGovern headlined. Dixon hoped that a good showing against Dougherty would lead to a third

Chapter 14. George Dixon's Second Act: A Career on the Skids

bout with Terrible Terry, but his effort was lacking, and the consensus of the newspaper writers was that Dougherty had the best of it. Dougherty was a former world bantamweight title claimant, but yet the fight didn't attract much ink, not even in Philadelphia, Dougherty's hometown.

Dixon fought twice more over the course of the next three weeks. A third meeting with Eddie Lenny on Lenny's turf in Chester, Pennsylvania, was deemed a draw—"Dixon's clever defense saved him from serious damage on several occasions"[11]—and then it was on to Findlay, Ohio, where 19-year-old Biz Mackey was making waves. Situated in northwest Ohio, Findlay was home to about 16,000 people.

Little is known about the Dixon–Mackey fight other than the fact that Dixon quit in the fifth round. Little Chocolate was then being handled by Joe Dunfee, a former boxer from Syracuse. Dunfee's version of events was that the referee, a local bartender, looked the other way as Biz Mackey violated every "thou shall not" in the Queensberry code and that Dixon finally had enough and turned away in disgust. Dunfee further alleged that the fight was held in a room with no chairs and that Mackey's friends were allowed to crowd the ring and hang on to the ropes.[12]

It wouldn't be shocking to learn that Dunfee's tale was true. Strange developments informed prizefighting in the tank towns. However, the mere fact that Dixon quit, no matter the circumstances, was another stain on his legacy. "It's a shame to let him go around the country to be a chopping block for all sorts of fighters," rued a Buffalo writer.[13]

Despite the indignity, Dixon kept plugging along. On June 30, 1902, he reprised his six-round go with Tim Callahan in Philadelphia. "Callahan carried the battle into the enemy's camp from the outset, believing as all of Dixon's recent opponents do, that aggression will beat down the former champion quickly," said a reporter.[14] Opponents had little fear of letting their hands go as Dixon's retorts were so soft that he may as well have been wearing pillows. But Dixon wasn't overwhelmed by Callahan and had enough good moments to capture a draw.

Little Chocolate had come full circle. His comeback began in Philadelphia with a six-rounder against Tim Callahan, and now he had returned to meet him again for a payday that would keep the wolf from his door. This would have been a good time for him to hang up his gloves for good.

But he didn't.

* * *

Clash of the Little Giants

George Dixon sailed off for England on July 16, 1902. Shortly after his departure, it was reported that he would return in the latter part of September and take up residence in Cleveland where he had accepted a position as a boxing instructor for the Black Bass Athletic Club. But Dixon remained in England for almost three full years.

Several other African American boxers made forays to Great Britain during Dixon's day and then stayed over there for a good long while. Bobby Dobbs toured the British Isles between 1902 and 1909, plying the fair circuit between engagements at boxing theaters and arranging matches on the side. Early in his career, Dobbs was generally recognized as the lightweight champion of California. Frank Craig, the Harlem Coffee Cooler, set the template. Craig first came to England in 1894 and fought there almost exclusively for the remainder of his long career. Craig held the British version of the world middleweight title when he returned to the U.S. for a short stay in 1899, the inducement a date with the brilliant Tommy Ryan, who stopped him in the 10th round at Coney Island after which Craig was never the same.

George Dixon was extraordinarily active in England. He had 51 fights during this phase of his career, answering the bell for 514 rounds, the equivalent of two full careers for many high-grade modern-day boxers—and all of it compressed into only 33 months and this for a man who was so far past his prime that he risked permanent disability each time that he stepped into the ring. Moreover, George fought some of Britain's top guys. In addition to rematches with Pedlar Palmer, Will Curley, and Ben Jordan, he met future Hall of Famers Jim Driscoll and Owen Moran; had two encounters with the outstanding gypsy fighter George "Digger" Stanley; and had four bouts with rugged Morris "Cockney" Cohen, the British equivalent of Joe Bernstein. Hardly any of these fights attracted mention in the American press. Periodically, a bunch of these fights—typically just the results, no details—would be bundled into a news story about Dixon's goings-on across the pond.

In Britain, Dixon lost more fights than he won and received more draws than wins and losses combined, but he had some notable triumphs including back-to-back wins over Palmer and Cohen in bouts advertised for a world title. Many of his matches were contested at catch-weight. In December of 1903 he met Dai Morgan, said to be the best lightweight in Wales, in a 15-round bout in Morgan's hometown of Swansea. Despite being out-weighed by 14 pounds, Dixon was reputedly fresher at the finish. The contest was scored a draw.[15]

In December of 1903, a story in a Buffalo paper said, "Dixon went

Chapter 14. George Dixon's Second Act: A Career on the Skids

to England a physical wreck and practically penniless. Now he is strong and vigorous, has a bank roll and is enjoying great popularity."[16] But this report didn't jibe with an item that appeared the very next month in the *Baltimore Sun* which reported that good purses had become scarce. "Some time ago, the National Sporting Club made a sweeping cut in the purses, and the other clubs followed suit," it said. "As a consequence, the incentives were so small that the winner's end was not large enough to cover expenses." To make a go of it, a boxer had to find a backer with deep pockets, and "these people are scarce in England just now."[17]

When Dixon first came to England in 1890, he boxed before aristocrats dressed in evening clothes. Now he toiled in places identified with the working class. He made 11 appearances at Wonderland. A three-story building situated in the predominantly Jewish Whitechapel district in London's hardscrabble East End, Wonderland was a multi-purpose entertainment palace that was part music hall, part dime museum, and part boxing arena. Fights were held weekly there during Dixon's stay. All of Dixon's fights here with one exception (an eight-rounder with Pedlar Palmer) were six-round affairs pinned to deep undercards. Some of these fights, and many of Dixon's longer battles in England, had two-minute rounds.

In Northern England, the Wonderland equivalent was Ginnetts Circus in Newcastle. Here fights were usually scheduled for longer distances. Dixon had six fights here, three of which lasted 20 rounds. It was at this venue that he finally got the best of Palmer, winning a 20-round decision in their fourth and final meeting. By this time, England's celebrated "Box o' Tricks" was also well past his prime.

Dixon's last appearance in a British ring came on June 26, 1905. He fought a 10-round draw with veteran Joe Goodwin at a union hall in Manchester. He sailed for home later that summer, returning on the same ship as Big Tim Sullivan, who was in England for the Derby. When he arrived back in the States, he sheepishly admitted that the talk that he had straightened out his finances in Great Britain was a big lie. "I got such a small amount that I am sure I could go into any crap game and with a little luck with the bones in one evening I could come out of the place with more money than I got out of all the fights I had in England," he told a reporter.[18] Big Tim reportedly paid for his passage back home.

Regrettably, Dixon wasn't done fighting quite yet. On September 20, 1905, he fought Harlem Tommy Murphy before the National Athletic Club in Philadelphia. Tom O'Rourke handled the negotiations for Dixon. O'Rourke had washed his hands of Little Chocolate but purportedly felt an obligation to help him get back on his feet. Whether that was his true motivation or not, O'Rourke did Dixon no favors by thrusting him against Harlem Tommy who, although only 20 years old, was recognized as one of the top featherweights. Murphy toyed with Dixon in the first round and then knocked him out in the second, caving him in with a body punch.

Harlem Tommy Murphy, whose lineage was Irish, was the house fighter. Most of his fights were held under the auspices of the National AC, and he had built up a nice following. However, on this particular occasion and for one of the rare times in his life, George Dixon had the crowd in his corner. Many of his old friends turned up, and even the younger attendees joined in as Dixon was showered with a grand ovation as he entered the ring. His legend had grown during the three years that he was away, perhaps abetted by reports that he had regained much of his old form in England.

"His color was forgotten, no one appeared to notice that the dapper little fellow in the famous old faded bathrobe was other than a white boy," said a reporter for the *Boston Globe*.[19] His poor showing was disheartening.

In May of the following year, after a handful of exhibitions, Dixon landed a match in Gloucester, Massachusetts. His opponent, Billy Ryan, had only three wins to his credit in 16 documented fights. Dixon reportedly kept Ryan guessing throughout most of the 12 scheduled rounds, but there was an agreement in place that the bout would be scored a draw if both men were on their feet at the finish, and it lasted the full dozen.[20]

History would show that Dixon had one more fight left in him before he hung up his gloves for the final time, and it transpired on December 10, 1906, before a club in Providence, Rhode Island, where he was matched against a local man of little repute, Harry Kronski, whose ring name was Monk the Newsboy. They fought 15 rounds, and Dixon looked nothing like the Dixon of old. Some of his punches missed the mark by nearly a yard. He took a lot of punishment and grew weaker as the fight progressed, but he had too much pride to surrender and went out on his shield.[21]

It was an inglorious end to a glorious career for the man once championed as the fighter without a flaw. And more indignities awaited Little Chocolate before the Grim Reaper cut short his mortal life.

Chapter 15

Terry McGovern After the Fall

Terry McGovern and George Dixon both won world titles before their 20th birthdays, but their career trajectories were quite different. Those in the know could see that Dixon was special, but it took a while before an appreciation of him became more general. His decline wasn't linear as he had a knack for turning back the clock just as the knowing ones were about to write him off, but subpar efforts began to occur with greater frequency. When he was sent out to defend his featherweight title against McGovern, he was a decided underdog in the betting.

Terry McGovern's rise to celebrityhood, by contrast, was meteoric. Had he turned up 100 years later, one would have said that his ascent was Tysonesque. And his fall from grace was just as sudden, albeit his shocking smash-up at the hands of Young Corbett II was generally seen as the product of carelessness born of overconfidence, or the pernicious effect of his second career in vaudeville—too many nights in smoke-filled theaters when it behooved a prizefighter to keep regular hours and lead an active, outdoor life.

McGovern opened the next phase of his career against Dave Sullivan in Louisville on Washington's birthday, February 22, 1902. Sullivan, briefly the world featherweight champion, was renowned for his stamina. The previous year, in a Louisville ring, he had overcome a lot of adversity before storming back to stop the tough Pittsburgh veteran Jack McClelland in the 19th round. That performance factored into the pre-fight dope. If Sullivan could take the fight into the middle rounds—the bout was scheduled for 25—he figured to have clear sailing, or so it was postulated. Taking the fight into the middle rounds was the hard part. McGovern closed a 3/1 favorite.

The fight played out exactly the opposite of what was anticipated. Sullivan had the best of the early rounds and had McGovern in deep trouble in the fifth before Terry turned the tide sharply in his favor.

When the fight was halted in the 15th round, both of Sullivan's eyes were nearly shut, his lips were puffed, and his left ear was badly swollen whereas Terry had hardly a scratch.[1]

Sullivan was well-beaten, but he wasn't insensate when referee Bob Fitzsimmons, the club's honored guest, terminated the match. Because McGovern landed so many blows on Sullivan's face without knocking him unconscious, it was written that he had fallen back. He had set the bar so high on the way to his match with Young Corbett that anything less than a conclusive knockout was interpreted as a sign of erosion. But one thing that wasn't diminished was his drawing power. Large delegations from New York, Chicago, and Pittsburgh descended on Louisville for the bout, which was an advance sellout.

Within a few days, McGovern affixed his signature to the Articles of Agreement for a rematch with Young Corbett. The contract specified that the fight—"a boxing exhibition for scientific points" (wink, wink)—would be contested at 127 pounds with five-ounce gloves on or before October 15, 1902, before the club offering the best inducements.

The Nutmeg Club of Hartford, Connecticut, submitted the winning bid, but there was a snag. America was in the throes of what historians would call the Progressive Era. Across much of the country, reform candidates were being swept into office and that included Hartford, which had a new mayor who was receptive to the blandishments of the anti-prizefighting lobby. Charles A. Jewell, the president of the Hartford YMCA, issued this statement after attending the first McGovern–Corbett fight as a delegate of the Law and Order League: "My conviction that such things are brutal, degrading and of a bad moral influence has been confirmed."[2]

Rather than fight the mayor and his allies, the directors of the club elected to move the fight to New London, roughly an hour away. Located roughly equidistant between New York and Boston, the seaport city had adequate train service, could be accessed from New York by ferry, and most importantly had a climate more favorable to prizefighting.

The city council granted the club a license to stage the fight, but the council was overruled by the governor of Connecticut, George P. McLean, who ordered his attorney general to suppress the event. The fight was then acquired by the Southern Athletic Club in Louisville and set down on a new date, September 22, but with the same result. The governor of the Commonwealth of Kentucky, J.C.W. Beckham, was persuaded to have his attorney general issue an injunction against it. His petition was filed on September 16 with the fight only six days away. The

Chapter 15. Terry McGovern After the Fall

State Court of Appeals let the injunction stand (for the time being), and all the preparation that went into the event was all for naught.[3]

S.P. Thrasher, the national secretary of the Law and Order League, galvanized the opponents of the event in a letter he sent to all of the Louisville papers. In his letter, Thrasher wrote that he thought it important that the citizens of Louisville keep in step with their brethren in other cities in an age of sweeping reforms when "one part of the country pulsates to the sentiment of another."[4]

The prizefight was then shifted to Detroit. On December 11, 1902, McGovern and Corbett signed the Articles of Agreement in New York for a 10-round fight to be held before the Metropolitan Athletic Club on the 21st or 28th of January. The club was run by Billy Considine, who ran a gambling saloon in downtown Detroit that was something of an annex of his brothers' saloon at the Metropole Hotel in New York City. It was the favorite watering hole of the local sporting crowd and touring vaudevillians.[5]

McGovern was so anxious to avenge his loss to Corbett that he arrived in Michigan a few days before Christmas, setting up his training camp at a lakefront resort in Mount Clemons. Located roughly 25 miles from Detroit, Mount Clemons was known for its mineral baths. But Terry would be frustrated once again. Michigan's newly elected Republican Governor Aaron T. Bliss, a staunch Methodist, forbid the fight and ordered the county sheriff to take proper measures if the organizers attempted to circumvent his decree. Bliss was on firm legal footing. In Michigan, prizefighting was illegal, a felony for the combatants and a misdemeanor for anyone found guilty of abetting it.[6] The law was widely ignored with little fear of legal reprisal, but a fight such as McGovern–Corbett II was pushing the envelope too far.

There was talk of moving the fight across the Detroit River to Windsor, Ontario, Canada, but nothing came of it. During his stay in Michigan, which lasted three weeks, McGovern refereed two fight cards, both of which included future heavyweight champion Tommy Burns, who was still using his birth name Noah Brusso. Before he left town, Terry was presented with a $500 check as compensation for his time and aggravation.[7]

The orphaned prizefight finally found a home in San Francisco. The second meeting between Terry McGovern and Young Corbett II came off on March 31, 1903, 214 days after they were originally scheduled to have their do-over. After leaving Michigan, Terry had two stay-busy fights in Philadelphia, thrashing Joe Bernstein and scoring a fourth-round knockout over third-rater Billy Maynard, an old acquaintance from Brooklyn. Young Corbett was far more active during the interlude between McGovern I and McGovern II, going to post nine times, including successful title defenses against Kid Broad, the ubiquitous Bernstein, Austin Rice, and Eddie Hanlon.

Eddie Hanlon, a local boy, only 17 years old, had the crowd firmly in his corner when he challenged Young Corbett at San Francisco's Mechanics Pavilion. Corbett was the better man in most of the 20 rounds, but the referee thought it prudent to score the fight a draw. While Corbett should have gotten the decision, his performance left much to be desired. There were times, said the *San Francisco Examiner*, when he looked as limp as a dishrag.[8] He reportedly boiled off three pounds on the day of the fight to make weight, and his battle with the scales would be a recurrent theme leading into his rematch with Terrible Terry and beyond.

To keep his weight in check, Corbett's training regimen was heavy on roadwork. There wasn't much to see when reporters and fight fans visited his training quarters; he was usually out running. McGovern trained at Croll's Gardens across the bay on the beach at Alameda, the worksite favored by most of the area's top boxers. Terry was a whiz with the speed bag, mesmerizing onlookers as he banged away in perfect rhythm. Those that saw both fighters in the flesh were more impressed with McGovern, who attracted the vast majority of the small bets and closed a 10/7 favorite.

The rematch proved to be another fierce battle. Veteran referee Eddie Graney, who absorbed more than a few wayward blows, called it the hardest and fastest fight that he had ever refereed.[9]

Terry was knocked down for a "7" count in the opening frame, but opened a cut over Corbett's left eye during the milling. Corbett had him on the canvas again in round two, and both men were groggy at various times as the fight progressed. Round nine was a big round for Corbett, who landed a big right uppercut to the jaw that had McGovern all at sea. Two rounds later, the Denver boy applied the finisher. McGovern went down hard after receiving a right on the jaw and was counted out. He almost beat the count and would yelp that he had been robbed by the timekeeper, but his eyes were glazed when he got to his feet, and his grievance fell on deaf ears. "McGovern could not have been able to defend himself if given thirty seconds to recuperate instead of ten," wrote W.W. Naughton, the dean of West Coast boxing writers.[10]

The rationalizations for McGovern's setback in their first meeting

Chapter 15. Terry McGovern After the Fall

Terry McGovern (left) and Young Corbett II await the opening bell of their March 31, 1903, rematch in San Francisco. The man in the middle is referee Eddie Graney.

no longer held any water. Styles make fights, as they say, and Young Corbett II simply had the right style to dismantle Terry McGovern. It was a style predicated on strength and volume that was very similar to that of McGovern, but with one major difference: when things weren't going his way, Corbett kept his composure whereas McGovern, who knew only one way to fight, instinctively cranked up the intensity.

The fight was a commercial success, attracting an SRO crowd said to be a record for Mechanics Pavilion. "An immense crowd filled the streets for hours after the battle, discussing the merits of the contest," said the *San Francisco Call*. At the *San Francisco Examiner* building, a crowd said to be "fully 5,000" braved a heavy rain to scan the bulletins from ringside that were prominently displayed in the picture window. Young Corbett II was inundated with offers from theatrical companies and remained in the city for a few days as he sorted them out while taking a turn as an interlocutor at a minstrel show.[11]

McGovern's defeat put a dent in the economy of South Brooklyn. The Terry McGovern Athletic and Social Club had grown to about 300 members, and it was thought that virtually all of them had placed a wager on Terry. Shortly after the fight, a *New York World* reporter caught up with Terry's mother as she was harvesting eggs from the backyard chicken coops at her house, a house that Terry had purchased for her that sat only a few blocks from the home of her famous son. "I am not the only mother in South Brooklyn that is sorrowing because Terry lost the fight," she said. "There was a lot of money lost in this neighborhood... and there is many a poor mother and wife that will have to wear her last year's hat made over on account of it instead of the fine bonnet that she would have had if my son had won."[12]

Like a man who had fallen off a horse, McGovern thought it important to get right back in the saddle. He accepted a match with Abe Attell for early June at Fort Erie, Ontario, Canada, where Buffalo's leading promotional group had dropped anchor following the repeal of the Horton Law. But his manager Sam Harris had second thoughts, and believing his fighter needed more rest, he reneged on the deal.

It would be six months before McGovern returned to the ring. On September 26, 1903, he opposed Lew Ryall in Philadelphia in what would be his first of eight appearances at the National Athletic Club, which under the direction of promoter/matchmaker Jack McGuigan had become the premier boxing club in the city. Terry would return there two weeks later to oppose Billy Willis, who, like Ryall, was a local man of no great distinction. Terry was extended the full six rounds in both contests but won both decisively. He hurt his left hand in the Willis fight, but that did not keep Sam Harris from sending him back out 15 days later where he was matched tough against Chelsea blacksmith Jimmy Briggs, the New England featherweight champion, in a 15-round contest on Briggs' turf in Boston.

Briggs battled McGovern on even terms until he ran out of gas. Terry dominated the late rounds and was returned the winner, but he re-injured his left hand, and a year would elapse before he took on another fight that posed any significant risk.

Terry busied himself during the first nine months of 1904 with theatrical work—*The Bowery After Dark*, which now included Mrs. McGovern, was rewritten to include a reproduction of his fight with Frank Erne—with looking after his little stable of thoroughbred racehorses, and helping to advance the boxing career of his younger brother. Hughey McGovern, three years younger than Terry, was a capable bantamweight but one whose career would be devoid of a signature win.

Phil McGovern, the youngest of the three McGovern brothers, also boxed professionally but without great distinction.

Chapter 15. Terry McGovern After the Fall

Hughey McGovern had taken up residence in Philadelphia where Terry had his next three noteworthy fights beginning with an October 10 engagement with Eddie Hanlon, the West Coast Wonder Boy. The bout would be remembered for a sensational fourth round. Hanlon floored McGovern with a left to the jaw, but moments later Terry had him backed up against a ring post and was flailing away with nothing coming back in return. Hanlon had his hands dangling at his side when a police captain bounded into the ring and rescued him. "It was the most brutal scene ever enacted in a ring in this city," said a correspondent for an out-of-town paper who said the referee's inertia was a black eye for the sport.[13]

Two of the three fighting McGoverns: Hughey (left) and Terry, ca. 1903.

Another 12 months would elapse before Terry got back in the ring, and for a time it looked like his career was finished. In April of 1905, he abruptly cancelled the remaining dates of his tour and headed off to Hot Springs, Arkansas. The wide-open resort city in the Quachita Mountains, famed for its mineral baths, was a good boxing town when the race meet was in session—Tommy Ryan, Joe Gans, Abe Attell, and Young Corbett II made title defenses in Hot Springs—but McGovern wasn't drawn there by anything related to boxing, but for health reasons. He had been behaving oddly on the stage and was suffering from insomnia. Big Tim Sullivan, who was then vacationing in Hot Springs, took Terry in hand and accompanied him back to New York, where he was put under the care of a physician and arrangements were made to place him in a sanitarium.[14]

McGovern was under a tremendous amount of stress. His wife had taken ill and left the show, returning to Brooklyn to recuperate. He had suffered a parent's worse nightmare, not once but twice, losing a three-year-old daughter and a 12-month-old daughter to pneumonia. Reporters thought a large contributing factor in his strange behavior was the grief he felt at losing the featherweight title. Although McGovern also complained of headaches, no one then thought to connect his condition to ring damage.

McGovern was sent to Stamford Hall, a privately-run sanitarium located on a hill overlooking Long Island Sound in Stamford, Connecticut. Stamford Hall accepted patients remanded there by the courts and others who came of their own volition or at the behest of family and friends; the "volunteers," typically wealthy businessmen, were housed apart from the others, residing in one of the 12 little cabins rather than in the main building where security was tight. Most of the residents were not insane in the conventional sense, certainly not terminally insane, but people in need of rest and treatment for "nervous exhaustion," the medical term of which was neurasthenia. There were hundreds of these "wellness destinations" around the country in those days, the largest and most famous of which was Dr. John Kellogg's sanitarium in Battle Creek, Michigan.

Stamford Hall couldn't contain a man as restless as Terrible Terry McGovern. The day after his arrival, he darted away from an attendant and ran like a deer into the woods, making his way to a nearby town where he caught a streetcar to the railroad station and made his way back to Brooklyn.[15]

Back in Brooklyn, McGovern continued to act erratically, reinforcing the notion that he would never enter the ring again. He was barred from Belmont Park for being a perpetual nuisance. Beefs with bookmakers occurred with such frequency that the bet-takers in the betting ring petitioned the Pinkertons to put him on their blacklist.[16]

On July 28, 1905, Terry and Sam Harris and Young Corbett II were in attendance when Terry's younger brother Hughey fought Frankie Neil before a sellout crowd at the National Sporting Club in Philadelphia. Neil, from San Francisco, claimed the world bantamweight title and was making his first appearance in the East. To Terry's dismay, Hughey was in over his head and took a bad beating. Three days later, back home in Brooklyn, in the wee hours of the morning, McGovern was involved in a street fight with a railroad switchman named William Kennedy. According to a front-page story in the *Brooklyn Citizen*, Kennedy suffered "a fractured rib, a broken jaw, a bruised and discolored face, contusions of the body and lacerations of the head. It is said that Terry never

Chapter 15. Terry McGovern After the Fall

inflicted on an opponent in the ring the punishment he did on Kennedy, who makes the claim that McGovern displayed a spirit of cowardice and brutality by kicking as well as punching him." McGovern, who denied ever kicking a man, was arrested but released on his own recognizance after pleading "not guilty" and told to report back at his convenience.[17]

McGovern's career wasn't quite finished. He thirsted to win back his title and began his campaign by landing a bout with Harlem Tommy Murphy, who was fresh off his victory over George Dixon. They met on October 18, 1905, at the catchweight of 129 pounds. Harlem Tommy had previously won a newspaper decision over Hughey McGovern with Terry sitting ringside, so the match was personal for Terry, who reportedly trained with great dedication.

The fight was over in a flash, 122 seconds, but not before Murphy was on the deck six times. He made it to his feet each time, but the final punch, a right to the jaw, left him in such a bad way that it took five minutes before he was fit to leave the ring. Sportswriters who had written Terry off made an abrupt U-turn: "[He] has been resurrected," said a reporter for the *Globe*. "He is once more the McGovern who electrified the sporting world a few years ago by mowing down the best little fighters in the country."[18]

His marketability suddenly white-hot once again, Terry was matched against another charismatic ring personality, Oscar "Battling" Nelson, the Durable Dane. Nelson was from Chicago but had come to prominence out west in places like Butte, Salt Lake City, and San Francisco. He had accomplished what Terry had been unable to accomplish, knocking out Young Corbett II, not once, but twice. Famed for his ruggedness, the Battler had a tenuous hold on the world lightweight title and before the year was out would compete in one of the most hashed-over fights in boxing history, a fight-to-the-finish with Joe Gans in the evanescent boomtown of Goldfield in desolate Esmeralda County, Nevada.

The McGovern–Nelson fight, contested on March 13, 1906, at 133 pounds, was a huge commercial success, setting an attendance and box office record for a six-round fight. The Durable Dane opened a 3/1 favorite, but the odds sank when the New York contingent, reportedly 2,000 strong, arrived in Philadelphia. Among the notables at ringside were Harry Payne Whitney, John A. Drake, and John "Bet a Million" Gates, titans of the turf.

The first two rounds, marred by excessive clinching, were tedious and the crowd hissed loudly. "And then," said Robert Edgren, "presto—it became a kaleidoscopic series of shifting surprises, McGovern smashing away like a madman, Nelson nearly twisting Terry's jaw around to his back hair."[19] At the conclusion, the McGovern faction shouted "draw, draw" in hopes of influencing the newspaper writers and saving their bets, but the overwhelming consensus was that Nelson had a shade the best of it. Overall, the bout was rather disappointing as it took too long to heat up, but considering the odds, McGovern's performance hardly diminished his refurbished reputation.

There was a clamor for a rematch, and Parson Davies, who was then headquartered in New Orleans where he had purchased a poolroom, set about arranging it, intending to plant it in the city he now called home, but the bout never materialized. Instead, Harris arranged a match for McGovern with Jimmy Britt, a 10-round contest at Madison Square Garden.

A terror in the amateur ranks, Britt, born and raised in San Francisco, the son of a well-connected plumbing contractor, had transitioned seamlessly to the professional game, conquering faded luminaries Frank Erne and Kid Lavigne in his third and fourth pro fights. He had split two fights with Battling Nelson, winning the decision in their first meeting and then out-generaling the Durable Dane until Nelson found the mark and took him out in the 18th round in their rematch. He was managed by his brother, the voluble Willus Britt. It would be Jimmy Britt's East Coast debut—he hadn't fought east of Montana—and the first fight of importance in Gotham in nearly six years. Although the repeal of the Horton Law had put a damper on ballyhoo, the fight attracted considerable buzz.

McGovern was lax in his training amidst whispers that his mental state was deteriorating. "His trainers have lost control of him," said a story in the *San Francisco Call*. "Every chance he gets he breaks away from his training camp and generally lands at the race track."[20]

Terry entered the ring with a conspicuous band of flab around his mid-section but more than held his own with the San Francisco invader, who was troubled by a cut over his right eye that formed a lump and bled continuously from round two. Reporters were divided as to who merited the decision, but most sided with referee Tim Hurst, who was overheard saying that he thought McGovern had the edge in most of the rounds.[21] A versatile sports arbiter, Hurst was a former manager of the St. Louis Cardinals baseball team.

The fight violated a provision of the Frawley Law, which forbid charging an admission fee beyond the extra tariff dunned club members. Little clubs mocked the law with their little "smokers, but this

Chapter 15. Terry McGovern After the Fall

promotion, with tickets coyly marked 'associate membership certificate'" being hawked openly on the streets, pushed the envelope too far. At the conclusion of the bout, McGovern, Britt, and 13 others including Hurst and promoter Harry Pollack were arrested and hauled off to the police station where they were booked and released on $500 bond.

There was talk that the next fight for McGovern and Britt would be a rematch between them on Britt's turf in San Francisco. Both were gung-ho, but that wasn't going to happen. San Francisco, indeed the entire Bay Area, was picking up the pieces after the devastating earthquake, and prizefighting there was at a standstill. A club in Chelsea, Massachusetts, stepped up and inked McGovern and Britt for a 15-round contest, but the fight fell out, ostensibly over money issues. When the plug was pulled, McGovern and his wife and son were living in a cabin on Lake Ponpoosuc in the Berkshire Mountains of western Massachusetts. Terry's management thought it wise to get him out of the city.

During the summer of 1906, Terry's troubles mounted. On July 18, he was spotted in Norwalk, Connecticut, where, as he told a trolley conductor, he had come in search of a sanitarium to get "braced up." He did not find what he was looking for. Twelve days later, he appeared in court in Brooklyn on the complaint of a Coney Island policeman who said that McGovern, who was at the amusement park with friends, was accosting strangers and challenging them to a fight. On September 14, at a theater in Pittsfield, Massachusetts,

Grace McGovern, wife of Terry, and their son Joseph, pictured in 1909. Joseph passed away of an unspecified illness in 1938 at age 38, leaving his widowed mother childless.

where a play called *The Irish Pawnbrokers* was running, Terry objected to some of the dialogue with language so salty that several women got up and left, and he was told to never come back.[22]

Pittsfield was the closest town to his cabin by the lake where he had returned to prepare for a third meeting with his nemesis Young Corbett II. It was arranged for October 17 in Philadelphia.

Corbett's reputation had taken a big tumble since their last encounter. In addition to his losses to Battling Nelson, he had been the victim of a vicious knockout at the hands of Aurelio Herrera. In fact, his form was so bad that McGovern actually ruled a small favorite.

It was a match between has-beens that attracted very little news coverage west of Pennsylvania, but Terrible Terry and Young Corbett II put on quite a show. After six fierce rounds, both were covered with blood, and there was little to choose between them.[23] The fight was so good that it begged for yet another. Al Herford's Eureka Club in Baltimore out-bid other suitors for McGovern–Corbett 4, penciling it for the third week of January 1907.

The ink was barely dry on the Articles of Agreement when McGovern began acting strangely once again. On November 29, Thanksgiving, he was arrested in Washington, D.C., for "embroidering the atmosphere on Pennsylvania Avenue with too strenuous a variety of conversation."[24] He was hauled off to a magistrate and paid a $25 fine. Terry was in the nation's capital for the closing days of the Bennings race meet. A horse from his barn, Carmagnole, had run the previous day but was unplaced. Before leaving Washington, McGovern paid a visit to the White House. Accounts vary as to whether he actually got to meet with the president, but it would be written that Theodore Roosevelt gave him a cordial reception.

A few days later, back in Brooklyn, McGovern went off his rocker. On the morning of December 4, 1906, he ran through the streets in his neighborhood like a wild man, screaming incoherently at the top of his lungs as he kicked over curbside ash barrels. He had in his hand an unloaded revolver and in his pocket a shell from a battleship, live ammunition, given to him as a souvenir when he visited the Washington Navy Yard. The police were called, and he was removed in a paddy wagon to the psychiatric ward at Kings County Hospital. Doctors there pronounced his condition incurable, attributing it to "softening of the brain," and on December 9 he was spirited away to Stamford Hall.[25]

To make matters even worse for the McGovern household, Terry was broke. At the behest of Robert Edgren, who was working on a story

Chapter 15. Terry McGovern After the Fall

about McGovern's misfortunes, Sam H. Harris and Joe Humphreys sat down and went through old bookkeeping ledgers to ascertain how much money had slipped through McGovern's fingers. They determined that Terry had earned $203,200 in a little more than 10 years (equivalent to more than $5.5 million in today's dollars). His ring earnings totaled $136,000 and he had raked in $67,200 on the vaudeville circuit and in royalties from motion pictures. In 1901 alone he reportedly made $95,000, nearly double the salary of the man in the White House. (A man's earnings went farther in those days when there was no income tax.)

Where did all the money go? His misadventures on the turf accounted for a major share of it. He lost $39,000 establishing his racing stable, including salaries to trainers, jockeys, stable hands, veterinarians, etc. On top of this, he reportedly blew $20,000 betting at the track plus an additional $25,000 on a bookmaking concession that sharpshooters took to the cleaners. His saloon was a money-loser to the tune of $5,000. Handouts to poor neighbors and friends amounted to $15,000, and another $15,000 disappeared in loans that went unpaid for which Terry kept no books. In his widely circulated article, Edgren noted that unlike other lost fortunes, it was not squandered on riotous living. McGovern had taken refuge in alcohol following the death of his children, but he was a solitary drinker who was loyal to his wife.[26]

After McGovern entered the sanitarium, Harris and Humphreys set about arranging a benefit for him. It came off on January 23 at Madison Square Garden, and it was a gala affair, the greatest reunion of old-time boxers and wrestlers and ring officials ever assembled under one roof. Prominent entertainers and politicians were there as well as a large delegation from Wall Street. Chorus girls hawked the playbill in the lobby, and there were so many for-fun matches between active boxers and wrestlers that the show lasted well past midnight. One of the highlights was this song, rendered by a 12-piece choral group:

> Terry, Terry, Terrible Terry, the world in praise of you'll sing,
> Terry, Terry, eyes of blue and merry, we all miss you, lad, from the ring,
> Terry, Terry, we'll never vary, your pals in springtime or fall,
> Of all the fighters, in this here Yankee land, you're the best little boy of them all.

The attendees were observed humming the chorus as they filed out of the arena.[27]

According to published reports, the benefit brought in $16,582.76, which included receipts from a memorabilia auction and donations from boxing fans in other cities. Expenses, including the premium paid on McGovern's lapsed life insurance policy and money used to cover the cost of his keep in Connecticut, amounted to $4,289.09, leaving a balance of $12,293.67, which was placed in a trust account.[28]

Two weeks before the benefit, Joe Humphreys visited McGovern at the sanitarium, where he conferred with Dr. A.J. Givens, the founder and headmaster, to find out Terry's chances of recovering from his affliction. When Terry first arrived there, Dr. Givens had been confident that he could be cured. "All this talk about his being hopelessly insane is bosh," he was quoted as saying. "He'll be the old Terry in four months and if he doesn't fight again, it will be because he doesn't want to. McGovern is suffering from the high pressure of modern life." Givens thought it was important that McGovern get his mind completely off boxing, and to this effect he denied Terry the use of any exercise equipment.[29]

Givens quickly changed his tune. "There is no hope," he reportedly told Joe Humphreys. "He is dead mentally now and it will not be long he is physically dead."[30] But that gloomy prognosis also proved wrong. On April 5, not quite four months from the day that he was admitted, McGovern was deemed healthy enough to live off the premises and continue his treatment as an outpatient. He took an apartment in Stamford and, encouraged by his caretakers, joined the YMCA to stay trim. He returned to New York in the summer, where his exercise consisted of working out with the New York Giants baseball team. The team's manager, John J. McGraw, was an old friend. Terry was under the illusion that he could carve out a second career as an infielder.[31]

Astonishingly, and ignominiously, Terrible Terry still had two fights left in him! In May of 1908, after working out with the Giants at their spring training camp in Marlin, Texas, McGovern had two fights spaced nine days apart for the National Sporting Club, the first in Philadelphia and the second at the club's branch in New York. His opponents were Thomas Loughlin (aka Young Loughey), a Philadelphia man, and Spike Robson, a transplanted Englishman from Newcastle who once had a claim on the British 126-pound title.

The most credible report of the McGovern–Loughlin fight was authored by Ed W. Smith, the sports editor of the *Chicago American*. McGovern "didn't do much," said Smith, "and he finished in a tired and wabbly condition."[32] The McGovern–Robson fight was another humdrum affair. Both bouts were largely ignored by the national press. And so, on May 26, 1908, the boxing career of the great Terrible Terry McGovern, the pride of South Brooklyn, had finally run its course.

Chapter 16

Little Chocolate in the Autumn of His Years

George Dixon attended Terry McGovern's benefit. Terry had attended Dixon's benefit seven years earlier, and Little Chocolate was returning the courtesy. He was included on the program, paired with Austin Rice in a sparring exhibition consisting of three one-minute rounds.

The former multi-division champion received a royal welcome when he was introduced to the crowd, but the affection that people held toward him was quickly leavened with pity. "As Dixon walked from the ring, having done his best to help the man who conquered him, it was a pathetic sight. His tottering legs could hardly carry him to the dressing room. As he walked away those near him knew he did not have money to buy his next meal," said Robert Edgren.[1]

That Dixon was in dire straits financially was old news. In 1900, the *Boston Globe* reported that Dixon owned a small wooden house in Malden "saved from the wreck of a fortune."[2] What had become of his fine home furnished with rare pieces of art? For that matter, what had become of Kitty, his "dutiful" wife? It had been six years since sportswriters had mentioned her name.

Despite his weakened condition, Dixon was able to hire on with a vaudeville troupe. He was brought on as an extra attraction to prop up a long-running musical variety show called *The 20th Century Maids*. But he was let go after the ensemble played Buffalo in March. During the summer there was talk of holding another benefit for him, but nothing ever came of it. In October, he was reportedly offered a permanent position as a greeter in the soon-to-be-opened nightclub inside the Baltimore hotel that Joe Gans had purchased with the receipts from his fight with Battling Nelson. Gans said that he hadn't yet tendered the offer to Dixon because he couldn't find him, but Little Chocolate had a different take on the matter, saying that Gans made no serious attempt to reach out to him and was merely exploiting his name to give his new business venture some advance publicity. Later on, a reporter told his readers that Dixon was in New York "living as best he can among people of his own color, who treat him very kindly."[3]

George Dixon would assert that the only man that never turned him down when he needed a favor was John L. Sullivan. During his fighting days, the Boston Strong Boy boastfully drew the color line. This was rationalized as being a good citizen as interracial fights were seen as tinderboxes of racial discord (and served a dual purpose for Sullivan by keeping Peter Jackson at bay; the "Black Prince" would have likely boxed rings around him). John L. casually tossed around the "n-word," even in correspondence to newspapers in letters intended for publication, but it was yet true that Sullivan was very fond of George Dixon, a fellow Bostonian. Way back in 1892, Sullivan invited Dixon along on a carriage ride through the streets of New Orleans. Little Chocolate, although initially reticent as he thought it prudent to keep a low profile in this bastion of Jim Crow, took Sullivan up on his offer, knowing that no one would dare insult him to his face when he was in the company of the great John L.[4]

It isn't known where Dixon spent Christmas in the year 1907, but this would be the last Christmas of his life. On January 4, 1908, he checked himself in to New York's Bellevue Hospital. Two days later, in the early afternoon, he died. His death was attributed to inflammatory rheumatism and heart disease, but most news stories cited only alcoholism. When he checked in, he gave his address as 258 West 41st Street and named his "person to contact" as M.A. Harrison, a man who also lived at that address. A soft touch who gave freely to friends and acquaintances in need, George Dixon was alone in his hospital bed when he drew his last breath. He was 37 years old.

A story in the *Washington (DC) Herald* painted a grim picture of Dixon's final days: "[Little Chocolate] died alone and deserted by the people who once shouted themselves hoarse over his victories and threw their hats into the air as they crowded about the ring to grasp his soggy gloves.... He had drifted into the tide of homeless wrecks that swirl around dark corners and deserted, lonely places. Men who used to know him pulled their hats over their eyes and hurried by when they saw him."[5]

When no one claimed his body at the morgue, Mike Newman, the manager of the Longacre Athletic Club, took charge of it and took the bier to the club on West 29th Street and Seventh Avenue, where it rested for two days in the gymnasium under a huge chandelier while he sought to locate Dixon's relatives in Boston. If the search turned up empty, the directors of the club were prepared to pay for a proper burial in

Chapter 16. Little Chocolate in the Autumn of His Years

Brooklyn, preventing his body from being buried with other indigents in a communal grave in Potter's Field.

Dixon was known to have a brother in Boston. In fact, his brother John was very well-known in the Hub where he was an orchestra leader and a member of a popular brass band.[6] In reaching out to John, it came to light that he had another brother living there and also a sister, an unexpected finding as he had never spoken about them in the company of white boxing writers—or, if he did, they did not consider it important enough to spoon it into their profiles of him. His siblings, said a story in the *Baltimore Sun*, "never raised a hand to assist him when he was broken in spirit and pocket and was living on the charity of those who remembered his former greatness."[7]

More than a thousand people came by the Longacre AC to pay their respects, many leaving an offering to defray funeral expenses. Tom O'Rourke and Terrible Terry McGovern were not among them. O'Rourke was in England with the wrestler Joe Rogers. McGovern was appearing on the stage in Detroit with his old nemesis Young Corbett II. The little skit between the former fierce enemies, now fast friends, spiced up *The 20th Century Maids*, ironically the same variety show that had briefly employed George Dixon.

On January 9, an undertaker from Boston took charge of the remains, and the casket was taken to Grand Central Station and from there to The Hub.

Promoter Al Herford offered this tribute: "[George Dixon] was the most honest, upright, conscientious fighter of the lot. He was also the greatest bantamweight fighter that ever donned a mitt."[8] In all things, said Parson Davies, Little Chocolate was "honorable and honest ... he was merciless with a foe, but after he had won he was as tender to his victim as a nurse would have been."[9] The great referee George Siler framed his eulogy as a cautionary tale: "It plainly showed that the so-called friends who stick so closely to a successful fighter, are the quickest to desert him at his downfall, or after he has outlived his usefulness in the ring." A boxer, said Siler, "will do well to follow the path in which Dixon strode, but only to the turning point, where the sign 'Downfall' can be seen. They ought not go an inch further."[10] John L. Sullivan, a reformed alcoholic who had morphed into a temperance crusader, touring the country giving speeches on behalf of the Anti-Saloon League, chimed in with this counsel: "I hope that many a young man will take the warning contained in Dixon's history and cut out the booze."[11]

Chapter 17

Terrible Terry's Psychopathology

Little was written about Terry McGovern in the months following his final prizefight. When his name appeared in the papers, it was a case of a sportswriter revisiting one of his famous battles. When the quiet was broken, the news was again disturbing. On July 8, 1909, the *Brooklyn Daily Eagle* reported that he had an altercation with a man in his neighborhood, leading to an arrest on a charge of public intoxication. His wife told the police that he hadn't been home for four days. He was persuaded to "go out in the country and have a good rest" and was taken to a sanitarium in Amityville, Long Island.[1]

In September, Terry's friends were relieved to learn that there was no truth to the rumor that he had died. However, it was reported that his mind was occasionally a blank and that at times he gave his attendants much trouble. Terry would spend seven months in confinement before he was deemed fit to go home. He had a job waiting for him as a manager (apparently a fancy title for a ticket taker) at the Grand Opera House, one of New York's largest vaudeville theaters, a job arranged for him by Sam Harris, who had a financial interest in the property. In February of 1911 he was named the house referee of a new fight club in Greenpoint, the neighborhood in Brooklyn where he had several of his earliest fights.[2] That same month, he was reportedly dying in his room at the swank Arlington Hotel in Hot Springs. His ailment was a close secret, and he wasn't expected to live another day.[3] The story was patently false.

In May of 1913, Terry returned to the stage, reprising his role as the virtuous bootblack in *The Bowery After Dark* with old foe Joe Bernstein as his foil. In this latest incarnation of the long-running play, the villain tries to sell his wife to a Chinaman, the keeper of an opium den, to feed his gambling habit.[4]

Barely a month after his final stage performance, he had a relapse.

Chapter 17. Terrible Terry's Psychopathology

In January of 1914, he checked himself in to a Manhattan sanitarium but left after a few days. Several days later, he was arrested on a charge of public intoxication. In court, he talked in a rambling and incoherent manner. Several weeks after that, he was found wandering the streets of Brooklyn. When the policeman asked him his name, he could not remember it. They recognized him at the station house where he spent the night. On March 14, 1914, he voluntarily went to the Central Islip State Hospital for the Insane on Long Island for an evaluation and was told that he should stay there three weeks.[5]

In April of 1915, McGovern was spied slouched in a ringside seat at an important featherweight contest between Johnny Kilbane and Benny Leonard at a Bowery concert hall. A reporter painted a sad portrait: "The frame that was once a bundle of springs and tingling nerves was flabby and the face that was once alight with the fighting spirit was blank and expressionless."

The reporter may have been biased by his preconceptions. There were still times when McGovern was sprightly, as would be true later that year in December when he refereed a three-fight card at East Hartford, Connecticut, staged in the same ring (but not the same building) where he lost his title to Young Corbett II. In New York, McGovern had been reduced to refereeing only charity fights—he got in Dutch with the regulators in 1912 when he punched a former State Boxing Inspector during an argument at Brooklyn's Gowanus Club—but he still picked up an occasional out-of-town gig, and on weekends he was often found umpiring a semi-pro baseball game in Brooklyn.[6]

Terry McGovern's last public appearances were prompted by developments in Europe. In the fall of 1917, roughly six months after the United States declared war against Germany, Terry appeared at New York fight clubs exhorting draft-age patrons to join the war effort by enlisting in the Army or Navy. McGovern was paired on these excursions with Kid McCoy, the former boxer famed for his corkscrew punch. Neither was an eloquent speaker, but their "plain, forceful talks" reportedly got good results.[7]

In December of 1917, Terry took ill while visiting the troops at the Fort Upton boot camp in eastern Long Island. He was hospitalized and recovered quickly, but his days were numbered. On Wednesday, February 20, his wife and two friends brought him to Kings County Hospital. Two days later, on the morning of February 22, as 10,000 troops from Fort Upton were gathering in Manhattan to march in the Washington's Birthday holiday parade, he died in his Brooklyn hospital room with his wife and 19-year-old son at his bedside. Some papers identified the cause of death as pneumonia, others as Bright's disease, and the *Evening World* cited acute indigestion.

Terrible Terry McGovern was only 37 years old, the same age as George "Little Chocolate" Dixon when he drew his final breath. They were both old men when they left this world although their birth certificates said otherwise.

Chapter 18

Funerals and Monuments

Before George Dixon's coffin left the Longacre Athletic Club, there was a brief service conducted by two ministers, one Black and one white. In Boston, the funeral for him was held at the Charles Street African Methodist Episcopal Church. The most prominent "colored" church in the city, the Charles Street AME, then situated on Beacon Hill, had served as a gathering place for abolitionist crusaders such as Frederick Douglas and Sojourner Truth and was a transit point on the Underground Railroad. The memorial service was conducted by the Rev. T.W. Henderson, who was assisted by pastors from four other Black churches. The attendees represented both races. "White and black mingled in common sorrow," said a story in the *Boston Post*.[1]

According to the *Globe*, the funeral was the largest ever held in Boston for a man of color; there were "at least 2000 inside the church and fully as many others were outside, unable to gain admittance." The hearse, trailed by 10 carriages, left the church late because so many wanted one last look at the body. As a result, it was dark when the funeral procession reached Mount Hope Cemetery, and the burial had to be carried out by lantern light.[2] Joe Walcott was a pallbearer. Floral tributes arrived from as far away as Los Angeles.

Within a week after George Dixon's death, a committee was formed to erect a suitable monument. One of the first endowments was derived from a benefit held on January 26 at Miner's Bowery Theater. The star attraction was Joe Gans, who boxed a three-round exhibition with Elbows McFadden. Elsewhere, prominent fighters touring with vaudeville troupes, Terry McGovern and Young Corbett II prominent among them, joined the cause, soliciting donations at the end of their performances. Joe Humphreys took on the role of treasurer; Mike Newman handled the details of commissioning the sculpture.

On February 29, Newman entered into a contract with a sculptor in Quincy, Massachusetts. He would create a six-foot-six-inch bronze statue of Dixon in his fighting togs that would stand on a large slab of

Clash of the Little Giants

granite. The unveiling, "accompanied by appropriate exercises" would take place at the cemetery on Memorial Day.[3]

Dixon's relatives objected to the design, and the project was aborted. A simple but dignified headstone, albeit larger than those around it, was placed at his gravesite. However, a more ornate monument, a two-sided water fountain, was erected in New York City at the intersection of Eighth Avenue and Horatio Street in lower Manhattan. In the center of the round basin on the side facing the street—the side meant for horses— was an ornamental lamp post. The inscription read, "In Memory of George Dixon, Erected by His Friends, 1908."[4] The monument, dedicated on August 28, 1908, had a short life. It was torn down by the city as part of an urban renewal project on a date that wasn't recorded.

In recent years, Halifax has rediscovered its native son. A recreational center was named after him. A stone monument to Dixon sits outside the red brick building. Inside, two large portraits are displayed side-by-side on a wall. The portraits were unveiled on August 29, 2018. More recently, in an event timed to coincide with the 150th anniversary of Dixon's birth, a mural of him in a battle scene, painted on a container scavenged from a cargo ship, was unveiled on the grounds of the Africville Heritage Museum. The museum, opened in 2012, is housed in a replica of the community's old Baptist Church.

The short-lived George Dixon Memorial Fountain dedicated on August 28, 1908.

It was said of George Dixon that he had more friends in death than he had during the last few months of his life, when folks who once were thrilled to shake his hand now averted their eyes when they passed him on the street. More than a century after his death, Little Chocolate acquired new friends in the city of his birth.

Chapter 18. Funerals and Monuments

* * *

Terry McGovern's body "lay in state," as it were, for the better part of two days in the front parlor of his home at 205 Eighteenth Street in Brooklyn before it was transported to St. John the Evangelist Church for his high requiem funeral mass on Monday, February 25, 1918. The mourners that filed by his open casket represented every class of society, said the *Brooklyn Eagle*, "for the appeal of the fighting men to real men knows no distinctions."[5]

The church, founded in 1846 to serve the needs of Irish Catholic immigrants working on the Gowanus Canal, seated 1,300, but 2,000 reportedly crammed their way inside for the service. The funeral procession to Holy Cross Cemetery, consisting of more than 50 horse-drawn carriages, the first four of which held the floral arrangements, was said to be the grandest ever in South Brooklyn. Terry's casket was draped with a massive blanket of white roses and lilies of the valley, paid for by Sam Harris and George M. Cohan, who were among the honorary pallbearers. Among the faces in the gathering were the widow of the murdered gambler Herman Rosenthal and Charles H. Ebbets, the majority owner and president of the Brooklyn Baseball Club that would take the name Dodgers.[6]

As had been the case with George Dixon, friends of the late fighter talked about paying homage to him with a suitable memorial. But the idea never took flight. Nine years after McGovern's death, former state Senator William Heffernan, who had been a pallbearer at Terry's funeral, was said to be striving to revive the project. "At present there's only a very small slab of marble on his grave, with just his name on it," lamented Heffernan. "Even that is sunken into the ground and almost covered with weeds."[7]

In the late spring of 1918, roughly 15 weeks after McGovern's grand funeral, a writer for the *Bridgeport Telegram* authored this overwrought epistle: "[Terry McGovern's] memory will forever remain green in the hearts of boxing adherents the world over and until the day of judgment his achievements will reverberate down the corridors of time and redound to the plaudits of the younger generations."[8]

George Dixon's saga also played into a larger narrative, that of a man of color pushing against the barriers and insults hurled at people of his race. Terry McGovern never suffered Dixon's depredations, so his life was less amenable to rediscovery, but his saga too, although un-memorialized beyond that of words on a page, has a lot to teach us about the sporting life of an era swept into the dustbin of history.

Chapter 19

Necrology

"[Thomas] O'Rourke has lived his life in boxing and if there is any thing in connection with the sport of which he is unaware, it is not worth remembering."[1] This observation by a *New York World* reporter was made 15 years before O'Rourke died of a heart attack, the story of his sudden passing reading like a scene from a work of fiction.

O'Rourke had a lot of ups and downs, mostly downs, after his Big Three—Dixon, Walcott, and Sharkey—shook free of his grasp. He bought into the fool's gold of the White Hope craze after Jack Johnson won the world heavyweight title, and his two big guns Al Palzer and Fred Fulton never won a crossroads fight. Palzer was stopped in the 18th round by Luther McCarty in a fight billed for the White Heavyweight Championship of the World. Fulton, the Minnesota Plasterer, was knocked out in 23 seconds by Jack Dempsey, the Manassa Mauler, a man frequently described as a bigger version of Terry McGovern.

In 1921, O'Rourke was named a deputy commissioner on the reformed New York State Athletic Commission. He resigned his post the following year to become the matchmaker for the club that obtained the rights to promote boxing at the Polo Grounds. He was there for the big shebang (although forced into a secondary role by Tex Rickard), the September 14, 1923, fight between Dempsey and Argentina's Luis Angel Firpo, an event that attracted a paid crowd of 88,228 and a gate of $1.19 million. In his seventies, he kept his hand in as a licensed boxing judge.

When George Dixon fell on hard times, the press, which had previously written that O'Rourke had been very good for Dixon, now turned against him. He made a fortune out of Little George, said Robert Edgren, by working him like a gold mine, "and when he was whipped at last abandoned him like a gold mine that has 'petered out.'"[2] Late in his life, Dixon gave an interview in which he alleged that he once approached his former manager for a handout, and O'Rourke not only gave him the bum's rush, but attacked him physically, twisting his arm around his back in something of a hammer lock and nearly breaking it.[3]

Chapter 19. Necrology

Edgren came to reconsider his malevolent opinion of O'Rourke, writing that Tom was always a man of his word. (Without O'Rourke here to defend himself, it would be inappropriate to take sides, but this reporter can't help but be reminded of what the great heavyweight champion Larry Holmes purportedly said about his manager, the flamboyant Don King: "I knew he was ripping me off, but I also knew that I wasn't going to make more money with any other promoter.")

Considering all the years that Tom O'Rourke had been bound up in the fight game, one could say that when the Grim Reaper arrived to take him away, the setting could not have been more perfect. A Hollywood screenwriter could not have drawn it up any better.

On June 19, 1936, O'Rourke walked into Max Schmeling's dressing room at Yankee Stadium shortly before Schmeling and his seconds would leave the compartment for the long walk to the ring where Schmeling would meet the undefeated and seemingly invincible Joe Louis. This match—the first of their two meetings—was the match where Schmeling famously said, "I see something."

What he saw was that Joe Louis liked to double-up on his left and that he dropped his guard for a split second before coming with the second punch. That gave Schmeling just the opening he needed to sneak in a counter right, a punch he would land repeatedly before caving in the Brown Bomber in the 12th round in a stunning upset.

Schmeling would write that he discovered this flaw after procuring films of Louis's prior engagements and studying them for hours and hours, but that doesn't jibe with stories in the American press wherein the Big German credited Tom O'Rourke with giving him the key to unlocking the Joe Louis puzzle in a little conversation they shared moments before he was summoned to the ring.[4]

O'Rourke could not affirm his facilitation and bask in the glory. Max Schmeling left his dressing room that night, but O'Rourke did not. Right there in the bowels of Yankee Stadium—right at Schmeling's feet according to some reports—Tom O'Rourke, reputedly 83 years old, keeled over and dropped dead.

* * *

Tom O'Rourke lived more than twice as long as George Dixon. Little Chocolate predeceased him by 27 years. Joe Walcott also predeceased O'Rourke and the circumstances of Walcott's death are especially sad.

Like many fighters of the era, there's disagreement as to Walcott's actual birth date. But what's unusual about him is that even the date of his death is uncertain. Some say October 1, 1935, and others pinpoint October 4 of that year.

In 1901, Barbados Joe purchased an 11-room home in a fashionable district of Malden, Massachusetts, where he resided with his wife and their four young children and his mother-in-law. A close neighbor was rubber shoe manufacturer Elisha Converse, the wealthiest man in town.[5] But Walcott too would fall on hard times.

In February of 1918, six years and four months after his final fight, Walcott was found working as a fireman on a transatlantic freighter. A reporter found him while the vessel was docked in St. John's, Newfoundland, and told his readers that Walcott was in good spirits.[6] One suspects that this Walcott may have been an imposter, but the Walcott found working as a porter at Madison Square Garden in 1930 was definitely him. On fight nights Joe worked the graveyard shift, cleaning up the debris after the lights were dimmed and the crowd had filed out.[7] (A video clip of an interview with Joe Walcott conducted at Madison Square Garden surfaced in December 2019 on YouTube. The clip, a truly remarkable artifact, was from the library of Steve Lott, the protégé of Mike Tyson's late co-manager Jim Jacobs, who once owned the largest collection of rare fight films in the world. In the video, Walcott, seated in a broom closet, remembers his bouts with Choynski and Kid Lavigne and talks in general terms about the current crop of fighters: "Sometimes the boys box so bad I get a little disgusted.... You can't tell 'em anything because they think they know more than you.")

In August of 1932 Walcott was admitted to Bellevue Hospital after collapsing on the street with an apparent heart attack. Long a widower, he was then reportedly living in squalor in the unlighted, unheated cellar of a building on West 59th Street in New York City. At Bellevue, where he spent nine days, the diagnosis was arterial sclerosis and senile psychosis.[8]

The rags-to-riches-to-rags story of Barbados Joe Walcott intrigued some folks in Hollywood. That is why Walcott headed west in the fall of 1935 with a man who identified himself as a theatrical agent. A studio executive was interested in talking to Joe about a potential biopic. According to his sister, who lived in Philadelphia, Joe and his driver, whose name she did not know, left her home on September 7.

Somewhere in Ohio the two became separated, and Walcott disappeared. Months elapsed before his disappearance set off any alarms. In December of 1935, a reporter for the *Mansfield Journal* interviewed the

Chapter 19. Necrology

town's chief of police who was thought to be perhaps the last man to have seen Walcott alive. "He came to the police station one night [and told me] his partner was sick," said the Chief. "He wanted to know where the colored section of town was located, and I asked him if he had money for a room. I directed him to the district when he told me he could pay for his lodging. I know he was down there for a couple or three days."[9]

Three months later, on March 7, 1936, this headline appeared in the *Baltimore Afro-American*: "Joe Walcott Still Missing After 6 Months." By then, as it turned out, Barbados Joe was long dead.

The great Joe Walcott working as a porter at Madison Square Garden in 1932.

Back in early October of 1935, a man with no identification was found dead by the side of the road near Massillon, Ohio, 55 miles from Mansfield. An examination of the body indicated that he had been hit by a car. The man was buried in an unmarked grave in a little cemetery in the little town of Dalton in Ohio's Wayne County. Ultimately, through the dogged detective work of a man named Will Coreghin, a devoted boxing fan and boxing memorabilia collector from Defiance, Ohio, it was determined that the decedent was Joe Walcott.[10]

Coreghin arranged to have a headstone put on the unmarked grave. It reads, "Joe Walcott, World's Champion, 1872–1935." It's a nice, simple memorial, but doesn't begin to tell the story of Joe Walcott, the Barbados Demon.

* * *

A white male born in the decade 1871–1880 in the United States or in Great Britain had a life expectancy of about 40 years. This figure is misleading, however, because of the high rate of infant and child mortality. If a man reached the age of 20 with no underlying health conditions, he had a strong chance of living beyond the age of 70.

Most of the men who fought George Dixon and/or Terry McGovern were born in this decade. Their average age at death, based on information culled from BoxRec and other materials, was 58.9.

It's a small sample rendered smaller by missing pieces. Very few of those who challenged Dixon or McGovern on one of their vaudeville tours were of sufficient merit to command a mention in the sports pages when they died, and even some of their opponents in fights of major import fell into a rabbit hole when they left the sport.

Several notable boxers of this era lived to a ripe old age. Among former opponents of Dixon and/or McGovern, the Methuselah was Richard Henry Paul, who died in 1965 at age 90. A Londoner who boxed under the name Young Harry Paul, he was active from 1893 to 1906 and fought George Dixon at Wonderland in 1903.

Working down the scale from oldest to youngest, Billy Maynard (88), Brooklyn Tommy Sullivan (86), and Abe Attell (86) rank 2–3–4 behind the nonagenarian Paul. Sullivan and Attell both answered the bell for more than a thousand rounds, yet neither exhibited any signs of pugilistic dementia as they aged. Attell, according to *Miami Herald* sports editor Edwin Pope, could shadow-box with great alacrity when he was 80. (Shadow-boxing whenever he was cornered by a reporter was Attell's way of diverting the conversation away from his role in the 1919 Black Sox scandal.) Moreover, Attell, who married a woman of means and wintered in Miami Beach, was a drinker and party-goer his entire life, the worst kind of advertisement, said Pope, for clean living.[11]

Martin Flaherty lived a very clean life. In retirement, Flaherty and his wife established a health farm in Tewksbury, Massachusetts, near his boyhood home in Lowell, outfitting the large living room of the farmhouse with a boxing gymnasium that was patronized by many of the area's top prizefighters. At age 78 he was said to be in tip-top shape and bearing no scars of his fighting career other than his calloused and brittle hands.[12] Flaherty, who purportedly had 300 fights (*BoxRec* credits him with 78 totaling 960 rounds), lived to be 81.

Brooklyn Tommy Sullivan, Attell, and Flaherty were exceptions. Many ex-prizefighters died young, and many, whatever their age at death, were in bad shape financially and had serious cognitive issues and other health problems in their so-called golden years.

Cal McCarthy and Johnny Griffin died in their 20s. McCarthy's

Chapter 19. Necrology

death at age 26 was attributed to hasty consumption, a term then in vogue as a synonym for tuberculosis. Griffin, the Braintree Lad, who quit the ring to become a dentist but failed to complete his studies, was 29 when he was found dead in his room in a New York boardinghouse. The papers said he died of dissipation; in common with McCarthy, he was known to be a heavy drinker. Griffin died penniless and friendless, according to a story in the *Hartford Courant*.[13]

Six former opponents of Dixon and/or McGovern died in their 30s, including Johnny Reagan (35), Joe Gans (35), Tommy Warren (38), and Eddie Lenny (39). Pneumonia was listed as the cause of death in each instance. Reagan, Gans, and Lenny were said to be men of abstemious habits, but not Tommy Warren, who lived his life in the fast lane and reportedly died without a cent to his name.[14]

Eddie Santry was 42 years old when he died at the home of his mother in Chicago, his death attributed to nervous exhaustion. Five years earlier, Santry had been elected to the Illinois State Legislature, where his first action was to introduce a bill that would legalize 10-round bouts in Illinois, where professional boxing still existed in a legal gray area, a residue of the McGovern–Gans fiasco of 1900. Santry began behaving oddly after losing his bid for a second term in the statehouse and spent most of the last few months of his life in a mental hospital.[15]

George Monroe suffered a fatal heart attack at age 43. Terry McGovern's great rival when Terrible Terry was working his way to a title shot, Monroe passed away not quite 10 weeks after McGovern died. At the time of his death, Monroe resided in New Haven, Connecticut, where he had opened a boxing school.

British boxing luminaries Jim Driscoll and Digger Stanley were 44 years old when they drew their last breath. Stanley's age is approximate as his illiterate gypsy parents did not mark the date of his birth, and it wasn't recorded. Remembered in England as one of the first fighters to win a Lonsdale Belt outright, and the first bantamweight to accomplish this feat, Stanley purportedly died in poverty because of a gambling addiction.[16]

His death was attributed to stomach problems (likely cancer), whereas Driscoll fell victim to tuberculosis. Born in Cardiff to Irish parents, Peerless Jim was a huge star in Wales and especially beloved in Cardiff's Roman Catholic community. A crowd said to number more than 100,000 lined the street for his funeral procession.[17]

Young Corbett II was 46 when he dropped dead of a sudden heart

Clash of the Little Giants

attack on the sidewalk of a busy street in downtown Denver. Making weight was always a problem for Corbett during his fighting days, and when he left the sport, he got hog fat. After coming east to fight Terry McGovern, he lived primarily in mid–Manhattan to be near the theatrical agencies that arranged his vaudeville tours. He was in bad straits financially when he left New York for good in 1922, his train fare back home to Denver paid by gambler Charles Stoneham, the owner of the New York Giants baseball team. Slow horses and the "popping cork" were reportedly the main reasons for the hole in Corbett's pocket.[18]

Austin Rice, the Connecticut Iron Man, worked as a night watchman in a shipyard, as a milkman, and in a foundry after his career was finished. He died at age 48 when a wagon he was driving tipped over on him. Rice reportedly died penniless, having depleted what was left of his considerable savings on legal expenses in a failed attempt to prevent the execution of his son for a double murder committed during a robbery of a Washington, D.C., auto dealership. A benefit for his widow, said to be the biggest boxing carnival for charity ever held in Connecticut, reportedly raised $5,000 for her.[19]

Aurelio Herrera did not quite make it to his sixth decade, dying in a San Francisco hospital after a lingering illness at age 50. The year prior to his death, Herrera was sentenced to 30 days in jail for vagrancy in an Orange County, California, courtroom.[20] In death he became something of a cult figure. Boxing historians were drawn to the little knockout artist who reputedly trained on firewater and suffered many of the same indignities that were

Aurelio Herrera in his prime, ca. 1901.

Chapter 19. Necrology

tossed at his browner-skinned contemporaries. Herrera was routinely labeled a greaser by some sportswriters.

Those that lived into their 50s but died on the wrong side of the curve, meaning that they died before the average age at death of the boxers in this study, include Joe Bernstein, the Pride of the Ghetto. Bernstein, who answered the bell for a stupefying 307 rounds in 1899 alone, was 52 when he passed away at a Coney Island hospital in 1930.

Bernstein's death came 23 months after a big benefit was staged for him at the New Broadway Arena in Brooklyn. There were 12 four-round fights on the card, one of which featured the newly-crowned featherweight champion Tony Canzoneri. Bernstein, who married late and fathered two children in his 40s, was then a patient in an upstate sanitarium. Bad investments had wrecked his savings, and it was written that all he had left was his scrapbook.[21] An entry in it would have noted that he was the only man to take Terry McGovern to the limit in a 25-round fight.

When his career was finished, Sammy Kelly stayed involved in sports as the manager of Charles Stoneham's thoroughbred racing stable. A lifelong bachelor, Kelly died at age 52, three days after the death of his mother to whom he was very attached. He was delirious when she died and did not know of her passing.[22]

Oscar Gardner, the Omaha Kid, died on Christmas Day, 1928, at age 52. He spent the last several months of his life in a Minneapolis rest home. Fifteen days before his death, it was written that "the punishment he took in the ring is now making itself felt and he is a physical wreck with his mentality also affected."[23] It would be written that Gardner participated in 587 gloved battles, a number surpassed by only George Dixon.[24] Researchers at *BoxRec* have identified 142.

Ellwood McCloskey, who reportedly continued fighting after losing his sight in one eye in an industrial accident, went completely blind while still in his 20s. He and his wife ran a cigar store in Philadelphia, and he supplemented his earnings hustling peanuts and a little pamphlet telling of his ring exploits outside sporting events. He died at age 56 after a lingering illness.[25]

Eddie Hanlon, who died at age 56, was in and out of San Francisco hospitals the last few months of his life. Three years prior to his passing, he was arrested for disorderly conduct in Salinas, California. He told the judge that he had lost all of his money in a bad business venture and had come to Salinas looking for work. The judge, who remembered Hanlon from his fighting days, let him walk away free. Despite his various physical ailments, Hanlon reportedly remained mentally sharp. Reporters were amazed at his ability to remember the dates, places, opponents, and outcomes of all of his fights.[26]

Young Griffo lived to age 58, the mean age for boxers in this little study, but when he died, his worldly possessions consisted only of his clothing. Griffo, who was quite the hell-raiser during his years in Chicago, getting arrested at least 20 times for disorderly conduct while he was drunk, spent the last 10 years of his life residing in the storage room in the basement of a boarding house just off Times Square and spent his nights sitting on the concrete stoop at the back entrance of a Times Square movie palace watching the world go by. He was allowed to stay because he was then a meek soul, having quit drinking, and didn't overtly panhandle.[27] Griffo had a proper burial. Lore has it that he was buried in a silver casket paid for by boxing promoter Tex Rickard.

Solly Smith, recognized as the first boxer with a Mexican bloodline to win a world title and the first boxer from Los Angeles to achieve this distinction, had a starkly quieter send-off. In common with Barbados Joe Walcott, his body reposed for years in an unmarked grave until someone searching for it found it and saw to it that it received a headstone.

Smith worked as a roofer and a phone installer in retirement. His angels in his posthumous life were Dave Coapman, a purchasing manager for a Los Angeles medical center, and Bill Schutte, a University of Wisconsin–Whitewater librarian. Hobbyist boxing historians—Schutte is recognized within a tight little circle as one of the foremost authorities in the world on antiquarian prizefighters—they arranged to have a headstone placed over his grave. It was set down over his plot at East Los Angeles' Calvary Cemetery in 1981, 48 years after Solly's death at age 62.[28]

Abe Willis, recognized as the world bantamweight champion in Australia when he crossed the Pacific to fight George Dixon, lay in an unmarked grave in Orange, New South Wales, for more than eight decades until a great-granddaughter with a genealogical bent ferreted it out and rallied her extended family to fund a headstone to place upon it, building a family reunion around the consecration. In researching Willis, who died at age 67, his great-granddaughter learned that he had spent the last 11 years of his life in psychiatric hospitals.[29]

Oscar "Battling" Nelson, the Durable Dane, spent his end days residing with his wife in a seedy Chicago residential hotel before dying in an insane asylum at age 71. When he was remanded to the institution, he reportedly weighed only 80 pounds, and his mind was a complete blank.[30]

Harlem Tommy Murphy lived to age 73. In retirement he worked as a boxing instructor, sold insurance, and worked as a maintenance man in a Brooklyn shipyard. He passed away at the Brooklyn State Hospital where he had been a patient for many years. The facility was also known as the Kings County Lunatic Asylum.[31]

> Nat Fleischer, writing in 1924, nearly 30 years before Battling Nelson's passing, made this observation: There is hardly a retired fighter who does not believe that he can go out and whip the present-day crop in his class to a frazzle. Some of the cases really are sad. Terrific beatings taken on the head reduced some of the old boxers to a state of utter simplicity in so far as their mental processes are concerned.
>
> They hover around the offices of promoters like wraiths. They seek matches. They bring in their boxing paraphernalia and announce they are "ready to go." When boxing advances to where it ought to be it will take care of these unfortunates.[32]

Boxing has advanced, but the life stories of retired boxers, taken in the aggregate, have never stopped teeming with tales that ought to be a red flag for any young man contemplating a career in the squared circle.

Hall of Fame

George "Little Chocolate" Dixon and "Terrible" Terry McGovern were ushered into the International Boxing Hall of Fame in Canastota, New York, with the inaugural class of 1990. McGovern's road manager on the vaudeville circuit Joe Humphreys was named to the Hall in 1997 in the non-participant category, his selection based largely on his work as a ring announcer. Thomas O'Rourke followed him in 1999.

Dixon and/or McGovern exchanged blows with these Hall of Fame boxers during the course of their careers: Joe Gans, Jim Driscoll, and Abe Attell, all three entering the Hall with the inaugural class of 1990, Young Griffo (1991), Battling Nelson (1992), Owen Moran (2002), Young Corbett II (2010), and Frank Erne (2020). George Dixon's stablemate and frequent traveling companion Joe Walcott, the Barbados Demon, was part of the second class of IBHOF inductees along with Griffo.

APPENDIX I

Key Fights in the Boxing Career of George Dixon

NOTE: KOs include TKOs and corner stoppages. No distinction is made between referees' decisions and newspaper decisions.

Date	Opponent	Location	Result
11/01/1886 (debut)	Young Johnson	Halifax, NS	KO 3
03/21/1888	Patsy Kelley	Boston, MA	D 15
06/21/1888	Hank Brennan	Boston, MA	D 14
12/04/1888	Hank Brennan	Boston, MA	D 9
12/28/1888	Hank Brennan	Boston, MA	D 15
01/29/1889	Patsy Kelly	Boston, MA	W 10
10/14/1889	Hank Brennan	Boston, MA	D 26
12/27/1889	Eugene Hornbacher	New London, CT	KO 2
02/07/1890	Cal McCarthy	Boston, MA	D 70
06/27/1890	Nunc Wallace	London, ENG	KO 19
10/23/1890	Johnny Murphy	Providence, RI	KO 40
03/31/1891	Cal McCarthy	Troy, NY	KO 22
07/28/1891	Abe Willis	San Francisco, CA	KO 5
06/27/1892	Fred Johnson	Coney Island, NY	KO 14
09/06/1892	Jack Skelly	New Orleans, LA	KO 8
08/07/1893	Eddie Pierce	Coney Island, NY	KO 3
08/22/1893	Billy Plimmer	New York, NY	L 4
09/25/1893	Solly Smith	Coney Island, NY	KO 7
05/29/1894	Young Griffo	Boston, MA	D 20
01/19/1895	Young Griffo	Coney Island, NY	D 25
08/27/1895	Johnny Griffin	Boston, MA	W 25
10/28/1895	Young Griffo	New York, NY	D 10
12/05/1895	Frank Erne	New York, NY	D 10

Clash of the Little Giants

Date	Opponent	Location	Result
01/30/1896	Pedlar Palmer	New York, NY	D 6
06/16/1896	Martin Flaherty	Boston, MA	D 20
09/25/1896	Tommy White	New York, NY	D 20
11/27/1896	Frank Erne	New York, NY	L 20
01/27/1897	Torpedo Billy Murphy	New York, NY	KO 6
02/15/1897	Jack Downey	New York, NY	D 20
03/24/1897	Frank Erne	New York, NY	W 25
04/26/1897	Johnny Griffin	New York, NY	W 20
07/23/1897	Dal Hawkins	San Francisco, CA	D 20
10/04/1897	Solly Smith	San Francisco, CA	L 20
03/31/1898	Tommy White	Syracuse, NY	D 20
06/06/1898	Eddie Santry	New York, NY	W 20
07/01/1898	Ben Jordan	New York, NY	L 25
11/11/1898	Dave Sullivan	New York, NY	W DQ 10
11/29/1898	Oscar Gardner	New York, NY	W 25
01/17/1899	Young Pluto	New York, NY	KO 10
05/15/1899	Kid Broad	Buffalo, NY	W 20
06/02/1899	Joe Bernstein	New York, NY	W 25
07/11/1899	Tommy White	Denver, CO	W 20
08/11/1899	Eddie Santry	New York, NY	D 20
11/21/1899	Eddie Lenny	New York, NY	W 25
01/09/1900	Terry McGovern	New York, NY	L KO 8
06/23/1900	Terry McGovern	Chicago, IL	L 6
07/31/1900	Tommy Sullivan	Coney Island, NY	L TKO 7
08/16/1901	Young Corbett II	Denver, CO	L 10
08/23/1901	Abe Attell	Denver, CO	D 10
09/26/1901	Benny Yanger	St. Louis, MO	L 15
10/28/1901	Abe Attell	St. Louis, MO	L 15
12/19/1901	Austin Rice	New London, CT	L 20
01/17/1902	Joe Tipman	Baltimore, MD	D 20
01/24/1902	Eddie Lenny	Baltimore, MD	L TKO 9
06/30/1902	Tim Callahan	Philadelphia, PA	L 6
09/08/1902	Pedlar Palmer	London, ENG	L 15
09/29/1902	Will Curley	London, ENG	D 15
02/09/1903	Harry Ware	Northampton, ENG	D 20
04/11/1903	Spike Robson	Newcastle, ENG	L 20
06/01/1903	Jim Driscoll	location uncertain	L KO 5
11/09/1903	Pedlar Palmer	Newcastle, ENG	W 20

Appendix I. Key Fights in the Boxing Career of George Dixon

Date	Opponent	Location	Result
12/07/1903	Cockney Cohen	Newcastle, ENG	W 20
02/22/1904	Harry Mansfield	Plymouth, ENG	D 20
03/07/1904	Cockney Cohen	Leeds, ENG	L 15
03/06/1905	Cockney Cohen	Sheffield, ENG	D 20
09/20/1905	Harlem Tommy Murphy	Philadelphia, PA	L KO 2
12/10/1906	Monk the Newsboy	Providence, RI	L 15

Appendix II

Key Fights in the Boxing Career of Terry McGovern

Date	Opponent	Location	Result
04/03/1897 (debut)	Johnny Snee	Brooklyn, NY	L DQ 4
06/19/1897	Tommy Sullivan	Brooklyn, NY	W 10
06/05/1898	George Monroe	Yonkers, NY	W 20
06/11/1898	George Monroe	Coney Island, NY	KO 24
07/23/1898	Tim Callahan	Brooklyn, NY	DQ 11
08/04/1898	George Monroe	Brooklyn, NY	W DQ 7
08/20/1898	Tim Callahan	Brooklyn, NY	W 20
10/01/1898	Harry Forbes	Brooklyn, NY	KO 15
11/19/1898	Tim Callahan	Brooklyn, NY	KO 10
12/31/1898	Austin Rice	Brooklyn, NY	KO 14
01/30/1899	Casper Leon	Brooklyn, NY	KO 12
03/14/1899	Patsy Haley	New York, NY	KO 18
04/28/1899	Joe Bernstein	New York, NY	W 25
05/26/1899	Sammy Kelly	New York, NY	KO 5
06/08/1899	Billy Barrett	New York, NY	KO 10
07/01/1899	Johnny Ritchie	Tuckahoe, NY	KO 3
09/12/1899	Pedlar Palmer	Tuckahoe, NY	KO 1
12/22/1899	Harry Forbes	New York, NY	KO 2
01/09/1900	George Dixon	New York, NY	KO 8
02/01/1900	Eddie Santry	Chicago, IL	KO 5
03/09/1900	Oscar Gardner	New York, NY	KO 3
06/12/1900	Tommy White	Coney Island, NY	KO 3
06/23/1900	George Dixon	Chicago, IL	W 6
07/16/1900	Frank Erne	New York, NY	KO 3
11/02/1900	Joe Bernstein	Louisville, KY	KO 7

Appendix II. Key Fights in the Boxing Career of Terry McGovern

Date	Opponent	Location	Result
11/13/1900	Kid Broad	Chicago, IL	W 6
12/13/1900	Joe Gans	Chicago, IL	KO 2
04/30/1901	Oscar Gardner	San Francisco, CA	KO 4
05/29/1901	Aurelio Herrera	San Francisco, CA	KO 5
11/28/1901	Young Corbett II	Hartford, CT	L KO 2
02/22/1902	Dave Sullivan	Louisville, KY	KO 15
03/31/1903	Young Corbett II	San Francisco, CA	L KO 11
10/20/1903	Jimmy Briggs	Boston, MA	W 15
10/18/1905	Harlem Tommy Murphy	Philadelphia, PA	KO 1
03/14/1906	Battling Nelson	Philadelphia, PA	L 6
05/28/1906	Jimmy Britt	New York, NY	D 10
10/17/1906	Young Corbett II	Philadelphia, PA	D 6
05/26/1908	Spike Robson	New York, NY	D 6

Chapter Notes

Introduction

1. *Butte Inter-Mountain*, "The Ring," Feb. 16, 1901, p. 12.
2. Frank G. Menke, "McGovern In His Fistic Prime As Terrible As An Angry Tiger," *Richmond Times Dispatch*, Aug. 8, 1929, p. 15.
3. boxingcom/terry-mcgovern-the-year-of-the-butcher-part-two-the-dixon-of-old.html.
4. *New York Evening World*, "Referee Gave Verdict Against Joe Walcott," Nov. 11, 1903, p. 12; *Boston Globe*, "Ferguson Wins Bout. He Clearly Outclasses Joe Walcott," Nov. 11, 1903, pp. 1, 4; *Brooklyn Times Union*, "Wolcott Could Not Give Fifty Pounds, and Win," Nov. 11, 1903, p. 5.
5. Jimmy Breslin, *Damon Runyon*. New York: Tichner and Fields, 1990, p. 189.
6. Fleischer's account of the 1890 fight between George Dixon and Johnny Murphy for an athletic club in Providence, Rhode Island, serves as a good illustration. Fleischer writes that Dixon had to do all his fighting in the center of the ring, "so maneuvering his man to not get near the ropes (where Murphy's partisans awaited) with their black jacks and slug shots." (Nat Fleischer, *The Three Colored Aces*, Vol. 3 of the Black Dynamite series, 1938, p. 8). Far-fetched.
7. *Boston Globe*, "Boyle O'Reilly's Book," April 20, 1888, p. 4; John Boyle O'Reilly died in 1890 at age 46 after a long illness. More than 100 Catholic priests, many traveling long distances, attended his funeral Mass at his parish church in Charlestown. An inter-faith memorial service several weeks later at Boston's Tremont Temple likewise drew a large turnout at which members of the city's African American community were well-represented. (*Boston Globe*, "John Boyle O'Reilly Buried," Aug. 13, 1890, p. 12; *Boston Globe*, "Boston's Memorial to O'Reilly," Sept. 3, 1890. p. 4). O'Boyle's poems, speeches, and editorials were gathered into a book by his assistant James Jeffrey Roche that was published the year after O'Boyle's death. The foreword was by James Cardinal Gibbons, Archbishop of Baltimore.
8. Quoted in the *Baltimore Sun*, "Pretexts For Prize-Fighting," March 10, 1870, p. 2.
9. *Portland Oregonian*, "Boxing Versus Prize Fighting," Dec. 30, 1889, p. 6.
10. *Oakland Tribune*, "Dr. Dille on Indoor and Outdoor Amusements," Oct. 14, 1889, p. 5.
11. Quoted in the *Idaho Daily Statesman*, no title, Aug. 17, 1889, p. 4.
12. Margaret Frisbee, *The Fight of the Century: The Regulation and Reform of Prizefighting in Progressive Era America* (doctoral dissertation, https://digital repository.unm.edu/hist_etds/31). Frisbee astutely notes that women censured prizefighting on its brutality and immorality, whereas secular men were more interested in rooting out political corruption.
13. Quoted in John Betts, *America's Sporting Heritage, 1850–1950*. Reading, Mass: Addison-Wesley, 1974. The author of the quotation was the editor of a book published by the *New York Tribune*.
14. The noted historian Elliott Gorn and others have cited the influential role that *Police Gazette* publisher Richard Kyle Fox played in the development

of the modern sports page. "Large metropolitan dailies in New York, Chicago, San Francisco, and other cities learned from Fox's success, incorporating sensational reporting into the mainstream press and bringing regular sports coverage—in special sections with their own unique reportorial style—to the newspapers." (Elliott J. Gorn, *The Manly Art: Bare-Knuckle Prize Fighting in America*. Ithaca, NY: Cornell University Press, 1986, p. 133.)

Chapter 1

1. In his memoir, Albert Payson Terhune says that in those days virtually everything published under the byline of a well-known person was ghostwritten and that often the author didn't collaborate with his subject beyond getting his authorization. Terhune should know. He was the "Iron Man" of ghostwriters, producing hundreds of newspaper and magazine stories under the names of well-known people plus books credited to James J. Corbett and to Terry McGovern that had their genesis in ghostwritten newspaper serials. (Albert Payson Terhune, *To the Best of My Memory*. New York, Harper and Brothers, 1930; see especially Chapter 13, pp. 148–156).
2. Charley White, "Inside the Ring with the Great Fighters." *New York Evening World*, Aug. 30, 1911, p. 9.
3. *Boston Globe*, "Battles in the Ring," Sept. 22, 1887, p. 2.
4. James Jeffrey Roche, *Life of John Boyle O'Reilly*. New York: Cassell Publishing Company, 1891, p. 200; *Boston Sunday Post*, "Old Cribb Club of Boston the Most Select Organization That Ever Fostered Boxing," June 9, 1907, p. 18). The Cribb Club was reorganized in 1893. The treasurer was Captain Albert W. Cooke, the publisher of Boston's *Police News*. The secretary, who had a hand in the matchmaking, was Ben Benton who covered boxing for the *Boston Post* under the pen name Rob Roy.
5. *Detroit Free Press*, "Boston Happenings in the Aesthetic Center," Feb. 5, 1882, p. 13; *Swaunton Courier*, "A Pugilistic Club," March 3, 1883, p. 2.
6. Stephen Hardy, *How Boston Played: Sport, Recreation and Community, 1865–1915*. Boston: Northeastern University Press, 1982.
7. *Boston Daily Globe*, "Three Pairs of Fighters," Dec. 16, 1887, p. 2.
8. *Boston Daily Globe*, "'Fair Play' in Boxing," Jan. 25, 1888, p. 5; Blanchard served as the stakeholder for the Corbett–Mitchell fight. According to the *Boston Globe*, Blanchard's property holdings included a tributary of the Saguenay River in Quebec that was teeming with salmon. (*Boston Globe*, "River Owned by David H. Blanchard of Boston," Aug. 12, 1896, p. 10.)
9. *Boston Daily Globe*, "Four Lively Fights," Feb. 18, 1888, p. 6.
10. *Boston Daily Globe*, "Bantams Fight," March 22, 1888, p. 3.
11. *Boston Daily Globe*, "Fought to a Draw," Oct. 3, 1889, p. 3.
12. *Boston Daily Globe*, "Brennan's Bouts With Dixon," March 31, 1896, p. 21. See also Nat Fleischer, op. cit., p. 14. (Fleischer writes that after the fourth meeting, a pitched battle ensued between the partisans of the fighters that wasn't quelled until a police riot squad arrived and succeeding in routing the bloodthirsty mob (pp. 16–17). There is no evidence for this assertion in newspaper reports. Fleischer's five-volume *Black Dynamite* series, published in-house, hugely influenced future generations of boxing writers, notwithstanding the fact that the books are littered with dubious facts.)
13. *Brooklyn Daily Eagle*, "Hornbacher Defeats White," April 24, 1888, p. 1.
14. *New York Evening World*, "Knocked Out by Dixon," Dec. 28, 1889, p. 4.

Chapter 2

1. James Oliver Horton and Lois E. Horton, *Black Bostonians*. New York: Holmes and Meier, 1979.
2. Ray Stannard Baker, "The Color Line in the North," *Raleigh News and Observer*, Jan. 26, 1908, p. 5.

Notes—Chapter 3

3. Oscar Handlin, *Boston's Immigrants*. Cambridge, Mass: Harvard University Press, 1959, p. 52.
4. *Boston Sunday Post*, "Boxing," Feb. 17, 1895, p. 17.
5. *San Francisco Examiner*, "Godfrey's Gallant Defeat," March 14, 1891, p. 5. (A second George Godfrey, born Feab Williams, came along in the 1920s. A much bigger man than the original George Godfrey, Williams was assiduously avoided by Jack Dempsey, who used him as a sparring partner, and by Dempsey's successor Gene Tunney.)
6. *Brooklyn Citizen*, "The Ringside," Jan. 27, 1897, p. 7.
7. *Dayton Daily News*, "Kick On Jeff," Dec. 23, 1903, p. 8.
8. The word "pickaninnies" (often spelled without the "k") turns up frequently in advertisements for vaudeville shows. The word connoted an ensemble of Black boys employed as dancers and/or back-up singers.
9. Kevin Smith, *Boston's Boxing Heritage: Prizefighting from 1882 to 1955*. Charlestown, SC: Arcadia Publishing, 2002, p. 43.

Chapter 3

1. *Chicago Tribune*, "It Was a Drawn Fight," Feb 8, 1890, p. 3; See also Fleischer, op cit., p. 24.
2. *Sydney Referee*, "Nunc Wallace: Death of an Old-Timer, Some of his Battles," Oct. 12, 1912, p. 3.
3. *San Francisco Chronicle*, "America Wins Again," June 27, 1890, p. 10.
4. *Reynolds's Newspaper*, "Brutal Glove Fight in America," Nov. 2, 1890, p. 6.
5. *Brooklyn Citizen*, "Pugilistic Review," Feb 17, 1890, p. 6.
6. *New York Sun*, "The Battle Postponed," Feb. 6, 1891, p. 1.
7. *Ibid.*
8. *Brooklyn Daily Eagle*, "Dixon–McCarthy Fight Off," Feb. 6, 1891, p. 4.
9. *Brooklyn Citizen*, "Pugilistic Gossip, March 29, 1891, p. 3. See also Herbert A. Calkins, "Old Clippings Tell Story of Prize Fight That Shocked Troy Sixty Years Ago," *Troy Record*, Dec. 25, 1951, p. 12. Jere Dunn was best known for fatally shooting prizefighter Jimmy Elliott, a former opponent of John L. Sullivan, during an 1883 gunfight in a Chicago café. A jury acquitted Dunn of murder on grounds of self-defense. Despite his notoriety, Dunn in his role as a boxing referee was considered a man of unimpeachable integrity. For more on Jere Dunn, see "Jere Dunn Goes To Final Rest," *San Francisco Call*, June 28, 1906, p. 6.
10. Calkins, loc. cit.
11. *Saint Paul Globe*, "Pitiless and Rough," Feb. 14, 1889, p. 2.
12. *Chicago Inter Ocean*, "It Was Dixon's Battle," April 21, 1891, p. 6; see also *Boston Globe*, "At Dixon's Mercy," April 21, 1891, p. 2.
13. W.W. Naughton, *Kings of the Queensberry Realm*. Chicago: Continental Publishing Co; 1902, p. 40.
14. *Australian Star*, "Dixon v Willis," Sept. 15. 1891, p. 7. See also *Boston Daily Globe*, "Dixon's Left, it Brings Him Fame and Lots of Cash," July 28, 1891, p. 1.
15. *Philadelphia Times*, "Lyceum Theatre," Sept. 13, 1891, p. 10; *Montreal Gazette*, "Dixon at the Lyceum," Sept. 28, 1891, p. 8.
16. Commenting on Jim Corbett's theater engagements wherein he took on all comers, author Robert Cantwell made this observation: "A good deal of stagecraft was required in selecting likely looking challengers who were certain to lose and in avoiding ambitious and unknown aspirants who might really be able to fight." (Robert Cantwell, *The Real McCoy, The Life and Times of Norman Selby*. New York: Auerbach Publishers Inc., 1971, p. 43). If, perchance, the volunteer was perceived as a threat, there were ways to tilt the odds against him, such as outfitting him with heavier gloves or having the timekeeper modify the duration of a round. The various artifices originated among booth fighters plying the fair circuit in old England.
17. *Boston Globe*, "Why Not Professionals," Jan. 11, 1892, p. 2.
18. *Galveston Daily News*, "Opinions Of Experts And Odds in Betting," Aug. 29, 1892, p. 7.

19. *Brooklyn Daily Eagle*, "On a Hot Night," Aug. 1, 1890, p. 1.
20. *St. Louis Globe-Democrat*, "Dixon Arrives at New Orleans," Aug. 12, 1892, p. 9; *Kansas City Sun*, "J. Madison Vance Dead," Feb. 1, 1919, p. 1.
21. S. Derby Gisclair, *The Olympic Club of New Orleans: Epicenter of Professional Boxing, 1883–1897*. Jefferson, NC: McFarland, 2018.
22. *Chicago Tribune*, "It Was a Bloody, Wicked Battle," Sept. 7, 1892, p. 7. See also *Pittsburgh Dispatch*, "George Dixon Whips Skelly," Sept. 7, 1892, p. 7).
23. The Olympic Club went bankrupt in 1896 and its furnishings were auctioned off in a liquidation sale in May of that year. The club was re-formed, but a devastating fire on Dec. 6, 1897, put the final nail in the coffin. The land was subdivided into residential building lots. By then, prizefighting in New Orleans had fallen into a rut, the upshot of a fatal fight at a rival athletic club in December of 1894 that resulted in the death of a popular local fighter, Andy Bowen, who fell at the hands of Kid Lavigne. The sentiment to abolish prizefighting even had the support of Mayor Fitzpatrick, the third man in the ring for Sullivan–Kilrain.

Chapter 4

1. *San Francisco Chronicle*, "Seaside Gayeties," July 29, 1883, p. 1.
2. *Brooklyn Citizen*, "The Coney Island Athletic Club's Plans," May 3, 1892, p. 1.
3. *New York Times*, "M'Kane's New Paradise: Coney Island A Mecca For The Sluggers," May 10, 1892, p. 2.
4. *Brooklyn Daily Eagle*, "General Sporting Notes," May 14, 1892, p. 1.
5. *Buffalo Sunday Morning News*, "Featherweight Championship," June 19, 1892, p. 9.
6. *Pittsburgh Dispatch*, "Pugilistic Gossip," May 18, 1892, p. 8.
7. *Brooklyn Daily Eagle*, "Johnson No Match for the Colored Boy," June 28, 1893, p. 1.
8. *Boston Globe*, "Played For A Draw," March 21, 1893, p. 9; see also *Buffalo Commercial*, "Dixon Couldn't Do It," March 21, 1893, p. 10.
9. *Brooklyn Daily Eagle*, "Dixon In Three Rounds," Aug. 8, 1893, p. 2; *Milwaukee Daily Sentinel*, "Dixon's Easy Victory," Aug. 8, 1893, p. 2.
10. *Philadelphia Times*, "M'Grath Fights Gamely," Dec. 29, 1892, p. 6; see also *South Haven (KS) New Era*, "Most Brutal Exhibition," Dec. 31, 1892, p. 1.
11. *Boston Globe*, "Decision Against Dixon," Aug. 23, 1893, p. 6; see also *St. Louis Globe-Democrat*, "George Dixon Beaten," Aug. 23, 1893, p. 7.
12. *Boston Globe*, "The Realm of Sports" June 4, 1889, p. 7.
13. *Brooklyn Daily Eagle*, "Lively Fight Coming," Sept. 12, 1893, p. 2.
14. *New York Sun*, "Not In Dixon's Class," Sept. 26, 1893, p. 4.
15. *Los Angeles Herald*, "Solly Smith's Hard Luck," Sept. 26, 1893, p. 1.
16. *New York Times*, "Brooklyn Clergy Up in Arms," Sept. 24, 1893, p. 1.
17. *Ibid*.
18. *Ibid*.
19. *New York Times*, "Thunders of Denunciation," Oct. 9, 1983, p. 1.
20. *New York Times*, "Pastors or Sheriffs, Which," Oct. 18, 1893, p. 9.
21. *New York Times*, "M'Laughlin's Base Calumny," Oct. 5, 1893, p. 5.
22. *Ibid*.
23. *Brooklyn Times Union*, "Mul's Letter," March 13, 1915, p. 6.

Chapter 5

1. *New York Sun*, "Not in Dixon's Class," Sept. 26, 1893, p. 6.
2. *Kansas City Gazette*, "The Tiny Sullivan," March 13, 1894, p. 3. (Kitty Dixon was rumored to be Tom O'Rourke's sister.)
3. *Philadelphia Inquirer*, "Kentucky Rosebud Knocks Out Dixon," March 23, 1894, p. 3. Black boxers were often given exotic ring names. Another Philadelphia fighter, Willie Stokes, was billed as "Buffalo Sunflower."
4. *Elmira Star-Gazette*, "Dixon's Account of It," March 24, 1894, p. 1; *Buffalo Enquirer*, "Rosebud Challenges

Dixon," March 29, 1894, p. 8; see also William H. Rocap, "Twenty Years in the Ring; George Dixon Greatest Featherweight," *Philadelphia Tribune*, Sept. 26, 1914, p. 6. Walter Edgerton, aka Kentucky Rosebud, lived to be 75 or thereabouts; the exact date of his birth was unknown. After he retired, he was repeatedly in trouble with the cops for running a disorderly house, i.e., a combination bordello and gambling den.

5. *Boston Globe*, "Dixon and Griffo Fought Twenty Rounds," June 30, 1894, p. 4.

6. *Washington Times*, Dec. 19, 1894, "Griffo's Defiance to Dixon," p. 1.

7. *Philadelphia Times*, "The Dixon–Griffo Boxing Match," Jan. 21, 1895, p. 9.

8. *Boston Post*, "Rob Roy's Protest," May 30 1895, p. 3; see also *Brooklyn Citizen*, "Hard Fighting," May 28, 1895, p. 3.

9. *Boston Globe*, "Dixon Again," Aug. 27, 1895, p. 16.

10. *San Francisco Call*, "Fought To A Draw," Oct. 29, 1895, p. 5.

11. *Ibid.*

Chapter 6

1. *Buffalo Courier*, "He's A Tough One," Dec. 7. 1895. P. 9.

2. *Philadelphia Enquirer*, "Dixon Hardly A Has Been," March 18, 1896, p. 5. It would come out that Jerry Marshall was actually born in Chestertown, Maryland. He had his first 36 documented fights in Australia.

3. *Fall River Globe*, "Dixon and Flaherty Meet," June 17, 1896, p. 1.

4. *Boston Post* "Fought To A Draw," June 17, 1896, pp. 8, 15. In addition to being a newspaperman, Touhey was New England's most prominent wrestling promoter.

5. *Los Angeles Times*, "Sporting Record: A National Issue," Feb. 6, 1896, p. 2.

Chapter 7

1. *Boston Globe*, "Horton Boxing Law," Sept. 23, 1896, p. 2.

2. *Buffalo Times*, "Gossip of the Latest Happenings in Sport," Feb. 17, 1900, p. 6.

3. *New York Times*, "Slugging Matches Revived," Nov. 18, 1896, p. 4.

4. *Buffalo Enquirer*, "Tommy White Was The Versatile Youth," Feb. 17, 1912, p. 8.

5. *New York Sun*, "Dixon and White Draw," Sept. 26, 1896, p. 5.

6. *Brooklyn Standard Union*, "With The Boxers," Nov. 28, 1896, p. 8; *Buffalo Courier*, "Bad Day For Coons," Nov. 28, 1896, p. 9.

7. *Cincinnati Enquirer*, "Big Receipts at the Dixon–Murphy Contest," Jan. 25, 1897, p. 2.

8. *Philadelphia Inquirer*, "George Dixon and Jack Downey Draw," Feb. 16, 1897, p. 4.

9. *Buffalo Express*, "Erne Off For New York," Feb. 16, 1897, p. 11.

10. *Brooklyn Standard Union*, "Erne Defeated," March 25, 1897, p. 8.

11. *Philadelphia Inquirer*, "George Dixon Wins From Frank Erne," March 25, 1897, p. 4.

12. *New York Times*, "Dixon Pounded Griffin," April 27, 1897, p, 5; See also *Fall River Globe*, "Dixon The Winner," April 27, 1897, p. 5.

Chapter 8

1. *San Francisco Examiner*, "Aftermath of the Glove Contest," July 25, 1897, p. 22. Mechanics Pavilion was completely destroyed in the great earthquake and fire of 1906.

2. *San Francisco Call*, "Solly Smith is the New Featherweight Champion," Oct. 5, 1897; *Trenton Evening Times*, "At the Ringside," Oct. 15, 1897, p. 6.

3. *St. Louis Republic* Sunday Magazine section, "The Hoosier Baden-Baden," Aug. 9, 1903, pp. 1, 2. Several professional baseball teams held their Spring Training in West Baden, including the 1907 and 1908 pennant winning Chicago Cubs. West Baden remained a popular place for athletes to go and work out the kinks well into the 20th century. Joe Louis prepared for several of his title fights here.

4. *Buffalo Enquirer*, "Boxed A Draw," April 1, 1898, p. 6.
5. *Brooklyn Standard Union*, "Dixon Bests Santry," June 7, 1898, p. 7.
6. *Boston Globe*, "Son Of A Minister,' July 11, 1898, p. 9.
7. *New York Sun*, "Fighting," April 25, 1898, p. 10.
8. *Brooklyn Daily Eagle*, "Dixon's Colors Lowered," July 2, 1898, p. 4.
9. *Buffalo Times*, "George Beats Dave," Nov. 12, 1898, p. 6.
10. George Barton, "Oscar Gardner Greatest Fighter Ever Produced Here," *Minneapolis Star Tribune*, Feb. 5, 1928, p. 22.
11. *Cincinnati Enquirer*, "It's a Bad Decision," Nov. 30, 1898, p 4; *Boston Globe*, "Given To Dixon," Nov. 30, 1898, p. 9; Fleischer, op. cit., p. 91.

Chapter 9

1. Arthur T. Lumley, "Terry McGovern Dead Nine Years, No Monument Yet," *Brooklyn Daily Eagle*, Feb. 20, 1927, p. 37.
2. *Brooklyn Citizen*, "He is the Pride of South Brooklyn," Feb. 5, 1899, p. 5.
3. *Brooklyn Daily Eagle*, "Unfavorable Effect of the Gowanus Canal," April 24, 1887, p. 7.
4. *Joplin (MO) News Herald*, "Kilbane Only Son of Erin Holding Ring Title, But Irish Race Not on Wane," Dec. 13, 1914, p. 12.
5. *Brooklyn Union*, "The Prize Fighter of the Tax Office," Jan. 22, 1868, p. 2.
6. *Brooklyn Daily Eagle*, "Walks About The City," Nov. 25, 1888, p. 6.
7. *Brooklyn Daily Eagle*, "Boswycks Point a Moral," Feb. 24, 1893, p. 7. Brooklyn's leading club was the Crescent Athletic Club in the Bay Ridge section of the city. By 1907, the Crescent had 2,432 members and more than a million dollars in assets. Instruction was offered in 14 fields of athletics. (*Brooklyn Standard Union*, "Crescent A.C. Enjoys Very Successful Year, Jan. 18, 1907, p. 10.)
8. *Brooklyn Daily Eagle*, "Greenwood A.C. Bouts," April 4, 1897, p. 8.
9. *Brooklyn Daily Eagle*, "Dundee A Better Man Than Was McGovern," April 8, 1914, p. 22.
10. *Brooklyn Times Union*, "McGovern and Monroe Draw," May 6, 1898, p. 6.
11. *Brooklyn Daily Eagle*, "Munroe Is Counted Out," June 12, 1898, p. 30; see also *Rochester Democrat and Chronicle*, "Fighting," June 12, 1898, p. 18.
12. *Brooklyn Citizen*, "Fouled by Monroe," Aug. 5, 1898, p. 5; *Brooklyn Standard Union*, "Won On A Foul," Aug. 5, 1898, p. 7.
13. The Hesper Club folded in June of 1912. By then, according to an article in the *New York Sun*, the membership had become overrun with small stakes bookmakers and other petty gamblers. The clubhouse was raided by the police in April of that year. (*New York Sun*, "Rosenthal Twice Head of Hesper Club," July 17, 1912, p. 2.)
14. *Brooklyn Citizen*, "Tim Callahan Knocked Out," Nov. 20, 1898, p. 2.
15. *Brooklyn Times Union*, "McGovern and the Championship," Oct. 3, 1898, p. 6.
16. *Boston Globe*, "Made The Fight Of His Life," Jan. 1, 1899, p. 2.

Chapter 10

1. *Brooklyn Daily Eagle*, "Dixon Wins," Jan. 18, 1899, p, 14. Although no mention was made of it at the time, this bout was historic in that it was the first world title fight of the gloved era that pitted Black against Black. Pluto would claim that his two cornermen, whom he picked up in San Francisco, absconded with his purse. (*St. Louis Globe-Democrat*, "Pluto Being Used," Jan. 19, 1899, p. 5.)
2. *Brooklyn Times-Union*, "For the Bantam-Weight Championship," Jan. 27, 1899. p. 6.
3. *Brooklyn Daily Eagle*, "McGovern's Latest Success," Jan. 31, 1899, p. 12.
4. Otto C. Floto, "New Boxing Rules," *Denver Evening Post*, Feb. 19, 1899, p. 14.
5. *New York Journal*, "Greatest Fight in Years Seen at the Lenox Athletic Club," March 15, 1899, p. 6.
6. *Brooklyn Citizen*, "Terry McGovern Won," April 29, 1899, p. 5.

Notes—Chapter 11

7. *New York Sun,* "Terry McGovern Wins," April 29, 1899, p. 9.
8. *Buffalo Courier,* "George Dixon Got Decision," May 16, 1899, p. 9; *Boston Globe,* "Dixon Has Small Margin," May 16, 1899, p. 5.
9. *Lexington Daily Leader,* "Passing Of The Pugilist," July 28, 1898, p. 3.
10. *Pittsburgh Press,* "Dixon Still Champion," June 3, 1899, p. 5.
11. *Louisville Courier-Journal,* "Dixon Beats Sammy Bolen," July 4, 1899, p. 6.
12. *Boston Globe,* "Greatest Fistic Battle Seen in Denver," July 12, 1899, p. 1; *Chicago Tribune,* "Tommy White Meets Defeat," July 12, 1899, p. 4.
13. Joe Humphreys (as told to George B. Underwood), "Battles I Have Seen," *Buffalo Times,* Nov. 19. 1922. P. 76.
14. *Brooklyn Daily Eagle,* "Ritchie Knocked Out By Terry McGovern," July 2, 1899, p. 10.
15. *Chicago Inter Ocean,* "Palmer in Gotham," Aug. 6, 1899, p. 11.
16. *Wilmington Morning Star,* "Bantam Champion Of The World," Sept. 13, 1899, p. 1.
17. *Boston Globe,* "Bantams Struggling for the Championship," Sept. 12, 1899, p. 1.
18. Joe Humphreys, loc. cit.
19. *Los Angeles Times,* "America Forever: Knocks Out England in One Round," Sept. 13, 1899, p. 2.
20. *Brooklyn Daily Eagle,* "A Hot Time in South Brooklyn," Sept. 13, 1899, p. 13. Because the fight was over in record time, the motion pictures were a white elephant. Sam Harris claimed he lost $10,000. The 1988 heavyweight title fight in Atlantic City between Mike Tyson and Michael Spinks was reminiscent of McGovern–Palmer. Both were highly anticipated events that ended in a flash, stunning in their brevity.
21. *Boston Globe,* "Dixon Gets Only a Draw," Aug. 12, 1899, p. 3.
22. *New York World,* "Dixon The Winner in the Twenty-Fifth," Nov. 3, 1899, p. 6.
23. *Baltimore Sun,* "Dixon Defeats Lenny," Nov. 22, 1899, p. 6; see also *Brooklyn Times-Union,* "Two Good Fights at Coney Island," Oct. 2, 1899, p. 4.

24. *Philadelphia Enquirer,* "'Twas All M'Govern," Sept. 30, 1899, p. 4.
25. *Chicago Inter Ocean,* "M'Govern is Here," Oct. 9, 1899, p. 8. There was no Tom Figg; the author obviously meant James Figg, the 18th century bare-knuckle boxer widely considered the first heavyweight champion.
26. *Chicago Inter Ocean,* "Terry Puts out Two,'" Nov. 19, 1899, p. 11.
27. *St. Paul Globe,* "Greatest of the Age," Nov. 21, 1899, p. 5.
28. *Louisville Courier-Journal,* "M'Govern Wins Two," Dec. 19, 1899, p. 8. Walter "Freckles" O'Brien, who was from New Orleans, caught up with McGovern again on January 5, 1901, when Terry was appearing in that city. McGovern knocked him out in the third round on the stage of the Crescent Theater (*Louisville Courier-Journal,* "Another Victim For M'Govern," Jan. 7, 1901, p. 6). Curiously, O'Brien had accompanied Terry into the ring when he fought Joe Bernstein two months earlier in Louisville.
29. *Boston Globe,* "McGovern Again," Dec. 23, 1899, p. 8.

Chapter 11

1. *Philadelphia Times,* "Battle of the Midgets," Aug. 6, 1893, p. 9; Nat Fleischer, "The Three Colored Aces," p. 4.
2. In this regard, see Perry R. Duis, *The Saloon: Public Drinking in Chicago and Boston 1880–1920.* Urbana, IL: University of Illinois Press, 1983 (especially, chap. 4, pp. 114–142).
3. Thomas F. Keenan, "Over Four Hours," *Boston Globe,* July 21, 1887, p. 6; see also *St. Louis Post-Dispatch,* "The Weir-Havlin Mill," July 22, 1887.
4. *San Francisco Examiner,* "Sports of the Week," Dec. 3, 1888, p. 5; see also *Stockton Mail,* "A One-Sided Fight," Nob. 28, 1888, p. 2.
5. Damon Runyon, "Runyon Says," *Camden (NJ) Courier-Post,* Aug. 25, 1926, p. 25.
6. *Boston Globe,* "Dixon's Confidence," Feb. 5, 1891, p. 5.
7. O.O. McIntyre, "New York Day By

Day," *Charlotte Observer,* Aug. 13, 1936, p. 26.
　8. *Bangor Daily News,* "Fighters I Have Known," Feb. 26, 1907, p. 7.
　9. *New York Evening World,* "Dempsey Found At Last," June 16, 1893, p. 6; *St. Louis Globe-Democrat,* "Stood Dixon Off," June 18, 1893, p. 5.
　10. George Kibbe Turner, "Tammany's Control of New York by Professional Criminals," *McClure's Magazine,* Vol. XXXIII, June, 1909, pp. 117–134.
　11. *Buffalo Morning Express,* "Boxing Trust," Sept. 22, 1899, p. 9.
　12. *Ogden Standard,* "O'Rourke Never Developed Champs," May 8, 1917, p. 8.
　13. *Washington Post,* "Big Fights in Gotham," Feb. 19, 1905, p. 9.
　14. *New York Times,* "Jeffries Won the Fight," Nov. 4, 1899, p. 3.
　15. A resolution adopted by a consortium of Methodist preachers was especially strident in its opposition to the Horton Law. Upon leaving the Jeffries–Sharkey fight, said the epistle, "a motley crowd returned to certain portions of Manhattan and Brooklyn to make the night hideous with a saturnalia of vice and crime." (*New York Times,* "Prizefighting Attacked," Dec. 19, 1899, p. 11.)
　16. Robert K. DeArment, *Gunfighter in Gotham: Bat Masterson's New York City Years.* Norman: University of Oklahoma Press, 2013, p. 14.
　17. *Elmira Star-Gazette,* "A New Boxing Club," June 18, 1901, p. 6; see also, "Tom O'Rourke To Open Big Boxing Amphitheatre," Sept. 15, 1901, p. 8; see also *New York Times,* "Rose, Unshaken, Is To Be Accused," May 14, 1914, p. 4. Jack Rose went on to become an antigambling crusader, speaking before youth groups in churches and other places where he lifted the veil on the various tricks used by crooked gamblers. ("Tricks and Traps of the Underworld Which Beset the Unwary," *Portland Sunday Oregonian,* Feb. 2, 1913, p. 73.)
　18. *Buffalo Evening News,* "Tom O'Rourke Quits," Jan. 13, 1902, p. 6.
　19. *Chicago Tribune,* "Put Off Fight to Next Week," May 30, 1906, p. 10.
　20. *Kansas City Star,* "O'Rourke's Unknown," Oct. 18, 1892, p. 3.
　21. *Ibid.*
　22. *Boston Post,* "Clever Joe Walcott," Sept. 2, 1892, p. 3.
　23. Nat Fleischer, "The Three Colored Aces," Vol, 3 of *Black Dynamite,* 1938, p. 196; see also Nat Fleischer, "Joe Walcott, Caveman Of The Ring," *Hackensack Record,* Dec. 8, 1926, p. 17.
　24. *Boston Globe,* "Joe Walcott Knocks Out his Man in 15 Seconds," Aug. 23, 1893, p. 1.
　25. *Buffalo Enquirer,* "Tom Tracey Beaten," April 20, 1894, p. 8.
　26. *Boston Globe,* "15-Round Draw," March 2, 1895, p. 8.
　27. *Boston Globe,* "Killed By Joe Walcott," Oct. 18, 1904, pp. 1, 2; *Indianapolis Star,* "Weeps For Man He Shot," Oct. 31, 1904, p. 4; *Fall River Globe,* "Walcott Freed," Nov. 12, 1904, p. 1.
　28. *Los Angeles Times,* "David and Goliath of the Prize Ring," April 5, 1902, p. 5.
　29. *Butte Daily Post,* "Joe Walcott Meanest of all Fighters," March 23, 1903, p. 8.
　30. *Waterbury Evening Democrat,* "Walcott Quits O'Rourke," July 26, 1900, p. 1.
　31. *Boston Post,* "Walcott A Winner Over Larry Temple," Dec. 30, 1903, p. 3; *Indianapolis Star,* "Temple Knocks Out Walcott," Nov. 18, 1908, p. 9.

Chapter 12

　1. *Pittsburgh Daily Post,* "Featherweights To Meet To-Day," Jan. 9, 1900, p. 6; *Chicago Tribune,* "Local Opinions On The Fight," Jan. 10, 1900, p. 5.
　2. *Topeka State Journal,* "Phrenologist Fowler Says Terry McGovern Will Win," Jan. 6, 1900, p. 2; *St. Paul Globe,* "M'Govern To Win," Jan. 5, 1900, p. 5.
　3. *Boston Globe,* "After 800 Battles George Dixon, The Boston Boy, Retires from the Ring," Jan. 8, 1900, p. 5.
　4. *Pittsburgh Daily Post,* "The Great Train Robbery," Jan. 7, 1900, p. 8.
　5. *New York Times,* "McGovern Conquers Dixon," Jan. 10, 1900, p. 2; *Brooklyn Times Union,* "Dixon Finds M'Govern

Too Strong A Young Man," Jan. 10, 1900, p. 8.

6. *Chicago Tribune*, "Terence M'Govern, New 118-Pound Champion," Jan. 10, 1900, p. 5. Because Dixon wasn't knocked out in the conventional sense, some bookmakers were reluctant to pay off on the proposition that McGovern would knock Dixon out inside ten rounds, a popular wager. The bout's referee Johnny White came to the defense of those whose wagers were in limbo, asserting that all bets must be paid. (*Buffalo Times*, "Gossip of the Latest Happenings in Sport," Jan. 13, 1900, p. 6.)

7. *Brooklyn Times-Union*, "Walcott Into The Breach," Jan. 10, 1900, p. 8.

8. *Chicago Tribune*, loc. cit.

9. *Boston Globe*, "Dixon Passes," Jan. 10, 1900, p. 1.

10. *Buffalo Enquirer*, "Politician O'Dell's Wild And Rambling Ravings," Jan. 11, 1900, p. 4.

11. *Buffalo Review*, "Monster Benefit To Be Tendered George Dixon By His Many Friends And Admirers," Jan. 12, 1900, p. 2.

12. *Buffalo Times*, "George Dixon's Benefit," Feb. 22, 1900, p. 8.

13. *Ibid.*

14. Cross Counter, "Spendthrift Boxers Few And Far Between," Buffalo Evening News, Oct. 14, 1918, p. 11.

15. *Boston Globe*, "George Dixon, The Boston Boy Retires from the Ring," Jan, 8, 1900, p. 5.

Chapter 13

1. *Philadelphia Inquirer*, "Governor's Body Blow at Boxing," Jan. 5, 1900, p. 6.

2. *Chicago Tribune*, "Maher Wins The Fight," Nov. 17, 1896, p. 8; *Raleigh News and Observer*, "Roosevelt And The Fighters," Nov. 22, 1896, p. 3. There wasn't yet a general understanding that repeated head traumas could produce serious cognitive impairments that might not show up until much later in life. "Most persons who are 'knocked out' or 'put to sleep' as the poetic pugilists have it, are gently wafted into oblivion after some cuffings that leave no effects," insisted a writer for a Wisconsin paper in 1892. (*Milwaukee Daily Sentinel*, "Prize-Fighting," Sept. 8, 1892, p. 4.) A truer picture of this disturbing phenomenon emerges in Tris Dixon's well-researched *Damage: The Untold Story of Brain Trauma in Boxing* (Boston, Hamilcar, 2021).

3. *Boston Globe*, "Repeal Of Horton Law Causes Alarm," Jan. 4, 1900, p. 8.

4. *Ibid.*

5. *Waterbury Democrat*, "Lost Because No Boxing," March 15, 1901, p. 7.

6. *Miami News*, "Terhune A Fighter As Well As Writer Of Note," March 4, 1921, p. 22.

7. *Buffalo Enquirer*, "Managers of Boxing Clubs Now Looking to Other States," March 31,1900, p. 4; see also *Deadwood (SD) Pioneer-Times*, "Political Pugilists," April 13, 1900, p. 2.

8. *Baltimore Sun*, "Santry Down And Out," Feb. 2, 1900, p. 6.

9. 9. Leo Etherington, "Sporting Gossip Of The Week," *Deseret Evening News*, March 3, 1900, p. 10.

10. *St. Louis Globe-Democrat*, "Gardner Easy For McGovern," March 10, 1900, p. 7.

11. *Boston Globe*, "Only One Round," April 21, 1900, p. 8.

12. J.B. "Macon" McCormick, "Think M'Govern Can Lick Any Lightweight," *St. Louis Republic*, June 17, 1900, p. 16.

13. *Brooklyn Citizen*, "Frank Erne Is Still Champion," March 24, 1900, p. 8.

14. *Chicago Tribune*, "Erne Laid Low By The 'Terror,'" July 17, 1900. p. 4.

15. *Buffalo Enquirer*, "Croker and Terrible Terry," July 19, 1900, p. 4.

16. *Brooklyn Daily Eagle*, "Terry, The Tiger Cub, Wins," July 17, 1900, p. 6.

17. *Buffalo Enquirer*, "Terry M'Govern, The Featherweight Champion, Knocked Out Frank Erne," Nov. 17, 1900, p. 4.

18. George Siler, "Lasts For Seven Rounds," *Chicago Tribune*, Nov. 3, 1900, p. 7.

19. George Siler, "Gans–M'Govern Match Forecast," *Chicago Tribune*, Dec. 9. 1900, p. 17.

20. *Nashville Banner*, "FAKE! Cry Nearly All the Chicago Papers," Dec. 14, 1900, p. 10.

21. *Ibid.*
22. George Siler, "Mayor Forbids Boxing Planned," *Chicago Tribune*, Dec. 25, 1901, p. 6.
23. Quoted in the *Buffalo Courier*, "How Terry Beat Gardner," March 11, 1900, p. 27.
24. George Siler, "M'Govern Has Troubles," *Chicago Tribune*, March 17, 1901, p. 17.
25. *San Francisco Call*, "M'Govern, The Prize-Fighter, is Still 'Terry, The Terrible,'" April 30, 1901, p. 4.
26. For a time, Carillo handled the affairs of future heavyweight champion Jack Johnson, whose first fight after arriving in California was in Bakersfield. The partnership ended acrimoniously with Carillo suing Johnson over money allegedly owed to him. (*Bakersfield Morning Echo*, "Jack Johnson's Arrest Before Fight," Feb 7, 1903, p. 8; *Oakland Tribune*, "Signed Away His Earnings," Oct. 30, 1903, p. 4.)
27. *Pittsburgh Post*, "Aurelio Herrera's Death Recalls Great Bout With Terrible Terry McGovern When Mexican Mauler Almost Captured World's Feather Title," April 14, 1917, p. 16.
28. *Humboldt Times*, "Terry M'Govern Easily Bests Herrera at Mechanics Pavilion," May 30, 1901, p. 1.
29. *Knoxville Sentinel*, "Gotham's Latest Crusade With Terry M'Govern, The Pugilist, As A Leader," July 11, 1901, p. 8.
30. *Chicago Inter Ocean*, "Terry Praises Dixon," June 25, 1900, p. 8.
31. *Chicago Inter Ocean*, "Lou Houseman's Talk Of Boxers," Nov. 4, 1901, p. 20.
32. Robert Edgren, "Easterners Astounded by M'Govern's Defeat," *Miami Herald*, Feb. 5, 1933, p. 5.
33. Joe Williams, "Uppercut Proves History Making Punch," *Arizona Republic*, Feb. 23, 1926, p. 8. For sustained action compressed into a tight time frame, perhaps no title fight was comparably tumultuous until Marvin Hagler fought Thomas Hearns in Las Vegas in 1995.
34. *Houston Post*, "A Hero's Reception," Dec. 21, 1901, p. 3.

Chapter 14

1. *Buffalo Courier*, "George Dixon's Statement," Jan. 11, 1900, p. 9.
2. *Waterbury Evening Democrat*, "George Dixon, Fighter," May 5, 1900, p. 15.
3. *Sioux City Journal*, "Dixon Severely Beaten," June 24, 1900, p. 3.
4. *Philadelphia Enquirer*, "Sporting," April 15, 1901, p. 4.
5. *Los Angeles Express*, "Corbett Wins Decision," Aug. 17, 1901, p. 7.
6. *Indianapolis News*, "Pugilists' Affairs," Aug. 21, 1901, p. 6. Historian Louis Moore makes the case that white fight managers were always willing to loan money to their Black fighters, as this solidified their hold over them.
7. *St. Louis Post-Dispatch*, "Siler Gives Attell The Decision," Oct. 25, 1901, p. 8; *St. Louis Globe-Democrat*, "Attell Got The Decision," Oct. 24, 1901, p. 10.
8. *Chicago Tribune*, "Boxing Stopped in St. Louis," Nov. 17, 1901, p. 19.
9. *Washington Times*, "Dixon Strikes A Snag," Jan. 18, 1902, p. 5.
10. *Baltimore Sun*, "Dixon Knocked Out," Jan. 25, 1902, p. 6.
11. *Wilkes-Barre Dollar Weekly News*, July 12, 1902, p. 6.
12. *Buffalo Enquirer*, "Sporting Gossip," June 13, 1902, p. 4.
13. *Buffalo Times*, "Dixon's First Quit," June 12, 2002, p. 12.
14. *Brooklyn Times Union*, "Dixon and Callahan Box," July 1, 1902, p. 8.
15. *National Police Gazette*, "Little George Dixon, the ex–Featherweight Champion, is Boxing in Great Form," Jan. 23, 1904, p. 3.
16. *Buffalo Evening News*, "Great Record of George Dixon," Dec. 26, 1903, p. 16.
17. *Baltimore Sun*, "British Ring Gossip," Jan. 13, 1904, p. 9.
18. *Elmira (NY) Star-Gazette*, "Dixon Home And Is Broke," Aug. 25, 1905, p. 3.
19. *Boston Globe*, "All Wanted Dixon To Win," Sept. 21, 1905, p. 7.
20. *Fall River Evening Herald*, "Dixon Led All The Way," May 22, 1906, p. 2.
21. *Indianapolis News*, "Old George Dixon Defeated," Dec. 11, 1906, p. 7.

Chapter 15

1. *Indianapolis Journal*, "Terry M'Govern Won," Feb. 23, 1902, p. 7.
2. *Hartford Courant*, "Saw The Fight," Nov. 29, 1901, p. 8.
3. *St. Louis Globe-Democrat*, "Injunction Asked For," Sept. 17, 1902, p. 12; see also *Baltimore Sun*, "Protest Against Match," Sept. 15, 1902, p. 6.
4. *Louisville Courier-Journal*, "Up In Arms," Aug. 31, 1902, section 3, p. 1.
5. *Detroit Free Press*, "Billy Considine Dies 'Mid Peaceful Luxury," Feb. 17, 1932, pp. 1, 3.
6. *Fort Wayne Daily News*, "Pugilistic Game Like Opera Bouffe," Dec. 13, 1902, p. 7.
7. *Detroit Free Press*, "M'Govern to Box Bernstein," Jan. 23. 1903, p. 3.
8. *San Francisco Examiner*, "Eddie Hanlon and Young Corbett Fight to a Draw," Feb. 27, 1903, p. 3.
9. *San Francisco Call*, "Referee Graney Says M'Govern Was Counted Out," April 1, 1903, p. 3.
10. W.W. Naughton, "Corbett In Round Eleven," *Detroit Free Press*, April 1, 1903, pp. 1, 10.
11. *San Francisco Call*, "Thousands at Mechanics' Pavilion to see Great Battle," loc. cit.; *San Francisco Examiner*, "Examiner Fight Bulletins Were Loudly Cheered," April 1, 1903, p. 3.
12. *Baltimore Sun*, "Terry's Mother Tells," April 13, 1908, p. 9.
13. *Boston Globe*, "Punished Wickedly," Oct. 11, 1904, p. 7.
14. *Washington Evening Star*, "M'Govern Breaks Down," April 12, 1905, p. 6.
15. *New York Daily Tribune*, "McGovern Gets Away," April 18, 1905, p. 11.
16. *Detroit Free Press*, "Terry McGovern Barred From Belmont Park," May 11, 1905, p. 10.
17. *Brooklyn Citizen*, "M'Govern in Street Fight," July 31, 1905, p. 1; *Passaic Daily News*, "Terry McGovern Accused," Aug. 1, 1905, p. 5.
18. *Boston Globe*, "McGovern Is In Game Again," Oct. 19, 1905, p. 13.
19. Robert Edgren, "Battling Nelson Beat The 'Terror' in Oddest Fight," *New York Evening World*, March 15, 1906, p. 12.
20. *San Francisco Call*, "Britt Will Meet Terry McGovern Tonight," May 28, 1906, p. 3.
21. *Brooklyn Daily Eagle*, "McGovern, Though Out Of Condition, More Than Holds His Own With Britt," May 29, 1906, p. 7; see also *Pittsburgh Daily Post*, "Britt and M'Govern Fight To Draw," May 26, 1906, p. 8.
22. *Cumberland Evening Times*, "Terry McGovern A Wreck," July 19, 1906, p. 1; *Brooklyn Citizen*, "Warning for M'Govern," July 31, 1906, p. 5; *Berkshire Eagle*, "Bar McGovern From The Colonial Theatre," Sept. 15, 1906, p. 2.
23. *Indiana (PA) Gazette*, "Ancient Foes Meet," Oct. 18, 1906, p. 4.
24. *Washington Times*, "Terry's Escapade Costs Twenty-Five," Nov. 30, 1906, p. 13.
25. *Brooklyn Citizen*, "M'Govern Is Insane," Dec. 4, 1906, p. 1; *Buffalo Courier*, "M'Govern is Hopelessly Insane," Dec. 9, 1906, p. 27.
26. *Baltimore Sun*, "Money M'Govern Made," Jan. 15, 1907, p. 8.
27. *Brooklyn Citizen*, "I'm Sorry I Ever Left Denver," Jan. 24, 1907, p. 5; see also *Brooklyn Times-Union*, "M'Govern Testimonial Big Help To Family," Jan. 24, 1907, p. 5.
28. *Washington Post*, "Nice Sum For M'Govern," Feb. 8, 1907, p. 16.
29. *Buffalo Enquirer*, "Terry Never To Fight Again," Dec. 10, 1906, p. 8.
30. *Minneapolis Star-Tribune*, "Terry McGovern's Death Coming Soon, Says Doctor," Jan. 9, 1907, p. 8.
31. *Hartford Courant*, "Terry McGovern in Y.M.C.A Gym," April 10, 1907, p. 9; *Elmira Star-Gazette*, "Sport Gossip," June 4, 1907, p. 3.
32. *Butte Daily Post*, "Fighters Do Not Come Back," May 22, 1908, p. 6.

Chapter 16

1. *Baltimore Sun*, "Raised Purse For Dixon," Jan. 28, 1907, p. 8.
2. *Boston Globe*, "George Dixon, The Boston Boy Retires from the Ring," Jan, 8, 1900, p. 5.
3. *Paterson Morning Call*, "Gans Gives

Notes—Chapters 17, 18 and 19

Lift To George Dixon, "Oct. 30, 1907, p. 3; *Grass Valley* (CA) *Morning Union*, Dec. 19, 1907, p. 7; Clarence C. Cullens, "Followers of the Prize Ring Not Enthused Over The Recent Championship Affair in London," *Washington Evening Star*, Dec. 8, 1907, p. 55.

4. *Pittsburgh Press*, "Sullivan is George Dixon's Only Friend," Dec. 2, 1907, p. 12; *Boston Globe*, "Wouldn't Let Dixon be Jim Crowed," Feb. 9, 1908, p. 37.

5. *Washington Herald*, "Dixon's Last Count," Jan. 8, 1908, p. 8.

6. *Chicago Defender*, "Brother of World Champion Boxer, Dies," April 26, 1930, p. 6.

7. *Baltimore Sun*, "Dixon's Body Goes To Boston," Jan. 9, 1908, p. 10; see also Nat Fleischer, *Black Dynamite, vol. III*, pp. 121–22.

8. *Baltimore Sun*, "Talk Of George Dixon," Jan. 8, 1908, p. 10.

9. *Reno Gazette-Journal*, "Says Money Led to Dixon's Ruin," Feb. 4, 1908, p. 3.

10. George Siler, "Once A Hero; Dies A Pauper," *Chicago Tribune*, Jan. 12, 1908, p. 22.

11. *Louisville Courier-Journal*, "Sporting Men To Mark Grave," Jan. 12, 1908, p. 28.

Chapter 17

1. *Brooklyn Daily Eagle*, "Terry McGovern Held," July 8, 1909, p. 16; *Brooklyn Daily Eagle*, "McGovern to Sanitarium," July 15, 1909, p. 3.

2. *Pittsburgh Press*, "Terry McGovern's Mind A Blank At Times," Sept 11, 1909, p. 5; Robert Ripley, "'My Hardest Battle,'" *Vancouver Daily World*, Aug. 13, 1913, p. 12.

3. *Mathews (VA) Journal*, "Terry McGovern Dying," Feb. 16, 1911, p. 6.

4. *Brooklyn Citizen*, "The Bowery After Dark," Dec. 7, 1913.

5. *Brooklyn Standard Union*, "Terry M'Govern in Trouble Once More," Jan. 24, 1914, p. 1; *Grand Forks Herald*, "Terry M'Govern A Great Fighter," Feb. 21, 1914, p. 6; *Scranton Tribune*, "Terry M'Govern In An Asylum Again," March 16, 1914, p. 12.

6. *Salt Lake Tribune*, "Terry McGovern, Weary and Wan, Takes in Bout," May 10, 1915, p. 14; *Hartford Courant*, "Sammy Waltz Too Much For Tierney," Dec. 17, 1915; p. 19; *Brooklyn Daily Eagle*, "Warns Terry McGovern," Feb. 17, 1912, p. 2.

7. *Long Branch Daily Record*, "Two Boxers Are Patriotic," Oct. 16, 1917, p. 5.

Chapter 18

1. Harry B. Center, "George Dixon's Funeral," *Boston Post*, Jan. 10, 1908, p. 8.

2. *Boston Globe*, "Little George Dixon at Rest," Jan. 10, 1908, p. 7.

3. *Buffalo Courier*, "George Dixon's Memory Honored," March 1, 1908, p. 29.

4. *Camden Morning Post*, "Memorials to George Dixon," July 21, 1909, p. 7.

5. *Brooklyn Daily Eagle*, "Chums High and Low at Terry's Bier," Feb. 25, 1918, p. 18.

6. *Brooklyn Standard Union*, "M'Govern Laid To Rest In Plot At Holy Cross Cemetery," Feb. 25, 1918, p. 8.

7. Arthur T. Lumley "Terry McGovern Dead Nine Years, No Monument Yet," *Brooklyn Daily Eagle*, Feb. 20, 1927. P. 37.

8. *Bridgeport Telegram*, "McGovern's Son Visits This City For a Reunion," June 10, 1918, p.16.

Chapter 19

1. *New York Evening World*, "Many Reforms In Boxing Expected Under Gov. Miller's New Board," July 14, 1921, p. 16.

2. *Bangor (Me) Daily News*, "George Dixon's Finish Pitiful," Nov. 18, 1907, p. 7.

3. Robert Edgren, "Defends Feather Title for Ten Years," *St. Louis Post Dispatch*, Nov. 12, 1907, p. 16; *Pittsburgh Press*, "Sullivan Is George Dixon's Only Friend," Dec. 2, 1907, p. 12.

4. *Ironwood (MI) Daily Globe*, "Tom O'Rourke Was Ring Czar," June 30, 1936, p. 7; see also Harry Grayson, "A Tip To 'Smelling,'" *Wilmington (DE) News Journal*, July 20, 1966, p. 35.

5. *Boston Globe*, "Joe Walcott A Neighbor of Hon E.S. Converse," Aug. 17, 1903, p. 1.

Notes—Chapter 19

6. *Bangor Daily News,* "Joe Walcott Is Fireman On A Liner," Feb. 26, 1918, p. 10.
7. 'Lank' Leonard, "Joe Walcott, Once A Great Fighter, Now a Sweeper," *Brooklyn Citizen,* Jan. 18, 1930, p. 9.
8. *Washington DC Evening News,* "Joe Walcott, Ring Champ Of Old Days, Is Down But Refuses To Be Counted Out," Aug. 25, 1932, p. 40; *Boston Globe,* "Joe Walcott Discharged From Bellevue Hospital," Aug. 31, 1932, p. 19.
9. *Mansfield Journal,* "Famous Fighting Man, Last Seen Here, Missing," Dec. 12, 1935, p. 1.
10. Alan Goldstein, "Ohio Ring Historian Spends Vacations Digging Up Facts," *Baltimore Sun,* Aug. 3, 1964, p. 17.
11. Edwin Pope, "Abe Attell: A Bad Advertisement for Clean Living," *Miami Herald,* Feb. 8, 1970, p. 41.
12. *Newport (RI) Mercury,* "Martin Flaherty Still In Fighting Trim At 78, Longest Bout Was 60 Rounds," May 5, 1951, p. 5.
13. *Hartford Courant,* "Johnny Griffin Dead," March 13, 1899, p. 1.
14. *Houston Post,* "Tommy Warren Dead," Feb. 21, 1904, p. 24.
15. *Salt Lake Telegram,* "Vet Boxer Faces Mental Examination," Aug. 12, 1918, p. 4.
16. Thomas S. Rice, "Digger Stanley Dies After Long Career," *Brooklyn Daily Eagle,* March 26, 1919, p. 18.
17. *Ottawa Citizen,* "100,000 Watch As Boxer's Remains Borne To Grave," Feb. 25, 1925.
18. *New York Evening World,* "Young Corbett Says Good Goodbye To Great White Way," Feb. 13, 1922, p. 16.
19. *Hartford Courant,* "Austin Rice is Peddling Milk," Dec. 23, 1912, p. 16; *Norwich Bulletin,* "A Great Tribute to Austin D. Rice," Feb. 17, 1921, p. 3; *Norwich Bulletin,* "George Rice Hanged Friday at Washington," March 18, 1922, p. 5.
20. *Santa Ana Register,* "Former Ring Idol Serving 30-Day Sentence In Jail, Glories Of Past Vanished," Dec. 18, 1920, p. 6.
21. Ed Hughes, "Two Champions on Card of Bernstein at Broadway Arena Tonight," *Brooklyn Daily Eagle,* Feb. 23, 1928, p. 26.
22. *Brooklyn Times Union,* "Sammy Kelly Counted Out by Grim Reaper," May 30, 1923, p. 10.
23. *Pittsburgh Press,* "'Omaha Kid' on Death Bed," Dec. 10, 1928, p. 40.
24. *Dubuque (IA) Daily Times,* "Great Ring Record," Jan. 7, 1905, p. 6.
25. *Philadelphia Inquirer,* "Ellwood McCloskey, Noted Boxer Years Ago, Dies," March 5, 1927, p. 24; see also *Buffalo Times,* "Blind Man Enjoys Boxing," Dec. 16, 1908, p. 10.
26. *Salinas Morning Post,* "Hard Times Give Ex-Fighter Kayo Blow," July 27, 1939. p. 1; Prescott Sullivan, "The Low Down," *San Francisco Examiner,* Sept. 10, 1940, p. 18.
27. *Akron Beacon Journal,* "Young Griffo Is In Trouble Again," Sept. 8, 1909, p. 6; Mark Hellinger, "About Broadway," *New York Daily News,* May 8, 1927, p. 59; *New York Daily News,* "Fistiana Mourns Young Griffo," Dec. 18, 1927, p. 33.
28. Earl Gustkey, "Fight Fan Digs Into the Past, Emerges as the Graveyard Detective of Boxing," *Los Angeles Times,* June 11, 1986, p. D1.
29. Emily Bennett, "Family honours memory of boxer," *Central Western Daily News* (online edition), March 26, 2017.
30. Arne K. Lang, *The Nelson–Wolgast Fight and the San Francisco Boxing Scene, 1900–1914,* McFarland & Company, 2012, Chapter 14, pp. 148–157.
31. *New York Daily News,* "Thomas Murphy," Nov. 28, 1958, p. 42; Jack Cuddy, "Murphy Champions Of Near Champions: Held Attell To Draw In Goriest Fight," *Cumberland (MD) Evening Times,* Feb. 15, 1947, p. 6.
32. Nat Fleischer, "As We See It," *The Ring,* October 1924, p. 22.

Bibliography

Books

Allen, Oliver E. *The Tiger: The Rise and Fall of Tammany Hall*. Reading, MA: Addison-Wesley, 1993.

Aycock, Colleen, and Mark Scott. *The First Black Champions: Essays on Fighters of the 1880s to the 1920s*. Jefferson, NC: McFarland, 2011.

Barton, George A. *My Lifetime in Sports*. Minneapolis, MN: The Olympic Press, 1957.

Betts, John Rickards. *America's Sporting Heritage, 1850–1950*. Reading, MA: Addison-Wesley, 1974.

Brady, William A. *Showman*. New York: E.P. Dutton & Co., 1937.

Brown, Warren. *Win, Lose, or Draw*. New York: G.P. Putnam's Sons, 1947.

Brundage, W. Fitzhugh (ed). *Beyond Blackface; African Americans and the Creation of American Popular Culture, 1890–1930*. Chapel Hill: University of North Carolina Press, 2011.

Bushnell, R.A. *The San Francisco Irish 1848–1880*. Berkeley: University of California Press, 1980.

Cantwell, Robert. *The Real McCoy*. Princeton, NJ: Auerbach Publishers, 1971.

Chidsey, Donald Barr. *John The Great*. Garden City, NY: Doubleday, 1942.

Chudacoff, Howard P. *The Age of the Bachelor: Creating an American Subculture*. Princeton: Princeton University Press, 1999.

Deighty, Guy. *Noble and Manly: The History of the National Sporting Club*. London: Hutchinson, 1956.

Dixon, Tris. *Damage: The Untold Story of Brain Trauma in Boxing*. Boston: Hamilcar, 2021.

Dobbs, Brian. *Black and White: The Birth of Modern Boxing*. Sussex, UK: Pitch Publishing Ltd, 2021.

Duis, Perry R. *The Saloon: Public Drinking in Chicago and Boston 1880–1920*. Urbana, IL: University of Illinois Press, 1983.

Durso, Joseph. *Madison Square Garden: 100 Years of History*. New York: Simon & Schuster, 1979.

Early, Gerald. *The Culture of Bruising: Essays on Prizefighting, Literature, and Modern American Culture*. Hopewell, NJ: Ecco Press, 1994.

Fields, Armand. *James J. Corbett: A Biography of the Heavyweight Boxing Champion and Popular Theater Headliner*. Jefferson, NC: McFarland, 2001.

Flanagan, Maureen A. *America Reformed: Progressives and Progressivisms, 1890s–1920s*. New York: Oxford University Press, 2007.

Fleischer, Nat. *Black Dynamite: The Story of the Negro in the Prize Ring from 1782–1938*. Vol. 1–5. New York: C.J. O'Brien, 1938.

Fleischer, Nat. *50 Years at Ringside*. New York: Greenwood Press, 1969.

Fleischer, Nat. *"Terrible Terry" The Brooklyn Terror: The Fistic Career of Terrible Terry McGovern*. New York: Press of C.J. O'Brien, 1943.

Frisbee, Meg. *Counterpunch: The Cultural Battles Over Heavyweight Prizefighting in the American West*. Seattle, University of Washington Press, 2016.

Gems, Gerald R. *Windy City Wars: Labor, Leisure, and Sports in the Making of Chicago*. Boston: Scarecrow Press, 1997.

Gorn, Elliott. *The Manly Art: Bare-Knuckle Prizefighting in America*. Ithaca, NY: Cornell University Press, 1986.

Bibliography

Handlin, Oscar. *Boston's Immigrants*. Cambridge, MA: Harvard University Press, 1959.

Hardy, Stephen. *How Boston Played: Sport, Recreation, and Community, 1865–1915*. Boston: Northeastern University Press, 1982.

Hauser, Thomas. *The Black Lights: Inside the World of Professional Boxing*. New York: McGraw-Hill, 1986.

Horton, James Oliver, and Lois E. Horton. *Black Bostonians*. New York: Holmes and Meier, 1979.

Isenberg, Michael T. *John L. Sullivan and His America*. Urbana, IL: University of Illinois Press, 1994.

Kasson, John F. *Amusing the Millions: Coney Island at the Turn of the Century*. New York: Hill & Wang, 1978.

Laffoley, Steven. *Shadowboxing: The Rise and Fall of George Dixon*. Lawrencetown Beach, Nova Scotia, Canada: Portersfield Press, 2012.

Lardner, John. *White Hopes and Other Tigers*. Philadelphia: J.B. Lippincott, 1991.

McCabe, James D., Jr. *New York by Gaslight*. New York: Arlington Press, 1994.

Miletich, Leo N. *Dan Stuart's Fistic Carnival*. College Station: Texas A & M Press, 1994.

Moore, Louis. *I Fight for a Living: Boxing and the Battle for Black Manhood, 1880–1915*. Urbana: University of Illinois Press, 2017.

Morgan, Dan, and John McCallum. *Dumb Dan*. New York: Tedson Publishing, 1953.

Moyle, Clay. *Sam Langford: Boxing's Greatest Uncrowned Champion*. Seattle: Bennett & Hastings, 2012.

Musser, Charles. *The Emergence of Cinema: The American Screen to 1907*. New York: Charles Scribner's Sons. 1990.

Naughton, W.W. *Kings of the Queensberry Realm*. Chicago: Continental Publishing Co., 1902.

Nicholson, James C. *The Notorious John Morrissey: How a Bare-Knuckle Brawler Became a Congressman and Founded Saratoga Race Course*. Lexington: University of Kentucky Press, 2021.

Pollack, Adam J. *In the Ring with James J. Corbett*. Iowa City, IA: Win by KO Publications, 2007.

Putney, Clifford. *Muscular Christianity, Manhood and Sports in Protestant America, 1880–1920*. Cambridge: Harvard University Press, 2003.

Rader, Benjamin G. *American Sports: From the Age of Folk Games to the Age of Spectators*. Englewood Cliffs, NJ: Prentice-Hall, 1993.

Redmond, Patrick R. *The Irish and the Making of American Sport*. Jefferson, NC: McFarland, 2014.

Riess, Steven A. *City Games: The Evolution of American Society and the Rise of Sports*. Urbana, IL: University of Illinois Press, 1989.

Roberts, Randy. *Papa Jack: Jack Johnson and the Era of White Hopes*. New York: The Free Press, 1985.

Sammons, Jeffrey T. *Beyond the Ring; The Role of Boxing in American Society*. Urbana, IL: University of Illinois Press, 1988.

Sante, Luc. *Low Life: Lures and Snares of Old New York*. New York: Farrar Straus Giroux, 1991.

Smith, Kevin. *Boston's Boxing Heritage: Prizefighting from 1882 to 1955*. Charlestown, SC: Arcadia Publishing, 2002.

Somers, Dale A. *The Rise of Sports in New Orleans*. Baton Rouge: Louisiana State University Press, 1972.

Sutherland, Douglas. *The Yellow Earl*. New York: Coward-McCann, 1965.

Terhune, Albert Payson. *To the Best of My Memory*. New York: Harper and Brothers, 1930.

Thrasher, Christopher David. *Fight Sports and American Masculinity*. Jefferson, NC: McFarland, 2015.

Van Every, Edward. *Muldoon: The Solid Man of Sport*. New York: Frederick A. Stokes Company, 1928.

Ward, Geoffrey. *Unforgivable Blackness: The Rise and Fall of Jack Johnson*. New York: Knopf, 2006.

Welch, Richard F. *King of the Bowery: Big Tim Sullivan, Tammany Hall, and New York City from the Gilded Age to the Progressive Era*. Albany: State University of New York Press, 2009.

Wiggins, David K. *Glory Bound: Black

Athletes in White America. Syracuse, NY: Syracuse University Press, 1997.

Wiggins, David K. (ed). *Sport in America: From Wicked Amusement to National Obsession.* Champaign, IL: Human Kinetics, 1995.

Dissertations

Andrews, Matthew Philip, "A Carnival of Muscle": Popular Amusements and Popular Culture in Turn-Of-The-Century San Francisco, 1880–1920." (attp://dot.org/10,17615/hp9+-xz88)

Jason A. Winders, "'Fought the Good Fight, Finished My Course,' George Dixon Amidst the Rising Tide of Jim Crow America" (2016). *Electronic Thesis and Dissertation Repository. 4108.* http://ir.lib.uwo.oc/ca/eto/4108

Index

Numbers in ***bold italics*** refer to pages with illustrations

Abbott, the Rev. Lyman 44
Africville (Halifax, N.S.) 13
Africville Heritage Museum 144
American Derby 116
Armstrong, Bob 10
Athenian Club 15
athletic clubs (expansion of) 10, 65
Attell, Abe 70, ***117***, 128, 150
Austin, Sam C. 56

Bakersfield, CA 112
Barrett, Billy 71
Barry, Jimmy 31, 72
battle royals 24
Bauer, Paul 38
Baxter, Bill 39
Becker, Charles A. 90
Beckham, J.C.W. 124
Beecher, the Rev. Henry Ward 43, 45, 65
Bellevue Hospital 138, 148
Bennett, James Gordon, Jr. 27
Bennings racetrack 134
Benton, Ben (aka Rob Roy) 51
Bernstein, Joe ***73***, 109, 120, 125, 126, 140, 153
Bettinson, A.F. "Peggy" 77, 78
Biloxi, MS 36
Binney, Ed 23
Blakelock, Sam 77
Blanchard, David 15, 16, 18, 19, 164n8
Bliss, Aaron T. 125
Bolen, Sam 74, 75, 80
Bonner, Jack 23
Boston (The Hub) 10, 20
Bowery 40, 43, 108
The Bowery After Dark 108, 128, 140
Brady, William A. 87
Breslin, Jimmy 4
Briggs, Jimmy 128

British Boxing Board of Control 77
Britt, Jimmy 132
Britt, Willus 132, 133
Broad, Kid 109, 126
Broadway Athletic Club 55, 56, 58, 73, ***89***, 98, 100, 102
Brooklyn: athletic clubs 66, 168$ch9n$7; City of Churches 43, 44, 65; Democratic political machine 66; ethnic composition 65; Navy Yard 65; South Brooklyn 145
Burley, Charley 11
Burns, Tommy 90, 125
Butte, MT 113
Byers, George 22, 23

California Athletic Club 32, 57, 59, 85
Callahan, Tim 115, 119
Callan, Arthur 24
Canzoneri, Tony 153
Carnival of Champions 35 (*see also* Olympic Club)
Carr, Howard 65
Carrillo, Frank 112, 172n26
Carroll, Brooklyn Jimmy 65
Chambers, John Graham 7
Charles Street AME 143
Charlesbank Athletic Club 21
Charlestown (Boston) 84
Chicago 29, 111
Chicago World's Fair 49
Chickering, Elmer 14
Chiles, Frank 23
Choynski, Joe 22, 33, 93, 101, 102, 148
Churchill, Lord Randolph 27
Cleveland, Grover 54
Coapman, Dave 154
Coffroth, Jim 111
Cohan, George M. 69, 145
Cohen, Morris "Cockney" 120

181

Index

Colonel Creecy 35
Coney Island 9, 38, 43, 49, 55, 65, 66, 68
Coney Island Athletic Club 38, 39, 41, 42, 44, 45, 87
Connolly, Tommy 51
Considine, Billy 125
Considine, George 87, 88
Considine, John 87
Converse, Elisha 148
coon shows (vaudeville) 13
Corbett, Harry 112
Corbett, James J. 30, 32, 34, 40, 43, 53, 57, 59, 88, 90, 93, 101, 103, 104, 108
Corbett, Young II (William Rothwell) 114, 116, 123, 124, *127*, 130, 131, 134, 139, 141, 151, 152
Coreghin, Will 149
Courtney, John 45
Craig, Frank (Harlem Coffee Cooler) 120
Cribb, Tom 15
Cribb Club 15, 21, 23, 92, 164n4
Croker, Richard "Boss" 78
Croll's Gardens 126
Croot, Walter 52
Curley, Will 81, 120

Danforth, Tommy 17
Davies, Parson 29, 75, 90, 132, 139
Dawson, George 91
Delavan Hotel 88, 89, 96
Dempsey, Jack 146
Dempsey, Nonpareil Jack 65
Denver, CO 117
Dille, Dr. Elbert R. 7
Dixon, George *14*, *19*, *86*, *98*; benefit gala 101; debilitation and death 137, 148; Dixon the man 47, 74; early fights 14–16; estrangement and reconciliation with Tom O'Rourke 116, 121, 122, 146; funeral and burial 143; gravesite and monument 143, *144*; nickname derivation of 2; parents and siblings 13, 14, 139; relationship with John L. Sullivan 138; vaudeville days 134, 137; vs. Abe Attell (3-fight series) 117; vs. Abe Willis 33; vs. Ben Jordan 61; vs. Billy Plimmer 41; vs. Cal McCarthy (first fight) 26, second fight (28, 29); vs. Dal Hawkins 59; vs. Dave Sullivan 62; vs. Eddie Santry (3-fight series) 80, 118, 119; vs. Eugene Hornbacher 19; vs. Frank Erne (3-fight rivalry) 52, 57, 58; vs. Fred Johnson 39; vs. George Gardner 63; vs. George Siddons 40; vs. Hank Brennan (4-fight rivalry) 17; vs. Harlem Tommy Murphy 122; vs. Jack Skelly 37; vs. Joe Bernstein 74; vs. Johnny Murphy 27; vs. Kentucky Rosebud 48; vs. Kid Broad 74; vs. Martin Flaherty (first fight) 32, second fight (54); vs. Monk the Newsboy (farewell fight) 122; vs. Nunc Wallace 26; vs. Pedlar Palmer (at Madison Square Garden) 55, (rematches in Great Britain) 120, 121; vs. Solly Smith (first fight) 43; vs. Solly Smith (second fight) 60; vs. Terry McGovern anti-climactic rematch 106, 116; vs. Terry McGovern THE FIGHT (pre-fight analysis) 96, 97; vs. Terry McGovern THE FIGHT (round-by-round and rehash) 99, 100; vs. Tommy White (first fight) 56; vs. Tommy White (second fight) 75; vs. Young Corbett II 116; vs. Young Griffo (3-fight rivalry) 49–51; vs. Young Pluto 71; White Elephant saloon 100, 115
Dixon, Mrs. George (Kitty) 137
Dixon, John 139
Dobbs, Bobby 25, 120
Dobbs, Brian 14
Donnelly, Dan 3
Dougherty, Danny *86*, 118
Douglas, Frederic 1, 143
Drake, John A. 131
Driscoll, Jem 120, 151
Dunfee, Joe 119
Dunn, Jere 28, 29, 165n9
Dunn, Jim 65
Duran, Roberto 109

Earl of Lonsdale (Hugh Cecil Lowther) 26
Ebbets, Charles H. 145
Edgren, Robert 131, 134, 146, 147
Erie Canal 28
Erne, Frank 52, 106–109, 132

Farrell, Johnny 85
Figg, Tom 82
Firpo, Luis Angel 146
Fitzpatrick, John 35, 166n23
Fitzsimmons, Bob 30, 53, 57, 59, 88, 90, 124
Flaherty, Martin 59, 150
Fleischer, Nat 4, 5, 18, 63, 84, 91, 92, 95, 155, 163n6, 164n2
Floto, Otto 72
Foley, Larry 32, 48, 71
For Fame and Fortune 108
Forbes, Harry 70, 83, 115
Fort Upton 141

Index

Fowler, Orson 97
Frawley Law 132
Frisbee, Meg 8, 163*n*12
Fugitive Slave Act 13
Fulton, Fred 146

Gans, Joe 71, 101, 106, 109–111, 131, 137, 143, 151
Gardner, George 23, 65
Gardner, Oscar (Omaha Kid) 104, 105, 111, 153
Gates, John "Bet a Million" 131
Gay Morning Glories 104, *105*
Gilmore, Harry 31, 56
Ginnetts Circus 121
Givens, Dr. A.J. 136
Gleason, Jack 111
Gleason, Paddy 28, 86
Godfrey, George (Old Chocolate) 2, 21, *22*, 165*ch*2*n*5
Goodwin, Joe 121
Gorman, Johnny 36
Gowanus Canal 65
Gowanus Club 141
Grand Opera House 140
Graney, Eddie 126, *127*
Gravesend (Coney Island) 38, 69, 77
Gray, Billy 76
Green, George 60
Greenpoint (Brooklyn) 140
Greenwood Athletic Club 67, 68, 72, 79
Griffin, Johnny (Braintree Lad) 42, 51, 58, 60, 150, 151
Griffo, Young (Albert Griffiths) 46, 48, 49, 71, 154
Guillotte, Joseph 35

Haley, Patsy 73, 82, 83
Halifax, N.S. 13, 144; *see also* Africville
Hanlon, Eddie 126, 129, 153, 154
Hardy, Stephen 15
Harris, Sam H. 83, *86*, 87, 104, 128, 130, 135, 140, 145
Harrison, Carter, Jr. 111
Havlin, Johnny 84, 105
Hawkins, Dal 59, 63, 111
Heenan, John C. 28
Heffernan, William 145
Henderson, the Rev. T.M. 143
Herford, Al 110, 134, 139
Herget, John L. (aka Young Mitchell) 33
Herrera, Aurelio 112, 113, 134, *152*
Hertz, John 116
Hesper Club 69

Hill, Billy (aka Muldoon's Pickaninny) 23–25
Hoffman House 44
Hogan, Malachy 31
Holmes, Larry 147
Holy Cross Cemetery (Brooklyn) 145
Horton, George S. 56
Horton, James Oliver 20
Horton, Lois E. 20
Horton Law 55, 56, 88, 100, 102, 103, 110, 111, 128, 132
Hot Springs, AR 139, 140
Houseman, Lou 30, 31, 82, 113
Howell, Richard 89, 90
Hubbell, the Rev. Nathan 44
Humphreys, Joe 69, *86*, 112, 135, 136, 143
Hurst, Tim 132

Igoe, Hype 112
Ireland (immigration from) 20
Irish: in Boston 21; in Brooklyn 65, 66; as gambler-businessmen 8; inter-racial relations 20, 21; politicians 8, 9, 21; as prize-fighters and prizefight organizers 8, 9, 65; in San Francisco 32

Jackson, Peter 11, 22, 29, 30, 33, 48, 108, 137
Jacobs, Jim 148
Jamaica Racetrack 35
Jeffersonian Athletic Club 28
Jeffries, James J. 81, 87, 88, 90
Jewell, Charles A. 124
Johnson, Jack 22, 93, 146
Johnson, McHenry 22
Jordan, Ben 60–62, 120

Kearns, Tim 25
Keeley brothers (vaudevillians) 104
Kellogg, Dr. John 130
Kelly, Sammy 153
Kelly, Tommy 39
Kennedy, Eddie 95
Kennedy, Jim 58, 111
Kentucky Rosebud (Walter Edgerton) 25, 48, 114, 167*ch*5*n*4
Kilbane, Johnny 141
Kilrain, Jake 15, 22, 24, 27, 35
King, Don 147
Kings County Hospital 134, 141

Lakewood, NJ 96
Langford, Sam 11, 25
Langtry, TX 53

183

Index

Lavigne, George "Kid" 40, 49, 93, 106, 132, 148, 166*ch*3*n*23
Law and Order League 124
Lenny, Eddie 81, 105, 118, 119, 151
Lenox Athletic Club 55, 61, 62, 71–73
Leon, Casper 72, 81
Leonard, Benny 109, 141
Leonard, Mike 46
Lewis, Merton E. 102
Lipton, Sir Thomas 78
Long Island City 28
Longacre Athletic Club 138, 143
Lonsdale Belt 151
Lott, Steve 148
Loughlin, Thomas 136
Louis, Joe 147, 167*ch*8*n*3
Lumley, Arthur T. 35
Lyons, Harry 116

Mackey, Biz 119
Madison Square Garden 41, 52, 106, 135, 148
Maher, Peter 22, 63, 86, 102
Mahoney, Young 61
Mansfield, OH 148, 149
Marquess of Queensberry 18
Marshall, Jerry 53, 167*ch*6*n*2
Martin, Denver Ed 22
Martin, Harris 22
Mason, Charlie 83
Masterson, Bat 75, 89, 113
Maynard, Billy 126
Maywood, Charles 64, **86**
McAuliffe, Jack 29, 35, 36, 46, 49, 65
McCarthy, Cal 26, 49, 150, 151
McCarthy, Tim 15
McCarty, Luther 146
McClelland, Jack 123
McCloskey, Ellwood 105, 153
McCormick, J.B. "Macon" 106
McCoy, Kid 30, 141
McDonald, Mike 29
McFadden, George "Elbows" 111, 143
McGovern, Hughey 128–130
McGovern, Phil 78, 128
McGovern, Terry 64, **66**, **86**, **98**, **127**; benefit gala 137; career earnings (squandering of) 135; confined in sanitariums 130, 134, 136, 140, 141; end days and death 141, 142; funeral and burial 145; parents and siblings 69, 128; racetrack misadventures 130 135; refereeing 125, 141; sociopathy 130, 132–134, 140, 141; vaudeville days 103, 108, 139, 140, 143; vs. Aurelio Herrera 112, 113; vs. Austin Rice 70; vs. Battling Nelson 131, 132; vs. Billy Rotchford 82; vs. Brooklyn Tommy Sullivan 67; vs. Casper Leon 71; vs. Dave Sullivan 123, 124; vs. Eddie Hanlon 129; vs. Frank Erne (first fight) 107; vs. Frank Erne (second fight) 128; vs. George Dixon THE FIGHT (anti-climactic rematch) 106, 116; vs. George Dixon THE FIGHT (pre-fight analysis 96, 97; vs. George Dixon THE FIGHT (round-by-round and rehash) 99;vs. George Monroe (3-fight rivalry) 68; vs. Harlem Tommy Murphy 131; vs. Harry Forbes (first fight) 70; vs. Harry Forbes (second fight) 83; vs. Jimmy Briggs 128; vs. Jimmy Britt 132; vs. Joe Bernstein (first fight) 73; vs. Joe Bernstein (second fight) 109; vs. Joe Gans (backlash) 111; vs. Joe Gans (rumors of skullduggery) 110; vs. Oscar Gardner (first fight) 105; vs. Oscar Gardner (second fight) 111, 112; vs. Patsy Haley 72, 73; vs. Pedlar Palmer 78–**80**; vs. Tim Callahan (3-fight rivalry) 69, 70; vs. Tommy White 106; vs. Young Corbett II (first fight; shocking upset) 114, 123; vs. Young Corbett II (second fight) 124–126; vs. Young Corbett II (third fight) 134
McGovern, Mrs. Terry (Grace Smalley) 69, 78, 108, **133**, 142
McGrain, Matt 3
McGrath, Joe 41
McGraw, John J. 136
McGuigan, Jack 128
McGurn's handball court 31
McIntyre, O.O. 85
McKane, John Y. 38, 49
McLaughlin, Hugh "Boss" 45, 65, 66
McLean, George P. 124
Mechanics Pavilion 59, 111, 127, 167*ch*8*n*1
Menke, Frank 3
Meredith, the Rev. D.D. 44
Metropole Hotel 89, 90
Miller, "Swede" 59
Miner's Theater (Bowery) 40, 143
Mitchell, Charlie 43
Molloy, William 76
Monk the Newsboy (Harry Kronski) 122
Monroe, George 68, 104, 151
Moran, Owen 120
Morgan, Dai 120
Morgan, Dumb Dan 4
Morrissey, John 8, 28
Mount Hope Cemetery 143

Index

Muldoon, William 23, 24
Muldoon, William H. 45
Murphy, Harlem Tommy 121, 122, 131, 155
Murphy, Johnny 27
Murphy, Torpedo Billy 56
Murray, Jim 5
Muscular Christianity 6, 9, 10
Myer, Billy 29, 35

Nat Fleischer Award 5
National Athletic Club 122
National Sporting Club (London) 24, 52, 61, 77, 121, 128, 130, 136
Naughton, W.W. 126
Neil, Frankie 130
Nelson, Oscar "Battling" 131, 137, 154
New London, CT 19, 124
New Manhattan Athletic Club 51, 52
New Orleans 9, 35, 43, 44; see also Olympic Club
New York Times 43, 44, 46, 88
Newman, Mike 138, 143
newsboys 103
Newton, R.V. 44
North Judson, IN 29
Nutmeg Club 124

O'Brien, Dick 23
O'Brien, Freckles 83, 169*n*28
O'Brien, Hugh 21
O'Brien, Jack 23
Odell, Benjamin 99
O'Donnell, Steve 41
O'Leary, Dan 29
O'Leary, James Patrick 8
Olympic Club 34–37, 166 *ch*3*n*23
Ordway, Aaron P. "Doc" 77
O'Reilly, John Boyle 6, 15, 163*n*7
O'Rourke, Charlie 25
O'Rourke, Tom *19*, 83–95, 115, 116, 121, 146, 147

Palmer, Pedlar 52, *53*, 72, 76–79, 108, 120, 121
Palzer, Al 146
Park Slope (Brooklyn) 67
Paul, Richard Henry 150
Pelican Club (Boston) 17
Pelican Club (Brooklyn) 70
Pelican Club (London) 26
Pep, Willie 48
Perry, William 115
phrenology 97
pickaninnies 24, 165*ch*2*n*8

Pierce, Eddie 46
Plimmer, Billy 39, 41, 96
Pluto, Young 71, 168*ch*10*n*1
Police Gazette 17, 24, 35, 40, 56, 83, 84, 163*n*14
Pollack, Harry 132
Pollock, Johnny 79
Pope Edwin 150
Progressive Era 124
Puritan Athletic Club 28

Queensberry reformation 7, 10, 33, 77; see also Marquess of Queensberry

Reagan, Johnny 70
Reynolds, William H. 35
Rice, Austin 70, 118, 126, 137, 152
Rickard, Tex 146, 154
The Ring magazine 5; see also Fleischer, Nat
The Road to Ruin 108, 118
Ritchie, Johnny 76
The Road to Ruin 108, 118
Roberts, Randy 9
Robinson, Jackie 34
Robson, Spike 136
Roby, IN 30, 42
Rocap, Billy 90
Rogers, Joe 90, 139
Roosevelt, Theodore 100, 102, 103, 134
Root, Jack 23, 30
Rose, Jack (Jacob Rubenstein) 89, 170*n*17
Rosenthal, Herman 89, 90, 145
Rotchford, Billy 81, 113
Runyon, Damon 4, 85
Ryall, Lew 128
Ryan, Billy 122
Ryan, Paddy 28
Ryan, Tommy 50, 51, 120

St. John the Evangelist Church (Brooklyn) 145
San Francisco 9, 35
Sandburg, Carl 29
Santry, Eddie 61, 80, 104, 151
Saratoga, NY 8, 77
Schieren, Charles 46
Schmeling, Max 147
Schulian, John 5
Schutte, Bill 154
Scottish American Athletic Club 26
Seaside Athletic Club *44*, 46, 49, 50, 52, 106
Sharkey, Tom 81, 87, 88, 101

185

Index

Sheepshead Bay 38, 39
Siler, George **30**, 88, 107, 109–111, 117, 139
Skelly, Jack 35, 36, 40, 52
Slavin, Frank 85
Smith, Ed W. 136
Smith, Gardner J. 104, 105
Smith, Mysterious Billy 23, 50, 51, 93
Smith, Red 5
Smith, Solly 24, **42**, 47, 49, 62, 104, 154
Smith, Turkey Point Billy 82
Sousa, John Philip 79
Southern Athletic Club 124
sportswriters (circa 1900) 4
Stamford Hall 130, 134
Stanley, Digger 120, 151
Stoneham, Charles 151
Stowe, Harriet Beecher 30
Stuart, Dan 53, 57
Sullivan, Brooklyn Tommy 116, 150
Sullivan, Dave 62, 123
Sullivan, John L. 10, 15, 21, 22, 24, 25, 34, 35. 40, 44, 88, 103, 108, 115, 137, 139
Sullivan, Paddy 63
Sullivan, Spike 62
Sullivan, Timothy D. "Big Tim" 55, **56**, 63, 69, 86, 87, 121, 129
Sullivan, Tommy 67
Sweeney, Patsy 25

Talmage, the Rev. Thomas De Witt 43, 65
Tammany Hall 8, 44, 78
Tattersalls (Chicago) 82, 104, 105, 109, 111, 116
Temple, Larry 94, 95
Terhune, Albert Payson 104, 164*ch*1*n*1
Terry McGovern Athletic and Social Club 112, 127
Thomas, William (aka Kid Broad) 74
Thrasher, S.P. 125
Tipman, Joe 118
Touhey, George V. 54
Troy, NY 28, 29
Truth, Sojourner 143
Tuckahoe, NY 76, **80**
Tucker, Charles 118
Turner, George Kibbe 86

Tuxedo Club 90
Twentieth Century Athletic Club 111
The 20th Century Maids 137, 139
Tyson, Mike 148

Uncle Tom's Cabin 108
Underground Railroad 13, 143

Van Alstyne, the Rev. George 44
Vance, Madison J. 36
Vanderbilt Hotel 77
Van Heest, Johnny 49

Walcott, Joe 53, 58, 91, **92**, 99, 100, 143, 147: amateur days 91; disappearance and death 149; friendship with George Dixon 94; post-boxing employment 148; shooting incident 93; vs. George Gardner 93, 94; vs. Jack Hall 92; vs. Joe Choynski 93; vs. Kid Lavigne 93; vs. Larry Temple (3-fight series) 95; vs. Mysterious Billy Smith (6-fight rivalry) 93; vs. Tom Tracey 92
Ward, Jack 104
Warren, Tommy 85, 105, 151
Washington, Booker T. 1
Watson, Prof. Andy 24
Weir, Ike 17, 57, 84
West, Tommy 23
West Baden Hotel 60
West Baden Springs, IN 60, 72, 96, 167*ch*8*n*3
West Brighton (Coney Island) 38
West End Athletic Club 117
White, Tommy 56, 60, 105, 106
White Hope tournament 87
Whitney, Harry Payne 131, 132
Williams, Joe 114
Willis, Abe 154
Willis, Billy 128
Wonderland (London) 121
Woodward's Pavilion 60

Yanger, Benny 113, 115
YMCA 45

www.ingramcontent.com/pod-product-compliance
Ingram Content Group UK Ltd.
Pitfield, Milton Keynes, MK11 3LW, UK
UKHW042012140426
5217IPUK00015B/1137